MODERN WORLD HISTORY

Int_____nal Relations
from the First World
War to the present

Tony McAleavy

Humanities Inspector
for Gloucestershire

CAMBRIDGE
UNIVERSITY PRESS

For my mother and father

Published by the Press Syndicate of the University of Cambridge
The Pitt Building, Trumpington Street, Cambridge CB2 1RP
40 West 20th Street, New York, NY 10011-4211, USA
10 Stamford Road, Oakleigh, Melbourne 3166, Australia

© Cambridge University Press 1996

First published 1996

Printed in Great Britain at the University Press, Cambridge

A catalogue record for this book is available from the British Library

Library of Congress cataloguing in publication data applied for

ISBN 0 521 44575 2 paperback

Produced by Gecko Limited, Bicester, Oxon

Illustrations by Gerry Ball, Peter Kent, Stephen Ramsey

Picture research by Marilyn Rawlings

Acknowledgements
Cover, The Imperial War Museum; 4, Punch Publications; 6, 64, 82 Ullstein Bilderdienst; 8, 9, 18, 34, 37, 68, 81, 86–7 (background), 91, Imperial War Museum; 10, 11, 32, 78, 79, 107, 110, 132t, David King Collection; 13, 39, 42, 47, 48, 54, 74, 94l and r, 98, 101, 112, 115, 117, 125, 135, 139, Peter Newark's Historical Pictures; 14, 25, 31, 55 (© Solo Syndication), 63 inset (Solo), 69 (Solo), 137, 170, Centre for Study of Cartoons and Caricature, University of Kent at Canterbury; 15, 27, Illustrated London News; 16, 45, 52, 95, 99, E.T. Archive; 20, 26, 35, 38, 40, 50, 57, 77, 83, 111, 114, 120–1 and inset, Hulton Deutsch Collection; 22, Mansell Collection; 24, 36, 44, 53, 59, 60, 71, 126, 140, Bilderdienst Süddeutscher Verlag; 33, 46, 49, 62–3 (background), 75, 87 (inset), 97, 102, 109, 133, 142 (inset), 142–3, 143 (inset), 149, 150–1, 165, 167 (inset), 173 (background), Popperfoto; 43, 85, (Associated Press), 130, 132b (AP), 138 (AP), 168, 144, 159 (AP), 161 (AP), 164 (AP), Topham Picturepoint; 51, Roger Viollet, Pris; 52, 62 (inset), 67, 89, 106, 148, 154, 166–7 (background), AKG London; 70, Robert Hunt Library; 72, by courtesy of the National Portrait Gallery, London; 76, Wiener Library (© Bundesarchiv); 90, Rex Features/Sipa Press; 113, 118, 122, 127, 131, 141, 145, 147, 153, 155, 156, 157, 158, 160, 163, 171 (three pictures), 172, Camera Press; 136, Black Star (photo Gordon/Cranbourne).

Every effort has been made to reach copyright holders; the publishers would be glad to hear from anyone whose rights they have unwittingly infringed.

Contents

The origins of the First World War

In the late summer of 1914 the most powerful countries in Europe went to war. By the time the fighting stopped, four years later, 20 million people had been killed. Why did this disastrous war start? In 1919, the countries on the winning side met together and said that the war had been Germany's fault.

Was the war the fault of the German government?

Historians have identified a number of long-term and short-term causes of the war.

LONG-TERM CAUSE 1
THE RISE OF GERMANY

Until the middle of the nineteenth century Germany was divided into many separate states. The most important of these German states was a kingdom called Prussia. In the 1860s the leaders of Prussia wanted to unite Germany. France was unhappy about this and went to war against Prussia from 1870 to 1871. France was beaten and the victorious Prussian government was able to set up a new German Empire. This was a massive new state that included most German-speaking people. Wilhelm I, King of Prussia, was declared to be the emperor or Kaiser of Germany. His chief minister, Bismarck, became the powerful Chancellor of Germany.

Between 1871 and 1914 the economy of the new German state went from strength to strength. This was based on an amazing industrial revolution and by 1914 the output of German factories had overtaken the output of British factories. Chancellor Bismarck was very skilful. After 1871 he stopped the German government from getting involved in any more wars. France was the sworn enemy of Germany but Bismarck made sure that France remained isolated. As long as he was in charge of German foreign policy there was no danger of Germany going to war against Russia or Britain. This all changed when Germany got a new Kaiser – Wilhelm II – and Bismarck lost the chancellorship.

LONG-TERM CAUSE 2
THE NEW KAISER AND WORLD POWER

Now that Germany was the equal of Britain in terms of wealth and industry, some German people felt that their country should have a worldwide empire like Britain. One German who believed this was the new ruler of Germany, Kaiser Wilhelm II, who came to power in 1888. He made Bismarck retire in 1890. Wilhelm wanted a new, more aggressive approach to the rest of the world. He ended the friendly relationship that Bismarck had encouraged between Germany and Russia. As a result of his attitude other countries began to see Germany as a threat.

SOURCE A

L'ENFANT TERRIBLE !

CHORUS IN THE STERN. "DON'T GO ON LIKE THAT—OR YOU'LL UPSET US ALL!!"

A Punch cartoon suggests that the new Kaiser 'rocked the boat' with his aggressive foreign policy. Figures representing Russia, Britain, France and Austria-Hungary cower at the stern of the boat.

LONG-TERM CAUSE 3
THE ARMS RACE

After 1897 the German government started building up an enormous navy that could challenge the might of the British navy. The Germans knew that a worldwide empire would have to be defended by a worldwide navy.

The German government passed a law in 1900 ordering the building of a huge new fleet of 41 battleships and 60 cruisers. The British responded energetically to this threat by increasing the size of their navy. They introduced a new type of powerful battleship called a 'Dreadnought' in 1906. The Germans responded by building similar ships of their own. The British went on to order even more substantial battleships called 'Super Dreadnoughts'.

Other countries also took part in this arms race. The French increased their forces and by 1914 had an army of nearly 4 million soldiers. The Russians spent a fortune on military railways that were clearly designed to take troops to fight Germany and Austria-Hungary. Russian spending on its army was huge. People in Germany feared that this mighty force would one day flatten Berlin.

LONG-TERM CAUSE 4
THE TWO ALLIANCES

Germany signed a treaty of alliance with Austria-Hungary in 1879. The two states remained allies in the decades that followed. At first the only likely enemy of this alliance was France. However, Wilhelm's clumsy policy encouraged Russia to join forces with France. In 1892 France and Russia agreed to an alliance: if either country was attacked by Germany, the other state would go to war against the Germans.

The government of Britain began to look around for allies at the turn of the century. British politicians thought about an alliance with Germany against France and Russia. However, German policy under the Kaiser was so badly managed that Britain felt forced to look to France and Russia. Britain established friendly relations with France in 1904 and Russia in 1907. The link was not an official alliance but an 'entente' or understanding that the countries would try to work together. People talked of the Triple Entente: an anti-German grouping of France, Russia and Britain.

EUROPE, 1914 – THE TWO HOSTILE ALLIANCES

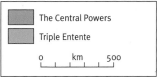

The Central Powers

Triple Entente

0   km   500

>> Activity

Look at the information on these two pages about four long-term causes of the First World War. For each cause explain in your own words:

a how it made war more likely;

b whether it shows that the German government was to blame.

The crisis in Europe: summer 1914

By January 1914 the situation in Europe was tense. Between January and August a number of short-term causes led to the outbreak of war.

>> Activity

1 Look at the information on page 7 about three short-term causes of the war. For each cause try to work out:

   a how it led to war;

   b whether it shows that Germany was to blame for the outbreak of war.

2 Using the information from pages 4–7 explain how far Germany was responsible for causing the First World War.

SOURCE B

The Archduke Franz Ferdinand and his wife leaving the townhall at Sarajevo shortly before they were assassinated by a Serb nationalist.

SHORT-TERM CAUSE 1
THE KILLING IN SARAJEVO

The city of Sarajevo in Bosnia was the centre of world attention in June 1914. Bosnia was part of Austria-Hungary but many of its people were Serbs who wanted to be ruled by the neighbouring state of Serbia. On 28 June 1914 a Serb called Gavrilo Princip shot dead the Archduke Franz Ferdinand, heir to the throne of Austria-Hungary, and his wife.

The killing of the Archduke was linked to a bitter dispute between Austria-Hungary and the state of Serbia. Austria-Hungary was looking for an excuse for a war against Serbia.

Austria-Hungary blamed Serbia for the murder and got ready to attack.

The system of alliances led to several other countries becoming involved in the outbreak of war between Austria-Hungary and Serbia. While Austria-Hungary was allied to Germany, Serbia was closely linked to Russia. The government of Austria-Hungary looked to Germany for help. Serbia expected Russian help. The Russians, in turn, hoped for support from France and Britain. In this way, the killing at Sarajevo made possible a wider war which would involve all the powerful countries of Europe.

SHORT-TERM CAUSE 2
THE GERMAN DECISION FOR WAR

In 1913 there had been another argument between Austria-Hungary and Serbia and Russia about how land taken from Turkey should be divided. This nearly led to war between the two alliances. It had not because the German government refused to support Austria-Hungary.

A year later the German policy changed. On 5 July 1914 the Kaiser gave his full backing for an Austrian attack on Serbia. Austria-Hungary would not have risked war without help from their more powerful ally. The German government knew that there was a good chance that Russia would go to war on the side of Serbia, and that the result would be a general war.

SOURCE C

The Austro-Hungarian ambassador to Berlin reported a discussion with the Kaiser on 5 July.

The Kaiser told me that we might rely upon Germany's full support. It was Kaiser Wilhelm's opinion that action must not be delayed. Should war break out between Austria-Hungary and Russia, Germany would stand at our side. Kaiser Wilhelm would regret it if we do not make use of the present situation, which is all in our favour.

In the following weeks of crisis the German government did more than offer support. It urged Austria-Hungary to make sure that war broke out. When Britain and Russia tried to get Austria-Hungary to negotiate, Germany told her ally to ignore these attempts to stop the war.

SHORT-TERM CAUSE 3
CONFUSION ABOUT THE BRITISH POSITION

The Germans were not sure whether the British would fight. If the British had made clear their determination to fight, the German leaders might have thought again about the war. The position of the British Foreign Secretary, Sir Edward Grey, was not complicated. Although Britain had links with France and Russia there was no official alliance. Legally, Britain was not bound to go war on the side of France and Russia.

As the crisis developed, senior civil servants urged Grey to say that Britain would definitely side with France and Russia. They hoped that an announcement like this would frighten the Germans into stepping back from war. Grey disagreed.

He wanted to try to avoid war by negotiating. Talks continued right up to 3 August when Germany attacked France via Belgium. At this point Britain stopped talking and, a day later, went to war.

SOURCE D

The Russian Foreign Minister, Sergei Sazonov, blamed Britain for not threatening war.

In 1914 Sir Edward Grey should have made a clear statement that Britain would stand by France and Russia. I insistently asked him to do this but he refused. He could have saved humanity from that terrible catastrophe.

The First World War

On 28 July Austria-Hungary declared war on Serbia. By 4 August Germany and Austria-Hungary (the Central Powers) were at war with Russia, France and Britain (the Allies). Generals in all countries were desperate to mobilise their troops; that is, to get them moving towards the frontier with the enemy. Rapid mobilisation reduced the time available for discussion and negotiation to virtually nothing.

Stalemate in the West

Each side expected the war to be short-lived. The German plan was for a quick knock-out blow against France. This nearly worked. The German army swept through Belgium and northern France. The German advance was finally stopped by the French army on the River Marne, not far from Paris . The Germans were driven back a little and a front-line was established. This front-line did not change very much for the following three years.

Attempts to break the stalemate led to enormous casualties. In 1916 the Germans tried to break through at the Battle of Verdun. They failed but in the fighting that went on between February and July there were about a million casualties. In the same year the British attacked on the River Somme. On the first day of the Battle of the Somme, 60,000 British troops were killed but the outcome was indecisive. In 1917 Britain once again tried to break through the German lines at a place called Passchendaele; there were half a million casualties. The result of this enormous suffering was that the British line moved forward only four miles.

Once the fighting had led to stalemate, the leaders had no idea how to end the war without losing face. Both sides looked for new allies to break the deadlock. Italy and Romania joined the Allied side and Bulgaria joined with the Central Powers. These new combatants did not end the war; quite the opposite. Each new player wanted some of the profits of war and was ready to fight until it got a 'fair share'.

A German poster from the First World War showing a heroic image of a frontline soldier. The poster was advertising a scheme to raise money for the German war effort.

The horror of the fighting is vividly conveyed in this painting, Gassed, by the British artist, John Singer Sargent. It shows a line of British soldiers blinded in a German gas attack.

The naval war and the Americans

There was no decisive victory in the war at sea. The only major naval battle took place in the North Sea in 1916 at the Battle of Jutland. Neither the British nor the German fleet was destroyed but afterwards the German fleet retired to port and did not venture out for the rest of the war. Unable to destroy the British navy, Germany turned to submarine warfare. The German submarines were known as U-boats. They attacked British shipping in order to try to cut off vital supplies.

The U-boat campaign helped to bring America into the war on the side of Britain and France. By 1917 U-boats were trying to sink any ship that might be trading with Britain. This involved attacks on American ships. The American government responded by declaring war on Germany in April 1917. The power and wealth of the USA greatly strengthened the position of the Allies.

While the USA entered the war on the Western Front, Russia was being defeated in the east. The war had been going badly for the Russians for some time. Revolution in Russia in 1917 led to a collapse of the Russian war effort and withdrawal from the war. Faced with total defeat, the new communist rulers of Russia agreed to all the German demands and signed the Treaty of Brest-Litovsk in March 1918. Under this peace treaty Germany dealt very harshly with Russia, taking control of huge areas of Russian territory.

German defeat and the armistice

Meanwhile, on the Western Front it took time for the American army to make a full contribution to the fighting. In March 1918 the Germans launched their last major offensive in the west. They tried to smash through to Paris before American reinforcements arrived in great force. After some successes the German attack petered out. By August 1918 the American reinforcements were in place and the allied forces were ready for a huge counter-attack. With the help of tanks the Allies made a decisive breakthrough. The German generals decided that they were about to be defeated and the German government asked the American President Wilson for peace. There was an agreement to stop fighting on 11 November 1918. This agreement was called the Armistice.

Discussion points

> Why were casualties so high on the Western Front?

> Why had Russia left the war by January 1918?

> How did the USA come to join the war? What difference did this make?

The Russian Revolution

Russia before communism

In 1917 Russia had been ruled for many years by Tsar Nicholas II. He was an autocrat; this meant that there were no limits to his power. The great majority of Russians were extremely poor peasants living in the countryside. A small but growing number of people lived in towns and worked in mines and factories.

In 1904–1905 Russia fought a war against Japan and lost. Defeat led to an attempted revolution in Russia in 1905. Tsar Nicholas only retained control by promising reforms. He set up a parliament for Russia called the 'duma'. This had little real power and it proved to be a great disappointment. Russia took part in the First World War and fought against Germany and Austria-Hungary. The war was a disaster for Russia and by 1917 many Russians were ready for another revolution.

WHY DID SOME RUSSIANS WANT A CHANGE OF GOVERNMENT IN 1917?

> The gap between rich and poor was enormous. Peasants and factory workers wanted a fairer deal.

> Ordinary people had no political power. They were angry that the Tsar could do what he liked and disappointed that the duma had no real power.

> Russians did very badly in the First World War. Russian armies were defeated by Germany.

> The war put a great strain on the Russian economy. Prices went up and food was scarce.

The storming of the Winter Palace in Petrograd by Bolshevik forces in November 1917. The Soviet artist created a romantic version of what happened. In fact, very little fighting took place and only six people were killed.

The two revolutions of 1917

Revolution first broke out in St Petersburg (known at the time as Petrograd) in March 1917. Shortages of bread led to strikes and riots in the city. Law and order broke down. The army mutinied and refused to help . Tsar Nicholas admitted defeat and abdicated on 15 March.

The Soviets and the Bolsheviks

Although the Tsar was no longer in charge, there was confusion about who would replace him. The duma set up a so-called 'provisional government'. Workers and soldiers in Petrograd established a governing committee or 'soviet'. Soon soviets were set up in other large towns. Both the provisional government and the soviets claimed to be in charge.

Among the revolutionaries was a group of communists known as Bolsheviks. The Bolshevik leader, Lenin, returned from exile to Petrograd in April 1917. Lenin and the Bolsheviks wanted to overthrow the provisional government. His slogan was 'All power to the soviets!' One of Lenin's most important colleagues was Leon Trotsky. He played a key role in the organisation of the Petrograd soviet. On the 6–7 November Bolshevik fighters, known as Red Guards, seized power in Petrograd. Soviets all over Russia followed the lead from Petrograd and took control of their local area. The Bolshevik revolution had begun.

The Treaty of Brest-Litovsk

At first, Lenin was convinced that the revolution would soon spread to the rest of the world. There was no need for a foreign policy because non-communist states were doomed. This belief encouraged him to make peace with Germany in 1918. Russia lost huge areas of territory under the treaty of Brest-Litovsk. Lenin was not concerned because he thought the settlement would soon be swept aside by a world revolution.

The civil war

The Bolshevik take-over was opposed by many Russians. In May 1918 fighting broke out between the Red Guards and anti-communist forces known as the 'Whites'. This was the start of a vicious civil war. In areas such as the Ukraine, Georgia and Siberia independent White governments were set up. The British, French, Americans and Japanese also sent forces to fight the Bolsheviks. The Bolshevik leader, Leon Trotsky, organised the Red Army very effectively. The Whites were divided among themselves and the foreign armies began to withdraw in 1919. By 1920 the civil war was over and the Bolsheviks had won,

World revolution?

Immediately after the Russian Revolution communists in other countries tried to copy the Russian example. Lenin encouraged this; he thought that without communist revolutions in other countries, revolutionary Russia would be destroyed. In 1919 an organisation known as Comintern (the Communist International) was set up by the Bolsheviks to encourage revolutionaries in other countries. There were many followers of communism in Germany. Communists briefly took power in Hungary but were overthrown in July 1919.

Lenin died in 1924. By this time there was no immediate prospect of a world revolution. Stalin took control of the Soviet Union and Trotsky went into exile in 1927. The new Soviet leader did little to encourage revolution abroad. Instead, he concentrated on transforming the Soviet Union into a powerful industrial country. However, all over the world, governments remained afraid of the spread of communist ideas.

An early Soviet poster celebrating Mayday and calling for workers of the whole world to rise up in revolution. A red flag, with its pole in Russia, encircles the globe. The anticipated world revolution did not occur.

Discussion points

> Why did many Russians want a new government in 1917?

> What part did Lenin play in the revolution?

> How successful were communists at spreading the revolution outside Russia?

Paris 1919

Britain, France and the USA won the First World War. In 1919 their leaders met together in Paris to decide on the future of Europe and the world. These leaders were known as the Big Three.

What were the motives of the Big Three in 1919?

PROBLEMS FOR THE WINNERS

The leaders of the victorious countries faced a number of complex problems:

> Germany had nearly defeated Britain, Russia and France single-handed. How could the winners make sure that Germany could not fight another war in the future?

> Communists had seized power in Russia. Communists wanted to destroy all other capitalist governments by workers' revolution.

> Central and Eastern Europe were in chaos. The royal families of Germany and Austria-Hungary had abdicated before the peace conference.

> The British and the French governments had entered into a number of secret treaties during the war. They had promised Japan special treatment in Asia. Under the Treaty of London of 1915 Italy had agreed to join the allies in return for the promise of gains from Austria-Hungary. Japan and Italy now expected to be given their rewards.

> Nationalists in Eastern Europe had set up new governments even before the war had officially ended. By early November 1918 there were new states in Yugoslavia, Poland and Czechoslovakia.

> The end of the war came more quickly than the allies had expected. The victorious allies had given little thought to the arrangements for the peace. When they did begin discussing the peace it became clear that the winners had very different views about the future.

Woodrow Wilson, US President

David Lloyd George, British Prime Minister

Georges Clemenceau, French Prime Minister

Differences between the Big Three

Perhaps the biggest problem faced at the peace conferences was the fact that the winning countries had very different views about what should happen next. The key players were the so-called Big Three. (The term 'the Big Four' is used when Italy is also included.) The differences between the Allies were hidden while the war was fought. The French and the British did not agree with many of Wilson's views. However, they had been desperate to make sure that the USA supported the war. During the war, they kept quiet in public, for fear that disagreement would limit the American war effort. Once the fighting had stopped the French and the British started to disagree with the Americans.

>> Activity

'Writing the peace treaties was never going to be easy.' Do you agree with this statement? Use the information in the table to support your answer.

A 'just peace' or reparations?

The American President Wilson was a very religious man. His aim was a just peace. He believed that God wanted him to make the world a better place. He disliked his allies in Britain and France. Wilson believed that politics was a simple matter of right and wrong. The European leaders were more concerned about selfish national interest than doing good. Wilson thought that Europeans had caused the war and it was America's mission to stop this happening again. In 1919 Wilson said, 'I do not mean any disrespect to any other great people when I say that America is the hope of the world. And if she does not justify that hope the results are unthinkable.' He thought that the old style of politics could be swept away if a new world organisation was set up called the League of Nations.

Wilson was a great believer in the idea of self-determination. This meant that each nation should have the right to decide for itself how it should be governed. Living far away in America, Wilson did not appreciate how difficult self-determination was in much of Eastern Europe. If Czechs and Germans and Slovaks lived together in an area, who had the right of self-determination? The opposite of self-determination was imperialism: the control of many nations by one powerful empire. The British and the French were imperialists. Their governments were very suspicious of talk of self-determination.

Britain and France wanted reparations from Germany. This was the payment of compensation for the damage caused in the war. Wilson was much less concerned about reparations. Britain and France had built up huge debts to pay for the war; they saw reparations as a way of getting rid of these debts. The USA did not have enormous war debts. Indeed, America was owed much of the money borrowed by Britain and France.

SOURCE A

Anti-German propaganda. An American recruitment poster of 1917 suggests that the German army was extremely brutal and must be stopped. After the war there was an argument about how far Germany should be punished for its actions.

The Fourteen Points

Woodrow Wilson made his own idealistic aims clear a year before the Paris conference. Speaking in January 1918, long before the war ended, President Wilson stated what he wanted as Fourteen Points.

SOURCE B

A summary of the Fourteen Points:

1   There should be no secret deals or treaties between states.

2   Countries should be free to send ships anywhere in the world without interference.

3   There should be free trade between countries.

4   The level of armaments should be reduced in each country.

5   The future of colonies should be reviewed and the wishes of local people taken into consideration.

6   Other countries should leave Russian territory.

7   The Germans should leave Belgium.

8   Alsace and Lorraine should be returned to France.

9   The Italian borders should be adjusted to bring Italian speakers into Italy as far as possible.

10   The different peoples of Austria-Hungary should be given their freedom.

11   Invading armies should leave the Balkan states.

12   Non-Turkish people in the Turkish Empire should be free to have their own governments.

13   An independent Poland should be set up. Poland should have access to the sea.

14   A League of Nations should be set up to preserve the future peace of the world.

>> How can you tell from the Fourteen Points that Wilson believed in the idea of self-determination?

SOURCE C

In January 1918 Wilson explained the thinking behind the Fourteen Points.

One principle runs through the whole program. It is the principle of justice to all peoples and all nationalities, whether they be strong or weak. Without this principle there can be no international justice. For this principle, the people of the United States are ready to devote their lives, their honor, and everything that they possess.

SOURCE D

Wilson knew that he disagreed with the French and the British. As early as 1917 he wrote a private note that said:

England and France have not the same views with respect to peace that we have by any means. When the war is over we can force them to our way of thinking because by that time they will, among other things, be financially in our hands.

SOURCE E

A HOME FROM HOME.

A British Punch *cartoon shows Wilson striding purposefully from America to Europe. His boots are decorated with the numbers 1–14: a reference to Wilson's famous Fourteen Points.*

The response of the European allies

The British and the French leaders did not agree with all the Fourteen Points. The French leader, Clemenceau, asked why Wilson needed as many as 14 when God had made do with only 10 commandments. The Fourteen Points attacked many ideas that the French and British held dear. They were also annoyed at what the Fourteen Points did not say. Wilson said nothing about the future of Germany and ways of making Germany pay reparations for starting the war.

SOURCE G

Lloyd George, Clemenceau and Wilson together in Paris. Clemenceau seems to be affectionately taking Wilson by the arm. In reality Clemenceau greatly distrusted the American President

SOURCE F

When the war was virtually over, on 29 October 1918, Clemenceau met Lloyd George. Now that the fighting had finished they could begin to express their disagreements with Wilson. According to one account, they discussed how far they agreed with the Fourteen Points.

Clemenceau: Have you ever been asked whether you accept the Fourteen Points? I have never been asked.

Lloyd George: I have never been asked either. We cannot accept the second point under any conditions; it means the power of the blockade goes. Germany has been broken almost as much by the blockade as by military methods. If this power is to be handed over to the League of Nations and Great Britain were fighting for her life, no League of Nations would prevent her from defending herself.

>> Activity

Britain and France did not like all of the Fourteen Points. Look at this list of British and French policies:

> They had made secret treaties before and during the war.

> They had powerful navies: the British Navy was the strongest in the world. These forces were sometimes used to stop the free movement of ships at sea.

> Both Britain and France ruled great empires that they wished to keep, regardless of the feelings of the local people.

Look back at Wilson's Fourteen Points. Which particular points do you think the British and the French governments disliked?

Clemenceau and a harsh peace

The French leader at Paris was Georges Clemenceau. His nickname was 'the tiger'. He was aware that most French people wanted revenge for the devastation of the war. The level of destruction was like no previous war and much of the bloodshed and destruction had taken place in France.

France had suffered greatly during the First World War. A quarter of all French men aged 18–27 had been killed. Another 4 million had been wounded. Much of north-eastern France had been devastated. The French government had borrowed huge sums of money to fight the war and was faced with an enormous debt. The French wanted Germany to pay for all these losses. They also wanted revenge for the defeat in the war of 1870–71 and the loss of Alsace-Lorraine.

Ideally the French wanted to break up Germany into a number of small, weak states. Failing this, Clemenceau called for Germany to lose the Rhineland, Saarland, Upper Silesia, Danzig and East Prussia. These areas included much of Germany's coal and heavy industry.

The French leaders disagreed very strongly with the USA over the question of compensation or reparations. The position of the USA was very different to France and Britain. For the two European countries, particularly France, the war had been an economic catastrophe. The USA had not suffered economically during the war and had no demands for substantial reparations.

SOURCE H

'Murderers always return to the scenes of their crime.' A French poster of the time which sums up French fears of further suffering and destruction should the Germans be allowed to attack France again.

SOURCE I

One eye-witness at the peace conference was a famous British economist called John Maynard Keynes. Keynes later wrote a description of the French leader, Clemenceau.

His approach was simple. He believed that Germans could understand nothing except intimidation. Germans have no honour, pride or mercy. You cannot negotiate with a German; you must dictate to him.

Politics was about power. Some lip-service was needed to the 'ideals' of foolish Americans and hypocritical Englishmen. It would be stupid to take too seriously Wilson's ideas about the League of Nations and self-determination.

SOURCE J

Mark well what I am telling you. In six months, in a year, five years, ten years, when they like, as they like, the Germans will invade us again.

We were attacked. We are victorious. We represent right, and might is ours. This might must be used in the service of the right.
Clemenceau, 1919

SOURCE K

André Tardieu, one of the French negotiators at Paris in 1919, was keen to take a hard line towards Germany.

France, like Britain and the United States, needs a zone of safety. Britain and America are naval powers and they create their zone of safety with their fleets and the destruction of the German fleet. France is unprotected by the ocean and must create its zone of safety by the occupation of the Rhineland area. To ask us to give up occupation of the Rhineland is like asking England and the United States to sink their fleets of battleships.

France has a unique experience of Germany. No one has suffered as she has. When dealing with Germany, it is France which must be heard.

Lloyd George and a compromise peace

Lloyd George was the British Prime Minister. He occupied the middle ground between France and the USA. Like Clemenceau he had to listen to public opinion at home. This had been influenced by a press campaign demanding harsh treatment for Germany. He was not personally anxious to punish the Germans severely. He was afraid that if Germany was too weak this would give France too much power in Europe.

The chief concern of Lloyd George was to make sure that the British Empire did not suffer as a result of the settlement. There was an early difference of opinion between Wilson and Lloyd George over the future of the former German colonies. Wilson hated imperialism and he wanted the colonies to be looked after by the new League of Nations until they became independent. Lloyd George wanted them divided up between the winning powers. Lloyd George wanted to make sure that South Africa, Australia and New Zealand were rewarded with nearby German territories. Both Britain and France also wanted a share of the former Turkish lands of the Middle East.

The British government team was suspicious of France. Traditionally, France had been an enemy of Britain. The British did not want a Europe dominated by France, any more than they wanted a German-controlled Europe. This was another reason for making sure that Germany was not too harshly treated. Lloyd George was also worried that a weak Germany would be unable to stop the spread of communism.

SOURCE L

A map illustrating and celebrating the worldwide British Empire. Lloyd George was determined to defend and preserve the empire.

>> **Activity**

Look back at pages 12–17. Explain in your own words:

a what each of the Big Three wanted at the Paris peace talks;

b how far the Big Three disagreed with each other.

The Treaty of Versailles

During the early months of 1919 the Big Three argued in Paris about the peace settlement. In June 1919 they finally agreed about how Germany should be treated. This settlement was called the Treaty of Versailles.

How far did the Big Three get what they wanted?

The League and self-determination

The peace talks began in January 1919. President Wilson wanted the Conference to set up the League of Nations as one of its first tasks. Britain and France agreed. The rules of the League of Nations were drawn up. These rules were known as the League Covenant. The Covenant was included in the Treaty of Versailles and in all the other peace treaties.

Wilson believed very strongly in self-determination for all peoples. Groups from all over the world made their way to Paris to argue that they should be allowed to set up their own nation-states. People ruled over by the French and British Empires demanded independence. The French and the British were unhappy at this. Wilson gave way to pressure from his allies. The idea of self-determination was not applied to the world empires of France and Britain. People such as Irish and Vietnamese nationalists, who had gone to Paris hoping for independence, left disappointed.

The mandates

Britain and France wanted control of German and Turkish colonies. The USA wanted these to be run by the League. Finally, a compromise was accepted. The colonies were divided up among the winning powers, but they agreed to look after these territories on behalf of the League of Nations. These lands were to be known as 'mandates' of the League of Nations. Through the mandates, Britain and France added considerably to their world-wide empires. The German colonies in Africa were divided among Britain, France and South Africa.

SOURCE A

A contemporary painting by William Orpen shows the German delegates signing the Treaty of Versailles. On the opposite side of the table sit Wilson, Lloyd George and Clemenceau, flanked by their assistants.

Then discussions began. Calm and unruffled on most points, bitter and stormy on three of the most important to France: the left bank of the Rhine, the Saar Valley and question of reparations. These three points took up long sittings and led to fierce debates. Mr Lloyd George would arrive at the meeting looking glum and announce, 'They will not sign.' He recommended to his allies a policy of extreme moderation.

André Tardieu, 1921

German loss of territory

In northern Europe new states were set up in Poland, Lithuania, Estonia and Latvia. Germany had annexed the three Baltic states from Russia a year earlier. In keeping with the idea of self-determination these small states now became independent. Clemenceau was particularly keen to ensure that Poland was large and powerful. He hoped that a strong Poland would weaken the future position of Germany. The new Poland took territory from Germany, Russia and Austria-Hungary. Former German land in West Prussia, Posen and part of Upper Silesia was given to Poland.

As a result there was a barrier or corridor of Polish territory that divided most of Germany from the German lands of East Prussia. This Polish Corridor was necessary if Poland was to have access to the sea in line with Wilson's Fourteen Points. The French wanted the largely German-speaking port of Danzig to be given to Poland. Lloyd George disagreed. Instead Danzig was turned into a 'free city'; this meant that it was not part of any state but was controlled by the League of Nations.

Each of the Big Three agreed that Alsace and Lorraine should be returned to France. Wilson had mentioned the return of Alsace-Lorraine in his Fourteen Points. The French also wanted to annex the nearby coal-rich district of the Saarland. Neither Wilson nor Lloyd George was prepared to give the Saarland to France. Instead it was decided that the area should be run by the League of Nations for 15 years, but during this time the French would have control of its coal-mines. Clemenceau had also wanted the large and wealthy Rhineland area of Germany to be permanently divided from the rest of the German state. A separate Rhineland would weaken Germany and form a barrier between Germany and France. The British and the Americans argued that this would be a mistake. The Germans would be so angry that afterwards they would demand revenge. Clemenceau eventually compromised. The Big Three agreed that no German soldiers should be allowed into the Rhineland and that it should be occupied by allied troops for 15 years.

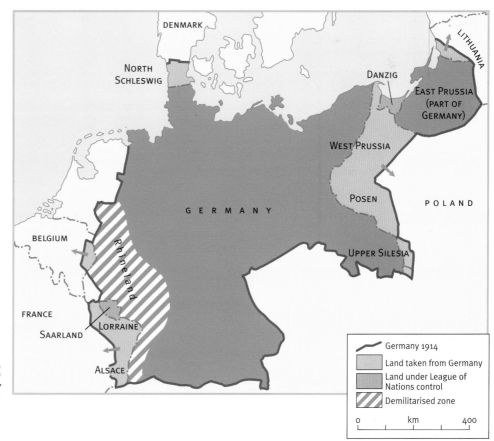

VERSAILLES AND THE TREATMENT OF GERMANY

German losses in Belgium and Denmark

Alsace-Lorraine and the Polish Corridor were the largest losses of German territory. In addition, Germany lost the small districts of Eupen, Moresnet and Malmédy to Belgium. The treaty ordered that there should be a plebiscite or vote in North Schleswig to see whether the local people wanted to stay in Germany or join Denmark. The result of the plebiscite was that North Schleswig became part of Denmark.

The French were successful in arguing that there should be strict limits on the armed forces of Germany. The treaty banned Germany from using tanks and armoured cars. There was to be no German airforce. The German army was limited to a mere 100,000 men. The German navy was to be limited to six battleships and there were to be no German submarines.

War guilt and reparations

The treaty made it clear that Germany was guilty of causing the First World War. This was stated in Clause 231 of the treaty. The idea of war guilt was used to justify the payment of reparations.

SOURCE C

Extracts from the Versailles Treaty:

Clause 231   The Allied governments affirm and Germany accepts the responsibility of Germany and her allies for causing all the loss and damage to which the allied governments and their nationals have been subjected as a consequence of the war imposed upon them by the aggression of Germany and her allies.

Clause 232   The Allied governments require and Germany undertakes that she will make compensation for all damage done to the civilian population of the Allied powers.

While the Americans agreed to go along with French ideas about war guilt, they differed wildly in their view of the right level of compensation. The French wanted Germany to pay an enormous $200 billion in reparations, the British argued for $120 billion and the American view was that the right figure was $22 billion. In the end the conference failed to agree and set up a Reparations Commission to look into the matter of the level of payment after the Treaty was signed.

SOURCE D

The French view of German guilt was reflected in the Allied statement to the German delegation June 1919.

In the view of the Allied Powers the war which began on August 1 1914, was the greatest crime against humanity and the freedom of peoples that any nation calling itself civilised has ever committed. Germany's responsibility is not confined to having planned and started the war. She is no less responsible for the savage and inhuman manner in which it was conducted. The conduct of Germany is almost unexampled in human history. No less than seven million dead lie buried in Europe because Germany saw fit to go to war. There must be Justice for the dead. There must be Justice for the people who now stagger under war debts. There must be Justice for those millions whose homes and lands German savagery has spoiled and destroyed.

SOURCE E

The treaty insisted that Germany should be largely disarmed. Here a German tank is dismantled in order to comply with the treaty.

Why did Wilson accept the treaty?

The American leader was unhappy with much of the treaty. Many British leaders were also concerned that the treaty was too hard on Germany. They went along with it because they thought the problems of the treaty could be sorted out at a later date. Wilson put much faith in the League of Nations. He thought that this organisation would be able to solve any arguments between countries.

SOURCE F

On 14 February 1919 Wilson wrote to his wife expressing his delight that the French and British had agreed to the setting up of the League of Nations.

This is our first real step forward. For I now realise, more than ever before, that once established, the League can arbitrate and correct mistakes which are in the treaty.

THE 14 POINTS AND THE PEACE TREATIES COMPARED

Achieved in full

7   Germany to leave Beligum

8   Alsace-Lorriane to be returned to France

10 Independence for the peoples of Austria– Hungary

13 Independence for Poland

Partially achieved

9   Italian borders to be settled

11 Invading armies to leave Balkans

14 An effective League of Nations to keep the peace

Not achieved

1   A ban on secret treaties between states

2   Free movement of ships anywhere in the world

3   Free trade between countries without import taxes

4   General disarmament

5   Greater independence for colonies

6   Non-interference in Russia

12 Independence for the non-Turkish people of the Turkish Empire.

>> Activity

Look back at what the Big Three wanted to achieve at the Paris peace talks. Read the information in this unit and work out how far Wilson and Clemenceau were successful in getting what they wanted.

The other peace treaties

Tómaš Masaryk, the first President of the Czechoslovak state created from the lands of the former Austria-Hungary.

The Paris peace conference was not simply concerned with Germany. The Big Three also made important decisions about the future of Austria-Hungary, Bulgaria and the Turkish Ottoman Empire. All these states had been on the losing side during the First World War. The plans for these territories were stated in a series of treaties signed between 1919 and 1923. All of the treaties included reference to the League of Nations as the organisation which would solve future problems between states. All of the defeated countries were initially ordered to pay reparations.

SAINT-GERMAIN: THE TREATY WITH AUSTRIA 1919

The peace settlement dealt with the two parts of Austria-Hungary in separate peace treaties. The agreement with Austria was known as the Treaty of St Germain and was signed in September 1919.

Terms of the treaty

Austria lost the South Tyrol and Istria to Italy and huge areas of land to three new states: Czechoslovakia, Poland and Yugoslavia.

The lands given to Czechoslovakia included some of Austria's wealthiest territories and over 3 million German speakers were placed in the new state.

Austria was reduced to a small mountainous country of 6.5 million people. A third of the population lived in the great city of Vienna.

Austria was forbidden from ever seeking unification or 'Anschluss' with Germany.

The Austrian army was limited to 30,000 men.

NEUILLY: THE TREATY WITH BULGARIA 1919

Bulgaria had also fought on the losing side. The Treaty of Neuilly was signed in November 1919.

Terms of the treaty

Land was taken from Bulgaria and given to Greece, Yugoslavia and Romania.

The Bulgarian army was restricted to no more than 20,000 men.

TRIANON: THE TREATY WITH HUNGARY 1920

While the peace talks were taking place, Hungarian communists seized power in Budapest led by Béla Kun. The signing of a peace treaty was delayed until Béla Kun had been overthrown and a right-wing government took over. The new ruler of Hungary, Admiral Horthy, was forced to sign the Treaty of Trianon in March 1920. The idea of self-determination led to the carving up of the old Hungary.

Terms of the treaty

Two thirds of Hungarian territory was given to Czechoslovakia, Yugoslavia and Romania.

The population of Hungary was reduced by these changes from 18 million to 7 million people.

The Hungarian army was limited to 35,000.

SÈVRES: THE TREATY WITH TURKEY 1920

The Ottoman family had ruled over a powerful Turkish Empire for many centuries. The Ottoman Empire had been in decline in the years before the First World War. The Turks fought on the losing side in the war.

Terms of the treaty

Turkey lost nearly all its land in Europe to Greece.

The lands of the Turkish Empire in the Arab Middle East were confiscated: France took charge in Syria and Britain took control in Palestine, Jordan and Iraq.

Turkey was to pay reparations.

LAUSANNE: REVISING THE TURKISH TREATY 1923

Many Turkish people were outraged by the treaty. A general known as Atatürk led a revolution and overthrew the Ottoman family in 1921. Once in power Ataturk used his armies to overturn the Treaty of Sèvres by force. As a result a new agreement, the Treaty of Lausanne, was signed in 1923.

Terms of the treaty

Turkey regained much of the land lost to Greece.

No reparations were to be paid.

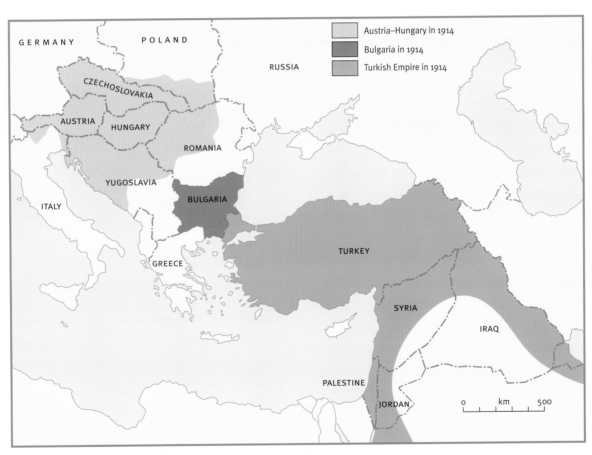

THE DISMEMBERMENT OF AUSTRIA–HUNGARY AND TURKEY

Discussion points

> What evidence is there that the winners tried to punish the losers through these treaties?

> How do you think the people of these countries reacted to news of these treaties?

Aftermath: the immediate

The peace treaties of 1919–23 created a new Europe. As the treaties were carried out, many problems emerged. There was political turmoil across central and Eastern Europe.

What was the immediate impact of the treaties?

The Weimar Republic

Defeat and the peace treaty brought chaos to Germany. In 1919 a new government was set up in the town of Weimar, and it became known as the Weimar Republic. The new government was attacked on all sides. Between 1919 and 1923 there were repeated attempts by both left-wing and right-wing militants to overthrow the new Weimar Republic. In January 1919 communist revolutionaries, called Spartacists, tried to stage a revolution in Berlin. In April communists tried to seize power in Munich. Both of these rebellions were smashed by armed and violent groups of ex-servicemen known as 'Freikorps' (Free Corps). In 1920 a Freikorps force attempted to seize Berlin. The army sympathised with the Freikorps and refused to fight them. This attempt at a right-wing revolution was eventually stopped by a strike by left-wing workers.

Attempts to pay the reparations bill after 1921 added to Germany's economic problems and helped to cause a huge level of inflation. At the same time a new political crisis created economic problems. The French invaded the Ruhr area in January 1923, on the grounds that the Germans were not paying their reparations. This was the centre of German industry. Germans responded with strikes – but this had the effect of doing more damage to Germany than to France.

The economic situation went out of control in 1923; inflation made banknotes virtually worthless. This was known as hyper-inflation. Pensioners lost their life savings. On 20 November 1923 one American dollar was worth 4 billion German marks.

SOURCE A

Hyper-inflation in Germany, 1923. A child plays with huge, worthless bundles of banknotes.

Another right-wing attempt to seize power was launched in November 1923. The leader of this rebellion was a militant nationalist called Adolf Hitler. The rebellion ended in fiasco in Munich after a few of Hitler's followers had been shot. Hitler was dealt with leniently and was imprisoned for a short time. By this time the economy of Germany had begun to recover and it seemed that stability was beginning to return to the country.

>> Activity

Describe in your own words how the Treaty of Versailles led to chaos in Germany.

consequences
of the treaties

TROUBLE IN EASTERN EUROPE
Anger in Hungary

The peace treaties created great bitterness and instability in Hungary. As in Germany, left-wing and right-wing militants tried to seize power. In 1919 the communist Béla Kun briefly set up a Soviet-style government. He was overthrown and Admiral Horthy, a right wing military dictator, came to power. He remained in charge until the Second World War. Under Horthy there was no democracy in Hungary.

Hungarians were horrified by the terms of the Trianon Treaty. Before the First World War Hungarians had controlled a huge, multi-national empire in Eastern Europe. In 1920 Hungary lost two-thirds of its pre-war territory. The lost land was given to Romania, Yugoslavia and Czechoslovakia. In each of these countries there was a Hungarian minority. After 1920 Hungarian foreign policy was completely dominated by a wish to 'get back' the lost lands. As a result, Romania, Czechoslovakia and Yugoslavia felt threatened. The governments of these three countries formed an alliance in order to protect themselves from the threat of a Hungarian invasion. This became known as the Little Entente.

Ethnic tension in Czechoslovakia

Czechoslovakia was the only new state in Eastern Europe that allowed free speech and democracy. There was great tension between different ethnic groups. The Czechs of the western part of the country were wealthier than the Slovaks of the east. Slovaks complained that they were treated as second-class citizens. Only 65 per cent of the population were Czechs or Slovaks. There were over 3 million Germans, known as the Sudeten Germans, and in many border areas the Germans were in a majority. Like the Slovaks, some Sudeten Germans said that they were not treated fairly by the Czechs.

War and revolution in Poland

Poland, with 30 million people, was by far the largest of the states set up by the treaties. The new Polish state was immediately involved in a series of brief wars with most of its neighbours. The Poles were not content with the borders set up in the peace treaties. Between 1918 and 1921 Poland fought against Germany, Czechoslovakia, Lithuania and the Soviet Union. These wars showed how difficult it was to impose the terms of the peace treaties. In 1920 the Poles defied the treaties and took control of the Lithuanian city of Vilna. By 1921 Poland had conquered a huge area of Belarus and Ukraine from the Soviet Union.

Polish politics were chaotic in the early 1920s. It seemed impossible to form a stable government and the country was close to civil war. The chaos came to an end in May 1926 when Marshal Pilsudski seized power and ended democracy in Poland.

>> Activity

How successful were the treaties in the new states of Hungary, Czechoslovakia and Poland? Describe in your own words the consequences of the peace treaties in each of these countries.

A harsh treaty?

The Germans were horrified at what they saw as the harshness of the peace treaty. They had hoped for milder terms in line with the Fourteen Points. There has been a lively argument since 1919 about the fairness of the Treaty of Versailles.

Was the Treaty of Versailles fair?

Germans had difficulty coming to terms with defeat. They had been proud of their army and were surprised and upset when Germany was defeated. Some said that people inside Germany – Jews, socialists and communists – had deliberately organised the surrender. They talked about the 'stab in the back'. The politicians who signed the armistice were called the 'November criminals'. Those Germans who felt that their country had been betrayed were appalled by the treaty. The section of the Versailles Treaty that most angered people in Germany was Clause 231 describing German 'war guilt'. They felt that it was wrong to put the entire blame for the war on their country. The payment of reparations was also deeply resented.

The Big Three had not allowed Germany to negotiate the treaty. The Germans were simply given the treaty and forced to sign it. This lack of discussion and consultation angered Germans who called it a 'diktat': a dictated peace.

The loss of German land was a severe blow. The fact that East Prussia was now separated by the Polish Corridor seemed unfair. Germans also resented bitterly the loss of their colonies in Africa.

SOURCE A

Count Brockdorff, the leader of the German delegation at Paris, set the tone for the national response to the treaty on 7 May 1919.

We are told that we should acknowledge that we alone are guilty of having caused the war. I would be a liar if I agreed to this. We are not trying to avoid all responsibility for this World War. However, we emphatically deny that the German people should be seen as the only guilty party. Over fifty years the imperialism of all European states has poisoned the international situation.

SOURCE B

Adolf Hitler was an obscure German corporal at the end of the war. In 1925 he expressed a common German view of the Treaty.

What I would like to do with the Treaty of Versailles! Each one of the points of that treaty is branded in the minds and hearts of the German people and sixty million men and women find their souls aflame with a feeling of rage and shame. A torrent of fire bursts forth as from a furnace, and a will of steel is forged from it, with the common cry – 'We will have weapons again!'

SOURCE C

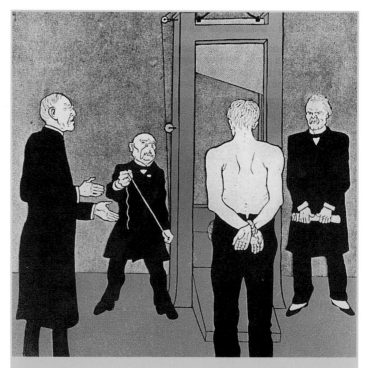

A German cartoonist sums up the common German view of the treaty. Wilson and Lloyd George look on as Clemenceau prepares to guillotine a figure representing Germany.

Conflicting interpretations

Some of the people on the winning side also thought that Versailles was quite wrong. One non-German critic of the Versailles Treaty was John Maynard Keynes. He had been a British official at Paris and later he became a very famous economist. Keynes left the Conference early, disgusted at the treatment of Germany. In 1920 he wrote a famous attack on the Treaty of Versailles. His book, *The Economic Consequences of the Peace*, was widely read. Many people in Britain, the USA and Germany agreed with Keynes.

SOURCE D

PEACE AND FUTURE CANNON FODDER

THE TIGER: "Curious! I seem to hear a child weeping!"

SOURCE E

John Maynard Keynes writing in 1920:

In my own opinion, it is not possible to lay the entire responsibility for the war on any single nation. By aiming at the destruction of the economic life of Germany this treaty threatens the health and prosperity of the Allies themselves. By making impossible demands it leaves Europe more unsettled than it found it.

Between 1920 and 1939 many writers and politicians in Britain and the USA agreed with the view of Keynes. As a result politicians, particularly in the British government, were ready to make concessions to Germany to try to improve on a flawed treaty. Since 1950 most historians have disagreed with Keynes and have taken a more sympathetic view of the treaty.

SOURCE F

A modern historian, Sally Marks, summed up her view of the Versailles Treaty in 1976.

The Versailles Treaty was severe, but it is amazing that it was not more so. Thanks to Wilson's insistence, Germany lost remarkably little territory, considering how thoroughly she had lost the war. True the colonies were gone, but the European losses were relatively modest. The real difficulty was not that the Treaty was exceptionally severe but that the Germans thought it was, and in time persuaded others that it was.

A cartoon produced in 1919 by the British artist, Will Dyson, predicts that the treaty was flawed and would lead to another world war. As the leaders of France, the USA, Italy and Britain leave the peace conference they notice a small child crying because he will have to fight in a future war. Prophetically, the cartoonist suggests that the next war might happen in 1940.

WAS THE TREATY OF VERSAILLES FAIR?

>> Activity

Keynes thought the treaty was unfair. Marks thought that it was fair.

1 Look at the points in the table. Work out which points fit in with the argument of Keynes and which ones fit in with the more recent view of Sally Marks.

2 Using these points and your wider knowledge explain whether you think that the Treaty of Versailles was unfair.

Clemenceau, Wilson and Lloyd George at the peace conference.
> *Was their treatment of Germany fair?*

ASSESSING THE TERMS OF THE TREATY

> It was wrong to put the sole blame for the war on Germany. Other countries had been aggressive in the years leading up to 1914. One of the causes of the war was imperialism; many countries, including Britain and France, had tried to build up world empires.

> The settlement removed only limited amounts of land from Germany. In places like Alsace-Lorraine and the Polish Corridor most people were not German-speakers and saw themselves as French or Polish.

> The treaty was unfair because it punished the people of Germany instead of the rulers of Germany. Reparations hurt ordinary Germans who were not guilty.

> German statements about the Fourteen Points were hypocritical. When Wilson described them in a speech in January 1918 the Germans made no reply. They only took the Fourteen Points seriously much later in the year when they had been beaten and were looking for the best possible terms. When Wilson was talking about the need for a just peace the Germans were busy defeating the Russians and imposing a brutal peace treaty on them. When they were winning, the Germans ignored fairness; when they were losing they demanded it.

> Germany was tricked because her government had been offered justice and fairness by Wilson when he made his speech about the Fourteen Points. When the Germans stopped fighting they expected to be dealt with under Wilson's terms. There was nothing about war guilt and reparations in the Fourteen Points.

> The treaty aimed to destroy the economy of Germany. This was a mistake that would do no-one any good. People throughout Europe would lose out if there were no successful German factories and businesses.

> The basic strength of the German economy was not destroyed by the Treaty of Versailles. Germany soon recovered its position as the most successful economy in Europe. In 1925 Germany was producing twice as much steel as Britain.

> The German Army was reduced in size but the leaders of the German Army were not removed. The army remained a powerful force in German society. The generals were ready and able to re-build German armed forces when the time was right.

The peace treaties of 1919–23

THE BIG THREE

The winners gathered in Paris in 1919 to decide on the future of Europe. The leaders of the victorious countries each had different objectives:

> **Woodrow Wilson, the US President,** wanted a fair peace. During the war he had called for a fair settlement in his famous Fourteen Points speech (January 1918). The USA had suffered much less than its allies in loss of life and economic damage. He accepted that Germany must be punished but he did not want this to be too harsh. He believed in self-determination – that every nation should have its own government.

> **Clemenceau, the French Premier,** called for harsh treatment of Germany. Much of the war had been fought in France and the level of damage was enormous. His aim was to weaken Germany so much that it would never again try to dominate Europe.

> **Lloyd George, the British Prime Minister,** wanted a middle ground between the French and American positions. He was more interested in the British Empire than events in Europe.

THE TREATY OF VERSAILLES 1919

This dealt with the future of Germany.

Germany was forced to disarm. The army was limited to 100,000. Tanks were banned and the navy was limited to six warships. German troops were banned from the Rhineland area, bordering France.

The territory of Germany was reduced. Alsace-Lorraine was returned to France. Poland gained West Prussia, Posen and part of Upper Silesia; Danzig was to be controlled by the League of Nations. A 'corridor' of Polish territory separated East Prussia from the rest of Germany. Small territories were given to Belgium, Denmark and Lithuania. The coal-rich Saarland was put under League of Nations control for 15 years and the coal mines were handed over to France for this period. Germany was forbidden from ever uniting with Austria. German colonies were confiscated.

Germany was ordered to pay huge compensation or 'reparations' to the winning powers. These payments were justified on the grounds that Germany was guilty of starting the war. A war guilt clause was included in this treaty.

THE OTHER PEACE TREATIES

Other treaties signed at the end of the First World War

> The Treaty of St Germain 1919 with Austria

> The Treaty of Neuilly 1919 with Bulgaria

> The Treaty of Trianon 1920 with Hungary

> The Treaty of Sèvres 1920 with Turkey. This was revised in 1923 and replaced by the Treaty of Lausanne.

Setting up the League of Nations

After the First World War a new organisation called the League of Nations was set up to solve arguments between countries in a peaceful way. The League was not a success and did not bring peace to the world.

Why was the League unable to ensure world peace?

The organisation of the League

The setting up of the League of Nations was written into the Treaty of Versailles and all the other treaties that were signed at the end of the war. The rules of the League, known as the League Covenant, formed part of each peace treaty. The League officially began its work in January 1920 when the Treaty of Versailles came into effect. Geneva was chosen for the League headquarters because it was in Switzerland, which had a long tradition of neutrality. Some officials worked permanently for the League in Geneva. They were known as the Secretariat.

The League set up a number of commissions and committees to deal with particular issues and problems. The most important commissions were those which dealt with disarmament and the running of the 'mandates' (the former German and Turkish colonies). The committees included the Health Organisation which campaigned to improve the health of people, particularly in poorer countries, and the International Labour Organisation which tried to improve conditions for working people.

The peace treaties not only set up the League but also established a group called the conference of ambassadors. The conference was supposed to have oversight of the way the peace treaties were put into effect. There was some uncertainty about which issues should be decided by the League and which should be sorted out by the conference of ambassadors.

All member states sent representatives to the League Assembly. This body met at least once a year. The League Assembly had no real power. Power in the League lay with a much smaller body known as the League Council. This was dominated by a few rich countries who were permanent members of the Council: Britain, France, Italy and Japan. In theory, decisions by the Council would be carried out by all member-states. Council decisions had to be unanimous: that is, all Council members had to agree. This rule made it difficult for the Council to take action if there was any disagreement among its members.

A European club?

Many non-Europeans were very unhappy with the way the Covenant gave power to the European countries of Britain, France and Italy. At the first meeting of the Assembly, non-Europeans criticised the rules of the League. The representatives from Argentina were particularly critical. They argued for a democratic League, with the Council elected by all the countries of the Assembly. These ideas were rejected and the Argentine delegation walked out.

Some non-European countries were worried that the League would be dominated by white people. The Japanese asked that the League should promise to oppose racial discrimination. The Americans and the British rejected this proposal. The Covenant took a very patronising view of people living in colonies. It considered that more 'civilised' states should have the job of looking after those 'peoples not yet able to stand by themselves under the strenuous conditions of the modern world'.

SOURCE A

Newton Rowell of Canada spoke at the first League Assembly in 1920 and was unhappy at the way some European countries had so much power on the League Council.

You may say that we should have confidence in the European statesmen and leaders. Perhaps we should, but it was European statesmanship, European ambition that drowned the world with blood and for which we are still suffering and will suffer for generations.

America says 'no' to the League

At first it was envisaged that the USA would be a member of the Council, but in the end America failed to join the League. Woodrow Wilson was a Democrat. The majority in the US Senate belonged to another party – the Republicans – and many of them disliked Wilson. There was a strong tradition of 'isolationism' in the USA: a belief that America should not get involved in international politics. Wilson was very stubborn and he failed to compromise or to persuade his opponents to support the League. In March 1920 the US Senate stopped the USA from joining the League. The absence of the USA greatly weakened the authority of the new League of Nations.

>> Activity

1 Explain the role of the following bodies within the League of Nations:

   a the Secretariat

   b the Assembly

   c the Council

   d Commissions and Mandates

2 Why were some non-European countries unhappy at the way the League of Nations was set up?

3 Why do you think the American decision not to join the League was a big blow to the organisation?

SOURCE B

THIS LEAGUE OF NATIONS BRIDGE WAS DESIGNED BY THE PRESIDENT OF THE U·S·A·

BELGIUM-FRANCE

ENGLAND-ITALY

KEYSTONE USA

THE GAP IN THE BRIDGE.

A British *Punch* cartoon comments on the American refusal to participate in the League of Nations.

> How does the cartoonist suggest that American absence was a great blow to the structure of the League?

Absent friends?

Forty-five states were founder-members of the League of Nations. These were all either victorious or neutral in the First World War. The defeated nations were not allowed to join immediately. As a result Germany, Austria and Hungary saw the League as a club for their enemies. The founders were frightened of the spread of communism, and the new Soviet Union was also not invited to join. Lacking American, German and Russian membership, the League could not really claim to be the voice of world opinion.

Tension between Britain and France

In the absence of other powerful countries, the League was dominated by Britain and France. These two countries had different views of how the League should work. The French wanted to make the League into a military alliance, with strict obligations on members to support each other. This was a result of the French obsession with the dangers of an attack on France by Germany. The British saw the League as a much looser, less formal organisation. The British resisted French demands for a stronger League. The British were finding it difficult to defend their own empire and had no wish to get involved unnecessarily in military conflicts anywhere else in the world.

SOURCE C

The British were very suspicious of the French. In 1919 George Saunders, a British official, criticised the French.

At the back of all this is the French scheme to suck Germany and everybody else dry and to establish French military and political control of the League of Nations. The French see the League of Nations as an organisation for the restoration of France to a supreme position in Europe and her maintenance in that position.

SOURCE D

In 1920 Marcel Cachin, a French politician, commented on the League without the USA.

The defeat suffered by Wilsonism in the United States strikes at the very existence of the League of Nations. America's place will remain empty at Geneva, and the two countries that dominate, France and Great Britain, are divided on almost every one of the topics to be discussed.

SOURCE E

A Soviet poster celebrating the work of the Communist International. This organisation was set up by Lenin to encourage world revolution. Fear of communism led to the exclusion of the Soviet Union from the League.

The French turn to direct action

By 1923 the French were unhappy at the League's inability to ensure Germany kept to the terms of the Treaty of Versailles. They were determined to make Germany pay reparations. The Reparations Commission announced in 1921 that Germany should pay £6,600 million over 42 years. The Germans, however, made only a small payment in 1922 and then stopped paying. The French were angry and took matters into their own hands.

The occupation of the Ruhr

On 11 January 1923 French and Belgian soldiers invaded the German industrial area of the Ruhr. This area was the heartland of the German economy. The occupation of the Ruhr did not work out well for France. The British and the Americans disapproved of the use of force. The people of the Ruhr refused to co-operate with the invaders and went on strike. Within a few months the French had to admit that direct action had not worked.

SOURCE F

French soldiers occupying the Ruhr set up a machine gun position in the centre of Frankfurt.

Collective security

Although the USA did not join the League, the ideas of Woodrow Wilson were central to its work. Wilson said that the League would provide 'collective security'. This meant that if a member state of the League was attacked, all other countries of the League would act together to stop the aggression. Collective security could make use of four possible weapons:

Discussion points

In practice collective security did not work very well in the 1920s and collapsed completely in the 1930s. Why do you think collective security often failed in reality?

1 The pressure of world public opinion

2 The use of trade sanctions

TRADE EMBARGO

3 Reducing the armaments of all countries to a minimum level

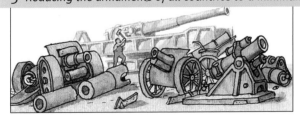

4 The use of force

World public opinion

Wilson believed in the power of public opinion. He felt that if ordinary people were allowed to speak out politicians would never go to war. Wilson claimed that if the League of Nations had existed in 1914 politicians would not have dared to start the First World War.

Looking back, the ideas of Wilson seem very naive. His talk of the power of world public opinion was based on a number of mistakes:

> In democracies like the USA people felt free to disagree with their government and could express a public opinion. Many other countries were not democratic and in these countries there was no such thing as a voice of public opinion.

> There was no evidence that ordinary people preferred peace and justice to war and injustice. Aggressive governments often had widespread support among the public.

> World public opinion did not always speak with one clear voice. What people wanted in France, for example, at the end of the war was very different from what most Americans wanted.

> Democratic government had to pay attention to public opinion in their country. Powerful undemocratic governments could ignore public opinion at home and abroad.

SOURCE G

Men and women employed in a munitions factory during the First World War. The League was committed to ensuring that nations would not need to make weapons of mass destruction.

Disarmament

The League was committed to disarmament: getting rid of weapons. Woodrow Wilson saw the arms race before 1914 as one of the causes of the First World War. The Covenant said that all members of the League should disarm.

SOURCE H

The Covenant of the League of Nations committed all members to disarmament.

Article 8 The members of the League recognize that the maintenance of peace requires the reduction of national armaments to the lowest point consistent with national safety and the enforcement by common action of international obligations.

The problem with this talk of disarmament was that it was so vague. The Covenant said that countries could keep a minimum level of arms needed for self-defence: it was not at all clear what this level was. A Disarmament Commission was set up to persuade countries to get rid of their weapons. The Commission had no way of forcing countries to disarm or checking that they had disarmed.

The use of sanctions and force

Perhaps the most important part of the Covenant were those articles that stated how the League would respond to future aggression. These ideas were found in Articles 11 and 16 of the Covenant: Article 11 said that the League of Nations would take action to stop war; Article 16 said that an attack on one member state would be seen as an attack on all League members. The League Council would decide on the appropriate punishment to use against the offending state.

The League had no army of its own. Instead, the idea was that all countries could act to help any other country if it was attacked. This turned out to be completely unrealistic. Every member state would first of all stop trade with an an aggressive country, and if this failed every country would supply soldiers for a joint war against the aggressive country. This assumed that goverments would be remarkably generous and would risk the money and lives of their own people in order to sort out a quarrel between two other countries. The threat of trade sanctions was weakened by the absence of the USA from the League. Members of the League knew that if they stopped trading, the USA could simply fill the gap.

SOURCE I

The full Assembly of the League in session, Geneva 1923.
> *How far could the League enforce its decisions?*

The Geneva Protocol

From the beginning, people were aware that the League was weak. The French, terrified as they were by the idea of a strong Germany, tried to give real military power to the League. However, Britain blocked moves in the early 1920s to improve the arrangements for the use of force. In 1923 a 'draft treaty of mutual assistance' was discussed. This was meant to make the threat of force more practical by saying that the League would only ask members to send troops to nearby conflicts. In 1924 a document called the Geneva Protocol was discussed. The Protocol set out clear rules for the peaceful arbitration of disputes. If countries did not follow these rules the League was entitled to use trade sanctions and force. The British government was not keen to get involved in other peoples' arguments. Britain was able to throw out the draft treaty. The British leader, Ramsay MacDonald, initially supported the Geneva Protocol. He fell from power in 1924 and the new government rejected the Protocol. Attempts to strengthen the military power of the League had come to nothing.

>> Activity

Use information from this unit to explain why collective security was unlikely to be successful.

Critics of the League

Focus

People in many countries disapproved of the League of Nations. Look at the following sources from four countries. What different criticisms did these people have of the League?

SOURCE J

An American called Lewis P. Showalter wrote an attack on the idea of the League in 1919. Showalter was an isolationist. The isolationists were successful in keeping the USA out of the League in 1920.

If there were twenty nations in the League we could control one-twentieth of our own affairs. If the Japanese would choose to send Japanese workmen over here to crowd out our workmen from our factories, mills etc., we could not say no. If the Japanese choose to come over here, seize upon our farms and homes, or take them by taxation, you could not say no, as you had signed your death warrant when you went into the League.

SOURCE K

An early Soviet view of the League as a club for fat Western capitalists. The slogan on the flag says 'Capitalists of the world unite'.

SOURCE L

William Hughes, the Australian Prime Minister, attacked proposals for the League in 1918.

I object altogether to President Wilson's scheme of a League of Nations. Where does it end? I don't know. He wants some sort of world-state, in fact a Utopia, in which all the nations would have to surrender some of their self-governing rights. There is to be an international police and there is to be a navy and an army, and so on, for this purpose. But it will not bear examination for ten minutes. It is a very obvious thing that no country will allow for a moment its vital interests to be decided by anyone but itself. Those who shout loudest for international arbitration will stand most rigidly on their own rights when a vital right is threatened. Let us ask ourselves if Great Britain would agree to interference by any council of nations as regards the size of her navy. Certainly not!

SOURCE M

Adolf Hitler speaking in 1928 expressed a common German view of the League:

Our people must be delivered from the hopeless confusion of international convictions and educated consciously and systematically to fanatical Nationalism. Belief in reconciliation, understanding, world peace, the League of Nations and international solidarity – we destroy these ideas. There is only one right in the world and that right is one's own strength.

The achievements of the League

The commissions and committees of the League did some good work. Refugees from conflicts were given vital help. A famous Norwegian explorer, Fridjof Nansen, worked for the League on the problems of prisoners of war stranded in Russia and he helped half a million men to return safely home. The International Labour Organisation (ILO) was led by an energetic and effective French man called Albert Thomas. Under his guidance the ILO encouraged many countries to improve working conditions for ordinary workers. The ILO is still in existence today and continues to campaign for workers' rights. The Health Organisation organised work on health matters, particularly in poorer countries. It worked successfully to reduce the number of cases of leprosy. Like the ILO the Health Organisation continues its work today as part of the United Nations Organisation (today it is known as the World Health Organisation).

SOURCE N

Prisoners at the end of the First World War. The League did valuable work helping such men to return home.

THE LEAGUE IN ACTION

> In 1920 the League dealt successfully with a dispute between Sweden and Finland. Both countries claimed control of the Åland Islands. The League decided that the islands should be given to Finland and this decision was accepted by Sweden.

> Throughout the 1920s the League administered the Saarland area of Germany and the Baltic city of Danzig with great fairness.

> The League was unable to find a solution to an argument between Poland and Lithuania over the town of Vilna. Poland had seized the town in 1920 in defiance of the peace treaties and the League was unable to persuade Poland to leave.

> In 1922 the League successfully organised a rescue plan for the Austrian economy.

> In 1923 Italy invaded the Greek island of Corfu. The League could not agree on what action to take. France did not want to annoy the Italian government and blocked firm League action. A settlement was eventually reached between Greece and Italy but the League took no part in negotiating this deal.

> Greece and Bulgaria came close to all-out war in 1925. The League took prompt action and ruled that Greece was at fault. Both sides stopped fighting and Greece agreed to pay compensation.

>> Activity

The League was not a complete failure. In the 1920s it had a mixture of success and failure. It had some sucess in dealing with disputes between smaller countries. Look at the table: The League in action. What evidence is there of a mixture of success and failure?

Reparations: the Dawes and the Young Plans

In early 1923, France had invaded the Ruhr area to make Germany pay reparations. Sending soldiers into the Ruhr solved nothing. The use of force did not make the Germans pay up. In November 1923 France was forced to agree to take part in a review of the reparations organised by an American banker, Charles Dawes. The Dawes Plan was agreed in April 1924.

THE TERMS OF THE DAWES PLAN

> There was to be a 2 year freeze on the payment of reparations.

> The level of German payments was scaled down.

> The USA offered huge loans to Germany.

> The French agreed to get their forces out of the Ruhr.

The consequences of the Dawes Plan

During the following five years the Germans paid a reparations bill of about $1 billion, and received American loans of about $2 billion. Germany did well out of the Dawes Plan. Much of the money from the American loans was spent on building new German factories. The French had wanted reparations in order to make Germany weak. The Dawes Plan helped Germany to become even stronger. As a result of the occupation of the Ruhr the Treaty of Versailles had been significantly altered in Germany's favour.

The Young Plan: 1929

The German government continued to complain at the level of reparations. The question of reparations was reviewed in 1929 by a committee led by an American called Owen Young. The committee produced the Young Plan. This considerably reduced the amount of reparations. The Young Plan was a considerable achievement for the German Foreign Minister, Stresemann. However, it did not bring peace and harmony to Germany. Extreme nationalists objected to the payment of any reparations and bitterly denounced the Young Plan.

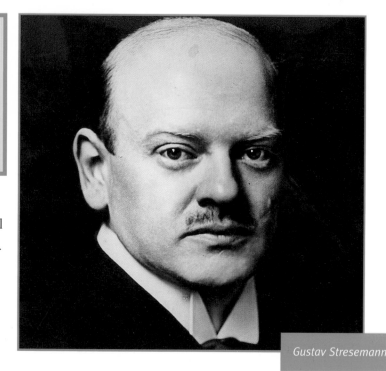

Gustav Stresemann.

After 1929 the Great Depression led to a great rise in unemployment in Germany and reparations effectively came to an end. In 1932 the participants in the Young Plan met to agree a conclusion to the sorry story of reparations. After a three-year freeze Germany was supposed to make a final payment. This payment was never made.

Discussion points

> How successful were French attempts to make Germany pay reparations?

> What was agreed in the Dawes and Young Plans? Who gained from these Plans?

> Why did the payment of reparations finally end?

The spirit of Locarno

In the 1920s there was much discussion and debate among the most powerful countries of the world. A number of international treaties were signed.

Did the agreements of the 1920s make the world a safer place?

Discussions in Washington 1921–2

The USA had refused to support the League of Nations. America ignored the League and organised conferences of its own in Washington in 1921 and 1922. The conferences concentrated on trying to limit tension in the Pacific Ocean between Japan and the USA. This was precisely the sort of dispute that the League was intended to sort out. The Washington Conferences showed the world the limits of the authority of the League. The Washington Treaty was signed in February 1922. The USA and Britain agreed to have navies of equal size. The Japanese navy was limited to three fifths of the size of each of the American and the British navies. The proportions of the navies were, therefore, set at 5:5:3.

SOURCE A

An American warship in the early 1920s. To comply with the Washington Treaty of 1922 the United States had to scuttle 30 warships, Britain destroyed 19 and Japan 17. France and Italy also agreed to limit the size of their navies. The League had no involvement in the Washington conferences.

The outcasts club together: Rapallo 1922

The British Prime Minister, Lloyd George, organised an international conference in Genoa in 1922. He wanted to find a solution to the argument between Germany and France over the payment of reparations and the level of German disarmament. The conference was a disastrous failure: the Americans refused to attend and the French and the Germans continued to disagree about reparations and disarmament.

Germany and Soviet Russia had not been invited to join the League of Nations. While the main conference was taking place at Genoa, the German delegation had discussions with the Soviets at the nearby town of Rapallo. A treaty was signed on 16 April between Germany and the Soviets. It became known as the Treaty of Rapallo. The two governments agreed to establish friendly relations, and secretly agreed to co-operate on military planning. News of the treaty and rumours of the secret military deal shocked the French government. The deal between Germany and the Soviet Union enabled Germany to get hold of most of the weapons banned under the Treaty of Versailles. As a result, the Treaty of Rapallo was a blow to the authority of the League of Nations.

>> Activity

1 Explain in your own words what was agreed in the Treaty of Rapallo and the Treaty of Washington.

2 For each treaty explain whether you think it made the League of Nations more or less powerful.

Locarno: 1925

After the failure of the occupation of the Ruhr, France looked for compromise with Germany. This search for compromise continued in 1925 when a major conference took place at Locarno, Switzerland. The key players at Locarno were the Foreign Ministers of France, Britain and Germany: Aristide Briand, Austen Chamberlain and Gustav Stresemann. The talks produced treaties that were greeted with wild enthusiasm. Many people saw Locarno as an end to the bitterness of the war and the start of a new period of peace in Europe. The three leaders won the Nobel Peace Prize for their work at Locarno.

SOURCE C

A German newspaper described the scenes at Locarno.

When the delegates arrived in their cars they passed through dense crowds. When the document had been signed, the Belgian, Rollin, went to the window, opened it and held the pact aloft. Loud cheers and prolonged applause arose from the street. Then came the speeches of Stresemann, Briand, Chamberlain, and finally, Mussolini. Soon afterwards the delegates left the building. The crowd shouted its approval, especially at the German delegates. Chamberlain, sitting in his car held a copy of the pact in his hand and received the cheers of the crowd.

Berliner Tageblatt, 1925

SOURCE B

The signing of the main Locarno Treaty, 1925. Stresemann can be seen signing on behalf of Germany. Despite the enthusiasm of people at the time, Locarno did not bring permanent peace to Europe.

THE TERMS OF THE LOCARNO TREATIES

> Under the main Locarno treaty Germany, France and Belgium agreed to accept their existing borders with each other as set up by the Versailles Treaty.

> Britain and Italy agreed to 'guarantee' the main agreement; this meant that Britain and Italy promised to take action if any of the three countries attacked each other.

> The main agreement and the guarantee did not apply to the eastern borders of Germany as laid down by the Versailles Treaty.

> Germany agreed to join the League of Nations.

> In separate treaties signed at Locarno, France promised to defend Belgium, Poland and Czechoslovakia if any of these countries was attacked by Germany.

In September 1926 the German delegates took their place at the League's Assembly Hall in Geneva. People saw this as a very historic and hopeful moment. They felt that the scars of the First World War were beginning to heal. The French leader, Briand, gave the Germans an enthusiatic welcome in his speech to the Assembly, saying, 'Away with rifles, machine guns and cannon! Make way for arbitration, conciliation and peace!' Locarno was seen as a symbol of a new period of peace and stability. Some talked enthusiastically about the 'spirit of Locarno'.

A minority of people were much more suspicious of the Locarno settlement. Behind his back, civil servants at the British Foreign Office made up a rhyme that expressed their view of the British Foreign Secretary:

'Good Sir Austen at Locarno,
Fell into a heap of guano.'

SOURCE D

Recent interpretations of Locarno have also been critical.

The League of Nations' commitment to collective security was devalued by Locarno. For, if collective security was in fact reliable, Locarno was unnecessary. If Locarno was necessary, the League of Nations was, by definition, inadequate to ensure the security of even its principal founding members. Locarno, hailed in 1925 as turning the corner towards permanent peace, in fact marked the beginning of the end of the Versailles international order.

H. Kissinger, 1994

>> Activity

Look at the following information about the effect of the Locarno settlement on Germany and France. Explain in your own words whether you think the Locarno treaties made the world a safer place.

LOCARNO: THE IMPACT ON GERMANY

> The main Locarno agreement said nothing about German frontiers in the east, and this encouraged German hopes to overturn this part of the 1919 settlement. Poland and Czechoslovakia were not allowed to take part in the main discussions and their representatives were invited to join only at the end in order to be told what the larger powers had decided.

> Each state saw the treaty differently. For Germany Locarno was the beginning of change to the Versailles Treaty.

> The Locarno settlement was a great triumph for the German Foreign Minister, Stresemann. After Locarno large amounts of American money were invested in Germany and this helped the Germans to improve their factories. Stresemann was not content with Locarno. He continued to ask for further concessions.

SOURCE E

Stresemann, the German Foreign Minister, expressed his real motives in a confidential letter written shortly before Locarno in September 1925.

In my view the foreign policy of Germany has for the short-term future three main objectives: First, a solution to the Rhine question favourable to Germany, and peace, without which Germany will not be able to regain its strength. Second, protection for the ten to twelve million Germans living under the foreign yoke. Third, the alteration of our eastern frontiers, so that we recover Danzig and the Polish Corridor. In the more distant future the reuniting of Austria with Germany.

French attitudes after Locarno

LOCARNO: THE IMPACT ON FRANCE

> The power of France to intervene in Germany was weakened by Locarno. The section forbidding invasion stopped France from repeating the 1923 occupation of the Ruhr.

> The French leaders continued to feel threatened and insecure after Locarno. They knew that sooner or later Allied troops would have to leave the Rhineland and that this would strengthen the German threat. This feeling of insecurity was expressed in the decision in 1927 to build the Maginot Line. Between 1929 and 1939 the French government spent a vast amount of money on the building of a huge line of fortifications along the border with Germany. This was the brainchild of a politician called André Maginot, and it was named after him.

SOURCE F

French pessimism was reflected in the building of the Maginot Line. It is also clear from this statement from a former French Prime Minister.

History eternally repeats itself. We have not finished with Germany. Any understanding with her is impossible, and England, whether she likes it or not, will be compelled to march with us at the moment of danger in order to defend herself.

Georges Clemenceau, 1928

SOURCE H

A French army recruitment poster shows troops stationed on the Maginot Line. The building of the Line was evidence of French insecurity.

SOURCE G

A modern historian has summed up French fears after Locarno.

The French position remained as brittle as ever. There was no firm entente with Britain. In 1928 the RAF drew up plans for a 'Locarno' war against France should she ever violate German territory. The Eastern alliances were a poor substitute. Germany, revived economically and secretly re-arming, had said nothing about her eastern frontier at Locarno. The French knew that when Germany was strong enough French security would once again be in the melting-pot.

R. Overy, *The Road to War*, 1989

>> Activity

French anxiety after Locarno led to yet another international agreement: the Kellogg–Briand Pact of 1928. Look at the following information about the Pact and answer these questions:

1 What was the Kellogg–Briand Pact?

2 How did the Pact show French anxiety about the future?

3 Why was the Pact virtually worthless?

The Kellogg–Briand Pact

In April 1927 Briand suggested that France and the USA should sign a pact promising never to go war against each other. This proposed agreement was meaningless because there was absolutely no possibility of war between America and France. However, Briand saw it as a way of symbolising the friendship between the two countries. The American government could see little value in the pact. The American Secretary of State was called Frank Kellogg. He eventually suggested that instead of an American–French agreement, all countries should be invited to sign an agreement not to go to war. On 29 August 1928 government leaders of 15 powerful countries gathered together to sign the Pact of Paris. This soon became known as the Kellogg–Briand Pact. It said that each participating country would not use warfare in order to get what it wanted. In the months that followed most countries in the world agreed to the Kellogg–Briand Pact. The Pact was worthless as it put no real obligations or restrictions on countries. Japan and Italy both signed the Pact but before very long they used war to get what they wanted and the Kellogg–Briand Pact was shown to be completely irrelevant.

SOURCE I

Aristide Briand. He was anxious to strengthen the position of France but the Kellogg–Briand Pact was of little practical value.

SOURCE J

The so-called Kellogg–Briand Pact was signed on 27 August 1928.

The High Contracting Parties solemnly declare that they condemn recourse to war for the solution of international controversies, and renounce it as an instrument of international policy in their relations with one another. The settlement or solution of all disputes or conflicts shall never be sought except by pacific means.

SOURCE K

Not everyone was impressed by the Pact. Stalin's comments about the Pact were dismissive.

They talk about pacifism. They speak about peace among European states. Briand and Austen Chamberlain are embracing each other. All this is nonsense. Every time that states make arrangements for new wars they sign treaties and call them treaties of peace.

Stalin, 1928

The rise of Hitler

Early life

Adolf Hitler was born in 1889 in Austria. On leaving school Hitler tried and failed to get a place in an art college. Unemployed and very unhappy, he lived in poverty in Vienna and Munich in the years before the First World War. His life was transformed by the outbreak of war. Hitler joined the German army and, for the first time, there was a sense of purpose to his life. For most of the war Hitler had a dangerous job as a messenger at the Front and he was awarded medals for bravery. He was horrified in 1918 when Germany lost the war. Like many Germans he felt that the Versailles Treaty of 1919 was very hard on Germany.

Although he hated communism, Hitler was impressed by the way communists were ready to use violence to get what they wanted. In November 1922 he said:

'The communists teach 'If you will not be my brother, I will bash your skull in.' Our motto shall be 'If you will not be a German, I will bash your skull in.' We cannot succeed without a struggle. We have to fight with ideas but, if necessary, also with our fists.'

After the war Hitler began his political life in the Bavarian city of Munich. In 1919 he joined and took over a tiny group called the German Workers' Party. Hitler was lazy but he was a brilliant public speaker. He appealed to the many ex-servicemen who were unhappy about Germany after the war. Slowly membership grew and in 1920 Hitler changed the name of the organisation to the National Socialist German Workers' Party (the term 'Nazi' is a shortened version of the German words 'National Sozialistisch' meaning national socialist). His followers deliberately got into fights with socialists and communists. In 1921 these Nazi street-fighters were organised into a private army called the 'Sturmabteilung' (the Storm Section or the Storm Troop) – the SA. They were also known as the brownshirts because of their distinctive uniforms.

A German crowd in Munich celebrating the outbreak of war in 1914. In it Adolf Hitler can be seen ringed.

November 1923: Hitler tries to seize power

Germany went through a great crisis in 1923. A French army occupied the industrial Ruhr area because Germany had not paid the reparations required as part of the Versailles Treaty. Germans went on strike as a protest against the French occupation and this led to many economic problems. The value of the German currency collapsed. People lost their life savings. Hitler decided that the time was right for a revolution.

On 8 November 1923 Hitler tried to use the SA to seize control of Bavaria. He planned to march to Berlin and force a Nazi government on the whole of Germany. This was a dismal failure. The event became known as the 'Beer Hall Putsch', because it began when Hitler used force to take over a meeting in a Munich beer hall. The next day, 9 November, the Nazi forces marched from the beer cellar and were stopped by armed police. The police opened fire, 16 Nazis were killed and the rest, including Hitler, then ran away. The revolution was over. Two days later Hitler was arrested.

After the Beer Hall Putsch Hitler was put on trial for treason. He made skilful use of the trial to win publicity and sympathy from German nationalists. He was treated leniently by the court; he was sentenced to five years in prison but he only served nine months. Hitler learnt a lot from his failed revolution. Afterwards he decided to concentrate on using legal means to get power.

Mein Kampf: 1925

While in prison Hitler wrote a book explaining his beliefs. This was called *Mein Kampf* or 'My Struggle' and was published in 1925. This book stated Hitler's basic ideas:

> The Treaty of Versailles was an unjust attack on the German nation and must be overturned.

> The leaders of the Weimar Republic were traitors because they had accepted the Treaty of Versailles.

> The Jewish people were the cause of many of Germany's problems. Jews were sub-human and were always trying to wreck Germany.

> Russian communism was wicked. Its leaders were Jews who wanted to destroy Germany.

> The German people needed more space or 'Lebensraum' (living space). This space should be taken from Russians and other non-German people of Eastern Europe.

The lean years

The Nazi Party was not very successful between 1925 and 1930. When Hitler came out of prison the German economy was beginning to recover. With jobs and more money people were less attracted to extremist nationalists like Hitler. The economic recovery, however, came to a very sudden end in 1930 as a result of the worldwide Depression. A return of unemployment and hard times caused a great upsurge in support for Hitler. Hitler finally took power in 1933. He was to remain Chancellor of Germany until his suicide in 1945 at the end of the Second World War.

This 1920s National Socialist German Workers' Party poster appealed to workers to vote for Hitler, the frontline soldier (Frontsoldaten).

Discussion points

> What was Hitler like as a person?

> Why do you think that Hitler's ideas were attractive to some Germans?

> Why did Hitler find it difficult to get support in the years 1925–30?

The Depression

One of the many Americans who was financially ruined as a result of the Wall Street Crash tries to sell his car for a very low price.

24 October 1929 was a fateful day in the history of the world. This was the day of the Wall Street Crash. The value of shares on the American stock market collapsed. People tried frantically to sell their shares before the prices fell even further. In one day no fewer than 13 million shares were sold. This was the start of an economic crisis that devastated the whole world.

What were the political consequences of the Depression?

THE ECONOMIC IMPACT OF THE DEPRESSION

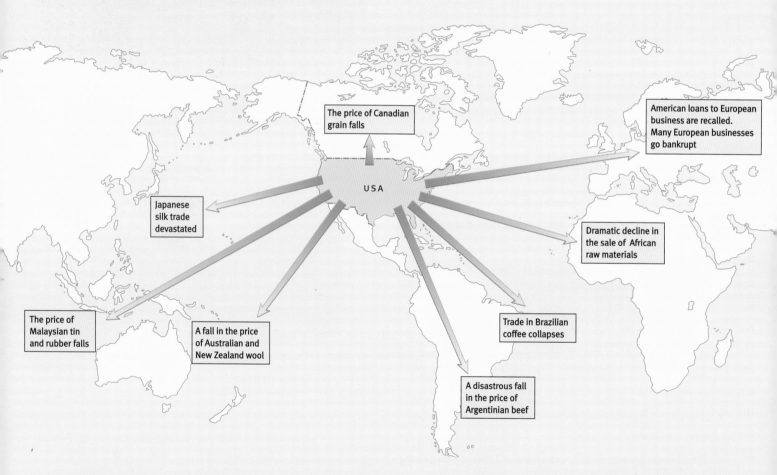

The price of Canadian grain falls

American loans to European business are recalled. Many European businesses go bankrupt

USA

Japanese silk trade devastated

Dramatic decline in the sale of African raw materials

The price of Malaysian tin and rubber falls

A fall in the price of Australian and New Zealand wool

Trade in Brazilian coffee collapses

A disastrous fall in the price of Argentinian beef

The depression began with the Wall Street Crash. This was a collapse of confidence among American investors. After Wall Street there was a dramatic slump in the USA. This had catastrophic results for the world economy. The world economy depended on the USA.

After Wall Street there was a worldwide economic crisis. Governments turned to protectionism: they imposed high import taxes to protect their own industries. This resulted in a further decline in world trade and widespread unemployment.

and international politics

The Depression and the USA

In the years before 1929 the American economy had grown at a dramatic rate. The USA was by far the most important manufacturing country in the world. On the eve of the Depression, the USA was producing 4.5 million cars a year, while Germany, Britain and France made less than half a million cars between them. Taken together, Britain, France, Germany, Italy, Japan and the USSR produced fewer manufacturing goods than the USA did by itself.

The national income of the USA fell by nearly a half between 1929 and 1932. American factories, which had become so successful, suddenly fell silent. Exports of cars fell from $541 million in 1929 to $76 million in 1932. Farmers were also badly hit: wheat exports fell from $200 million to a mere $5 million in 1932.

Isolationism

American foreign policy had been isolationist before the Depression. The US government became even more isolationist after 1929. Politicians were more interested in rebuilding the American economy.

In 1932 a new President was elected: F. D. Roosevelt. Under Roosevelt policy became even more isolationist. Roosevelt called for a New Deal for America. This New Deal policy was based on government spending on public projects and government help for businesses and farmers. Roosevelt needed the support of extreme isolationists in the US Congress to get support for his New Deal.

SOURCE B

Poverty in the USA during the Depression. A queue of poor black people wait for government handouts beneath a poster celebrating the wealth of some white Americans.

SOURCE C

Roosevelt made this statement shortly after becoming President in January 1933.

Our international relations, though vastly important, are secondary to the establishment of a sound national economy. I favour the practical policy of putting first things first.

America and the dictators

Lacking support from Washington, the leaders of France and Britain were encouraged to be cautious towards the dictators. Many American politicians said that America should be neutral if there was ever another war in Europe. This encouraged Hitler to think that Germany could be aggressive without much risk of war with the wealthy USA. American reluctance to get involved was seen during the crisis over Abyssinia in 1935. Mussolini was criticised by the US government for invading this African country but nothing practical was done to stop him. American companies greatly helped Mussolini by allowing a massive increase in the sale of American oil to Italy.

The Depression and Germany

In Europe the impact of the Depression was at its greatest in Germany. By 1932 German factories were only producing about 60 per cent of the output of 1928. By 1932 one out of every three of the working population was unemployed. The slump hurt farmers as well as factory workers. The income of German farmers fell by about half between 1928 and 1932. The result was massive discontent.

Democratic government was already in trouble before the Depression started. On both the left and the right, some German politicians had been unhappy for years with democracy. In addition, many senior army officers and civil servants disliked the rule of parliament. The Depression added a new sense of crisis to German politics. As early as 1930 emergency powers were given to the president that limited the power of the parliament or Reichstag.

Hitler's luck

The Depression was a tremendous piece of good luck for Adolf Hitler. Before the Depression his Nazi Party was very small. There were elections in Germany in 1928 and the Nazis won only 12 seats in parliament. Hitler's breakthrough came in September 1930 when the party won 107 seats and became the second largest party in Germany. At the same time, there was an increase in support for the communist party. As people lost their faith in democracy they turned to the two parties that wished to destroy parliament. Although deadly enemies, both Nazis and communists agreed that democracy was weak and worthless.

As unemployment rose in Germany there was an increase in street violence between gangs of Nazis and communists. The Nazis made further progress in the elections of July 1932 when they won 230 seats and became the largest party in the Reichstag. Hitler's appeal was based on the problems of the Depression; most of his supporters were impressed by the way his propaganda called for 'Work and Bread'.

SOURCE D

A Nazi election poster showing a heroic image of a German farmer. The poster promises voters 'Work, Freedom and Bread'.

Hitler takes over

Hitler was now in a powerful position. There were further elections in November 1932. The Nazis lost a little ground but remained the single largest party. Although he did not win an outright majority, Hitler was able to do deals with other parties and he became the Chancellor of Germany on 30 January 1933. After elections in March 1933 Hitler took complete control. Democracy came to an end on 23 March 1933 when the Reichstag passed the so-called 'Enabling Law'.
This gave Hitler the power to introduce future laws without the agreement of the Reichstag. Hitler was now the dictator of Germany.

SOURCE E

Hitler's appeal to the German people was very straightforward. He could offer them a simple explanation for all their problems. This is an extract from a proclamation he made on 1 February 1933, the day after he became Chancellor:

More than fourteen years have passed since the unhappy day when the German people, blinded by the promises of enemies at home and abroad, lost everything. Since that day of treachery, God has withheld his blessing from our people. Arguments and hatred spread among us. Within four years, unemployment must be finally overcome.

SOURCE F

One historian has assessed the results of the Depression for Germany.

Without the Depression Hitler would not have come to power. Mass unemployment reinforced all the resentments against Versailles and the Weimar democracy that had been smouldering since 1919. Overnight the National Socialists were transformed into a major political party; their representation in the Reichstag rose from 12 deputies in 1928 to 107 in 1930.

Anthony Adamthwaite, *The Making of the Second World War*, 1977

German rearmament

Hitler's rise to power did not lead to immediate war between Germany and other states. However, in October 1933 Hitler showed his contempt for the Versailles settlement by withdrawing Germany from the League of Nations. At the same time he withdrew Germany from the Disarmament Conference that had been meeting at Geneva since 1932. In the following two years he concentrated on strengthening his position in Germany and rearming Germany.

In February 1933, days after he came to power, Hitler instructed the German general, von Fritsch, to end German disarmament and to 'create an army of the greatest possible strength'. This was a breach of the Treaty of Versailles. Germany began a remarkable increase in its level of weaponry that was to gather momentum during the mid-1930s. By July 1933 tanks were being produced. By 1934 Germany was making aircraft and warships. The airforce did particularly well from the first days of rearmament. The production of military aircraft rose from 36 planes in 1932 to 1,938 planes in 1934 and 5,112 planes in 1936. In 1935 Hitler introduced conscription and began to increase massively the number of German soldiers. The limits on German power in the Treaty of Versailles had been completely overturned.

SOURCE G

Hitler surveys a massive Nazi rally. Once in power he committed Germany to rearmament.

The Depression and Britain

In Britain the Depression wrecked traditional manufacturing industries. The production of textiles fell by two thirds. Shipbuilding collapsed: in 1933 British yards were producing only 7 per cent of the amount produced in 1914. Between 1929 and 1932 iron and steel production halved.

At the time London was the most important financial centre in the world and the pound was a key currency in international trade. In 1931 the value of the pound was reduced and it was no longer linked to the price of gold. These changes were a blow to British pride and further evidence that Britain was losing its place as a great power. At the time of the Wall Street Crash, Britain was ruled by a Labour government. The crisis undermined the position of the government and led to a split in the Labour Party. The Prime Minister, Ramsay MacDonald, left the Labour Party and set up a coalition government with largely Conservative support.

Caution and cuts in defence

After the Depression, British leaders became very worried about the British Empire. They were not convinced that Britain was rich enough to defend its far-flung Empire. Above all, the government became convinced that they could not afford to fight two wars at the same time – one against Japan to defend the Empire in Asia and another to stop the rise of German power in Europe. Since the Empire was the first priority, the financial crisis encouraged the British government to take a very cautious approach to Germany.

Ramsay MacDonald responded to the Depression by cutting public spending. The result was a dramatic reduction in spending on defence in the early 1930s. It was not until 1936 that British spending on defence began to rise again. This further weakened Britain's ability to stand up to Hitler. Full-scale rearmament did not occur until 1938.

Cuts in defence spending coincided with a huge increase in German spending on weapons. By 1936 the German air force was close to overtaking in size that of Britain. British generals and admirals became very pessimistic about how well Britain could do in a war.

SOURCE H

Poverty in Britain in the 1930s. An unemployed man stands on a street corner in Wigan, northern England.

The Depression and France

The Depression took longer to have an impact on France because the French economy depended less on international trade. However, when the slump did start in France it had a very damaging effect. After 1933 French industry went through a great crisis. As late as 1938 France had still failed to restore the level of national income to that of the 1920s.

As in Britain, the slump had an impact on defence. With a huge debt for money borrowed during the First World War and war pensions the French government could not give its armed forces adequate weapons. The production of new aircraft fell and compared very badly with output in Germany. In one year, 1937, the French built 370 military aircraft while the Germans built 5,606.

The economic problems added to the bitter social divisions that existed in France. Unemployment trebled between 1931 and 1935. The membership of the French Communist Party rose dramatically at the same time. The Communist Party began to do very well in elections. The crisis also led to a great surge in extreme right-wing political support. A right-wing demonstration in Paris during February 1934 turned into a riot in which 14 people were killed. The deep divisions between left and right in France between 1933 and 1936 stopped the French government from standing up to Hitler.

SOURCE I

Unemployed French workers protesting in Paris, 1930. Their banner calls for 'Work or Bread'. The Depression in France heightened tensions between left- and right-wing extremists.

SOURCE J

The Nazi leader, Goebbels, speaking in April 1940, looked back to the early 1930s as a time when France failed to take firm action against Germany.

In 1933 the French Prime Minister should have said: 'Hitler cannot be tolerated. Either he disappears or we march!' But they didn't do it. They left us alone and they let us slip through the danger zone, and we were able to sail around all dangerous reefs. And when we were done, and well armed, better than they, then they started the war.

>> Activity

Look back at pages 46–51. Explain in your own words the link between the Depression and the following problems:

a The USA became more isolationist and did little to stop Hitler and Mussolini

b The extremist Nazi Party came to power in Germany

c The British government became less willing to fight a war in Europe.

d France became a weak and bitterly divided country.

Crisis in Manchuria

The authority of the League of Nations collapsed in the 1930s. Japan invaded the north Chinese province of Manchuria in 1931. Japan was criticised by the League but little was done in practice to drive the Japanese out of Manchuria.

Why did the League fail to stop Japan?

The rise of Japan

In 1853, after centuries of isolation, the peace of Japan was disturbed by the arrival of the American navy in Tokyo Bay. The arrival of the wealthy, well-armed Westerners was a great shock to people in Japan. They were both impressed and worried by their American visitors. In 1868 a group of angry 'samurai' or warrior nobles seized control of the government. They were determined to change Japan so that, unlike many other Asian lands, their country would not be taken over by Westerners. To resist Western armies the Japanese government was determined to make Japan as rich and powerful as Britain or America. In the late nineteenth century the Japanese government built up a strong economy and established a well-educated workforce. As a result the Japanese were able to build armaments as powerful as those of America and Europe.

Victory over Russia

The push for modernisation was so successful that in 1904 Japan was able to wage war against Russia. To the astonishment of the world the Japanese had defeated Russia by 1905. The Russian navy was convincingly beaten and its main fleet was sunk. Japan had arrived as a powerful nation.

Having defeated a great European country the Japanese government expected to be treated as an equal by other powerful states. In particular, the Japanese government wanted an empire in Asia. This empire could supply raw materials for the increasing numbers of Japanese factories. The Western nations were very unhappy at the idea of a Japanese empire. This was a threat to their own interests in Asia. The argument about a possible Japanese empire centred on China.

In the First World War Japan joined forces with Britain and France and declared war on Germany. Japanese forces occupied all the German territories in the Pacific. The Japanese government also used the war to start to build up an empire in the area of China known as Manchuria. The Japanese were disappointed by the 1919 peace settlement. They were on the winning side and they expected more rewards than they got. This led to a great sense of resentment towards Britain, France and America.

SOURCE A

A Japanese painting celebrating the defeat of the Russian navy at Tsushima in the war of 1904–5.

SOURCE B

Japanese troops interrogating a Chinese prisoner in Manchuria. The League did little to stop the Japanese occupation.

Attack on Manchuria

The army was a very powerful force in Japan. In the 1920s the power of the army grew to a point where politicians could no longer tell soldiers what to do. Army officers wanted to increase Japanese control in Manchuria. The army took the initiative in September 1931 when they organised an armed clash with Chinese forces in Manchuria. War followed. Japan won the war in Manchuria and set up a puppet government.

The invasion of Manchuria was a clear test of the League and collective security. Both China and Japan were members of the League. Would the League use economic sanctions or war to stop the Japanese take-over? In fact, the League did virtually nothing. A group known as the Lytton Committee was sent to Manchuria to find out what was happening. It took months to carry out its work, by which time Japan was firmly in control. Eventually it criticised both Japan and the government of China.

The League Council accepted the Lytton Committee Report. It criticised Japan but did not recommend a trade ban or the use of force. Even though the League did little Japan was not prepared to accept any criticism and left the League in 1933.

SOURCE C

The failure to take firm action over Manchuria was a great blow to the image of the League of Nations. People who expected the League to keep the peace began to despair. The English newspaper, the Manchester Guardian, *expressed a widespread concern about the failure of the League in Manchuria in December 1931.*

The League Covenant [the charter of the League setting out its principles] can apparently be ignored with impunity. Japan has ignored it by invading Manchuria; the nations represented on the League Council have ignored it by refusing to insist on the withdrawal of Japanese troops. The Covenant has failed to save China from aggression as completely as a signed and ratified treaty failed to save Belgium from German aggression in 1914. The Great Powers, despite all their fine gestures, have to their great shame not even seriously protested against, let alone resisted, such a state of affairs.

The failure of the League

>> **Activity**

1 Read Source E. Explain in your own words what this interpretation says about why no other country was ready to stop Japan taking over Manchuria.

2 Does the information on page 55 on other countries' reactions to the invasion of Manchuria support the interpretation in Source E, or does it suggest additional reasons why Japan was not stopped?

SOURCE E

Gaetano Salvemini was an Italian historian. Writing in 1954 he described Western attitudes towards the crisis in Manchuria.

In the Far Eastern crisis of 1931 and the following years, Japan and China, owing to their great distance from Europe, might as well have been on the moon. If a man sees a cat crushed under a car, he loses his appetite; yet the same man can calmly eat his breakfast while reading in his morning paper that thousands of men, women and children have been engulfed in some terrible earthquake. The Japanese Government could count on the ignorance of people too busy with difficulties at home to be bothered about events in remote lands. People's minds in both America and Europe were with the economic depression that had started in 1929 and was at its worst in 1931–2.

SOURCE D

THE DOORMAT

Both of the cartoons on these two pages were produced by the British artist, David Low. In this picture the League is shown as a doormat and a Japanese officer walks over it.

The missing powers

Two powerful countries with an interest in this part of Asia were not members of the League. These were the USA and the USSR. The USSR was worried about the actions of the Japanese. The move in Manchuria was seen as a challenge to Soviet power in East Asia. However, the government of the USSR was busy at the time, dealing with chaos at home as peasants were forced to live on new collective farms. In addition, the USSR had no allies who might join forces against Japan, and Soviet leaders were not ready to act alone.

Some members of the American government were appalled by the Japanese aggression. However, President Hoover believed in isolationism and did not want to get involved in the conflict between China and Japan. As a result the USA refused to support the idea of economic sanctions against Japan. This greatly weakened the ability of the League to threaten trade sanctions. Members of the League knew that if they refused to trade with Japan the USA might simply carry out the trade instead.

The sympathetic powers

Italy and Germany were important members of the League. They were happy with Japanese aggression. Italy was not interested in the Far East but, like Japan, was keen to build up its own empire. Germany had investments in China, but its main concern was to see if the Japanese would get away with the use of force. As a result, Italy and Germany offered no opposition to Japan.

The worried powers

The French were completely preoccupied with the German threat in Europe. While they disapproved of Japanese actions the French had no wish to get involved in a war in Asia. The use of French and British forces against Japan would weaken defences against Germany in Europe. In public the French government condemned Japanese action; in private messages were sent to the Japanese to let them know that France sympathised with the difficulties faced by Japan in China.

Members of the British government were in a difficult position. They did not feel that the British navy was in a position to take on the Japanese. The advice from military leaders was that a war with Japan might be disastrous. Vital parts of the British Empire – India, Singapore and Hong Kong – could well be lost if fighting broke out between Britain and Japan. British businesses did considerable trade with Japan and the government was unwilling to lose the trade. Although the British government was worried about Japan it was not prepared to take firm action.

SOURCE F

Japan is shown here as a gangster defying the judges of the League.

> How can you tell that the artist was not impressed by the way the League dealt with Japan?

Mussolini and Italian

Mussolini in military uniform.

Italy before Mussolini

Italy had many political problems in the years after the First World War. Italians felt cheated. About half a million Italian soldiers had been killed in the war. Italians expected payment for this sacrifice from the peace settlement. However, the peace treaties were a great disappointment because the Italians failed to get all the land they expected. It became known as the 'mutilated peace'. At home there were deep divisions between those who supported the ideas of the Russian Revolution and those who hated socialism and communism. Few people respected the Italian parliament. Five governments were formed between 1919 and 1922 and none of them was able to take control of the situation.

Mussolini: the man

Benito Mussolini was born in 1883. Before the First World War he had been a socialist journalist. He left the socialist party because he supported the war and other socialists did not. In 1919 Mussolini began to organise gangs of angry ex-servicemen into a powerful political force. They were known as 'fascists', because they belonged to a 'fascio' or armed squad. The fascists soon got a reputation for attacking and beating up their enemies. Mussolini loved parades and uniforms. The fascist fighters wore distinctive black shirts. Throughout his early political career he kept changing his policies. He was ready to drop any belief that got in the way of his search for power. Once in power, Mussolini encouraged Italians to look up to him as a special leader with extraordinary powers. He was called 'duce', which is the Italian for 'leader'.

The fascist take-over

Mussolini came to power in 1922. His followers staged a dramatic march on Rome to get publicity and to show how strong they were. Italy was in chaos. The king of Italy turned to Mussolini because he thought the fascists would improve law and order and stop Italy turning towards communism. At first the fascists did not have complete control and had to share power with other parties. After rigged elections in 1924 Mussolini strengthened his grip on power. The leader of the rival Socialist Party was murdered. From 1925 Mussolini began to rule Italy as a dictator. In 1926 all other parties were banned. Leading communists and socialists were imprisoned.

Some were murdered. Widespread use was made of propaganda to convince Italian people that Mussolini was an almost super-human leader. Posters were put up throughout the country saying, 'Mussolini is always right'. The voting laws were changed in 1928 so that only fascist men could vote, and the only permitted candidates were fascists. Not surprisingly, Mussolini did well in the elections that followed. In 1929 Mussolini came to an agreement with the Pope about the place of the Catholic Church in Italy. In return for giving the Church special privileges Mussolini made sure that the Church would not challenge fascism.

fascism

The dead bodies of Mussolini and his lover, Clara Petacci, displayed hanging from a garage after they had been tried and executed by Italian partisans in Milan in 1945.

Discussion points

> Why do you think some Italian people turned to Mussolini in the early 1920s?

> How did Mussolini strengthen his power in the 1920s?

Mussolini goes to war

By 1930 the fascist revolution at home was largely over. In the 1930s Mussolini looked to foreign policy for further triumphs. In 1935–6 Italy invaded and conquered Abyssinia (modern Ethiopia). He made an agreement to work with Hitler in 1936; the link between Germany and Italy was called the Rome–Berlin Axis. In 1940, when it looked as if Germany was going to win the Second World War, Mussolini joined forces with Hitler and went to war against France and Britain. The war was a disaster for Mussolini. His forces were defeated in North Africa by Britain and the USA. By 1943 Italy itself had been invaded. Mussolini was overthrown by other fascists and imprisoned. Hitler sent German paratroopers to rescue him. For the last two years of the war Mussolini ruled part of northern Italy, but real power lay with the Germans. He was captured and killed by anti-fascist fighters in April 1945 and his dead body was put on public display in Milan.

THE KEY IDEAS OF ITALIAN FASCISM

> Italians should take a fierce pride in their country.

> War is good for a country. Young Italian men should be ready to fight.

> Italy should establish an empire in Africa.

> No other political parties are allowed.

> Communism and socialism are the enemies of fascism.

> Democracy is useless. Italy needs a strong powerful leader who can tell people what to do.

> The place of women is at home. Italian women should have as many children as possible.

> A great country should be self-sufficient. The government should tell firms what to produce to bring this about.

The conquest of Abyssinia

Italy conquered Abyssinia in 1935–6. Some historians see a direct link between the crisis over Abyssinia and the outbreak of world war in 1939. In 1977 a British historian called Anthony Adamthwaite wrote: 'If there was a turning-point on the road to war it was the Abyssinian crisis of 1935-6. The crisis was the major step towards war.'

What were the results of the invasion of Abyssinia?

The search for an empire

In the late nineteenth century Italy tried to conquer the African state of Abyssinia (known today as Ethiopia). The attempt ended in disaster. In 1896 the Abyssinians destroyed an Italian army at Adowa. The Abyssinians castrated the Italian prisoners of war taken at Adowa. The battle stopped Italy for a while but after Adowa many Italians wanted to take revenge.

Mussolini looks south

By the early 1930s Italy was suffering from the Depression. Mussolini wanted a successful war to strengthen his position at home. He was also disturbed by the rise of Hitler. Hitler was planning to dominate central Europe, so Mussolini decided to look south and make Italy a great Mediterranean power. This led him to think about an Italian return to Abyssinia.

SOURCE A

Extracts from statements by Mussolini in 1935:

Whatever it costs, I will avenge Adowa. We have been patient with Ethiopia for forty years. Now, we have had enough!

The Stresa Front

France and Britain were keen to stop Italy joining forces with Germany. In return, they seemed ready to give Italy a free hand in Africa. In April 1935 Mussolini met the French and British prime ministers in the Italian town of Stresa. They condemned German breaches of the Treaty of Versailles. People began to talk about the Stresa Front: an anti-German grouping of Italy, Britain and France. The Stresa agreement was vague: the declaration talked only about the need to 'keep the peace in Europe'. Mussolini understood this to mean that France and Britain would not object to the Italian use of force outside Europe. Mussolini thought that in return for supporting France and Britain in Europe he would be allowed to attack Abyssinia without any

The Anglo–German Naval Agreement

The British government greatly weakened the Stresa Front in June 1935. Britain signed a treaty with Germany over the strength of their navies. This fixed the size of the German navy at 35 per cent of the British navy. The agreement allowed Germany to have submarines. The French and the Italians were annoyed by the Naval Agreement. They had not been consulted and the agreement was in breach of the Versailles Treaty.

Invasion

The Italian attack on Abyssinia began on 3 October 1935. Symbolically, one of the first Italian actions was the bombing of the town of Adowa, scene of the Italian defeat in 1896.

Britain and France were caught in a dilemma. They did not want to annoy Mussolini, but they also wanted to support the League of Nations and the idea of collective security. Abyssinia was a member of the League of Nations. The League condemned Italian action and imposed a trade ban. However, the ban did not include the trade in oil and petrol. This was crucial. As long as the Italians had petrol they could continue the war. Limited sanctions did not work.

Italian troops say farewell to their families at Rome railway station before departing for Abyssinia in 1935.

The Italian invasion of Abyssinia.

The Hoare–Laval Pact

The reaction of the French and British governments was half-hearted. In December 1935 the British Foreign Secretary, Hoare, had secret talks with Laval, the Prime Minister of France. They designed a compromise, known as the Hoare–Laval Pact, under which Abyssinia would have been divided in two, with Italy given the richer part. The war was going badly for Mussolini and he might have accepted the deal. However, the details of the Pact were leaked to the press. There was uproar in Britain. People saw it as a surrender to Italian aggression. The Pact was scrapped and Hoare was forced to resign.

After the failure of the Hoare–Laval Pact Britain and France took a tougher line against Italy. In March 1936 they finally decided to ban the sale of oil and petrol to Italy but by this time it was too late. In May 1936, before the oil and petrol ban had started properly, Italy won the war. The League had failed and on 15 July all the sanctions against Italy were ended.

>> Activity

1 What happened at the Battle of Adowa?

2 Why was Mussolini keen to conquer Abyssinia?

3 What was the Stresa Front? What was the Anglo-German Naval Agreement?

4 What was the Hoare–Laval Pact? Did it succeed?

5 Why do you think the sale of oil and petrol was important to the Italian army in Abyssinia?

SOURCE E

Hailie Selassie, addressing the League of Nations in June 1936. Despite his passionate pleas, the League was unable to stop the Italian conquest.

After Abyssinia

The League of Nations was broken by the Abyssinian crisis. Afterwards no one took it seriously. The failure of the League was highlighted by Hailie Selassie, the Abyssinian emperor, who made a passionate speech to the League Assembly after his country had been conquered.

SOURCE C

Extract from Hailie Selassie's speech to the League Assembly, 30 June 1936:

I was defending the cause of all small peoples who are threatened with aggression. Ethiopian warriors asked only for means to defend themselves. On many occasions I have asked for financial assistance for the purchase of arms. That assistance has been constantly refused me. The problem is a much wider one than that of Italy's aggression. It is the very existence of the League of Nations. God and history will remember your judgement. Are states going to set up a terrible precedent of bowing before force? What reply shall I have to take back to my people?

SOURCE D

The Italian government showed its contempt by sending a sneering message to the League. On 30 June 1936 the new Italian Foreign Minister, Count Ciano, responded defiantly to the speech of Hailie Selassie.

Italy views the work she has undertaken in Ethiopia as a sacred mission of civilisation, and proposes to carry it out according to the principles of the Covenant of the League of Nations. Italy will consider it an honour to inform the League of Nations of the progress achieved in her work of civilizing Ethiopia.

A discredited League

In the crises that followed Abyssinia, the League was completely helpless. When the Spanish Civil War broke out in 1936 Germany and Italy sent help to the anti-government side. The Spanish government appealed to the League: the League did nothing. In 1938–9, as the Second World War drew close, the League played no part in serious attempts to avoid conflict. When war broke out in September 1939 none of the countries involved bothered to tell the League that a war was taking place.

SOURCE F

Litvinov, the Soviet Foreign Minister, described the failure of the League in a speech to the League Assembly in September 1938.

The League was created as a reaction to the world war. Its object was to make that the last war, to safeguard all nations against aggression, and to replace the system of military alliances by the collective organisation of assistance to the victim of aggression. In this sphere the League has done nothing.

Germany and Abyssinia

Hitler was deeply interested in the crisis in Abyssinia. He wanted to know how far Britain and France would go to stop the Italians. He not impressed at the confused and feeble response of the democracies.

SOURCE G

A German newspaper commented unfavourably on the way the British had behaved over Abyssinia.

The English like a comfortable life, compared to us Germans. They avoid sustained effort, if possible. After the war, the British masters of the world thought that they had earned a rest. Today the Italians have complete control over Abyssinia. The League and the London government know that only the use of great force can drive the Italians out of Abyssinia, but they are not prepared to use such force.

Münchener Zeitung, May 1936

SOURCE H

Britain's anxiety to avoid war led Hitler to despise the British.

The modern British Empire shows all the marks of decay and unstoppable breakdown. Britain will regret her softness. It will cost her the British Empire.

Adolf Hitler, 1936

The fall of the Stresa Front

After Abyssinia the British and French governments hoped to re-establish a good relationship with Italy. Mussolini had different ideas. He had been annoyed by what he saw as British and French double dealing. Instead he turned to Hitler. The German leader had not interfered over Abyssinia. In January 1936 Mussolini thanked Hitler and made it clear that he was happy for an increase in German control over Austria. This was a significant development. In 1934 Mussolini had opposed German expansionism towards Austria. The Stresa Front against Germany had collapsed.

The Axis and the Anti-Comintern Pact

By November Mussolini was talking of a new force in European politics – a linking together of the fascist states of Italy and Germany called the Rome–Berlin Axis. Later in the same month the leaders of Germany, Italy and Japan signed the Anti-Comintern Pact (Comintern was the Soviet organisation whose job was to spread communism world-wide). On one level the Anti-Comintern Pact was simply an agreement to work together against communism. As far as Hitler was concerned it was much more important than that; it was a step towards an alliance of those countries that wanted to take land off their neighbours.

THE BENEFITS OF THE ABYSSINIAN CRISIS FOR HITLER:

> The League was unlikely to stop German aggression any more than it had stopped Mussolini.

> The anti-German Stresa Front fell apart.

> The crisis provided Hitler with an opportunity for his first act of aggression – the sending of German troops into the Rhineland area.

> The Rome–Berlin Axis and the Anti-Comintern Pact strengthened the position of Hitler.

>> Activity

Explain in your own words the consequences of the Italian conquest of Abyssinia. In your answer you should mention:

a the reputation of the League;

b the advantages of the crisis for Hitler.

The rise and fall of the League of Nations

THE ESTABLISHMENT OF THE LEAGUE

> The idea of a League of Nations was discussed by American, British and French politicians during the First World War, as an organisation that would prevent future war.

> The American President, Woodrow Wilson, was very keen on the idea of the League. He was very idealistic but not very practical about how the League should work.

> The League was set up as part of the Treaty of Versailles, 1919. It began work in 1920. Its headquarters was in Geneva, Switzerland.

> The plan was that the League would bring peace to the world through a system called 'collective security'. Collective security meant that the members of the League would act together to punish and stop any country that attacked another state. This punishment could be either economic sanctions: a ban on trade with an aggressor country; or military action: the use of war.

THE ORGANISATION OF THE LEAGUE

> Decisions were taken by the Council. This small group was dominated by a few powerful countries who were permanent members. At first the permanent members were Britain, France, Italy and Japan. Other countries took it in turns to have temporary membership of the Council.

> At first it was expected that the USA would be a leading member of the League. President Wilson had a disagreement with the US Senate about the League. In 1920 the Senate refused to let the USA join the League.

> Any decisions taken by the Council had to be unanimous: every member of the Council had to agree before any action could be taken.

> All member states could send representatives to the Assembly. This was a place to discuss the problems of the world. It had little real power.

THE WORK OF THE LEAGUE

The League was responsible for several organisations that did good work in a number of fields. These organisations still exist today as part of the United Nations and included:

> The Refugee Organisation which helped the victims of war;

> The International Labour Organisation which tried to improve working conditions;

> The Health Organisation which encouraged schemes to improve healthcare.

Burying the war dead, 1918. The League was intended to prevent the repetition of scenes like this.

SUCCESSES IN PEACE-KEEPING

The League made some progress in solving arguments between states during the 1920s. Often the success stories involved arguments between smaller countries:

1920: an argument was settled between Finland and Sweden about the Åland Islands;

1922: the League rescued Austria from a financial crisis;

1925: action by the League stopped war from breaking out between Greece and Bulgaria;

1926: Germany joined the League as part of the Locarno settlement;

1934: the Soviet Union became a member of the League.

THE LEAGUE! PAH! FANCY SUGGESTING NATIONS COULD UNITE FOR *PEACE*.

A David Low cartoon criticising the League's failure to take effective action during the Spanish Civil War, 1936.

FAILURES IN PEACE-KEEPING

From the beginning, the League found it difficult to stop powerful countries from attacking other states. The weakness of the League became clear to the world in the 1930s:

1923: Italy seized the Greek island of Corfu. The League could not agree on any action;

1931: Japan attacked the Chinese province of Manchuria. The League did little and Japan remained in Manchuria. Japan did not like being criticised by the League and left the organisation in 1933;

1934: Hitler had despised the League since it was set up. A year after he took power, Germany left the League;

1935: Italy invaded Abyssinia. The League tried to stop Italy through the use of economic sanctions. These did not include a ban on the sale of oil and they failed. After this the League was not taken seriously.

WHY DID THE LEAGUE FAIL?

Some powerful countries were not members
The League was greatly weakened by the refusal of the USA to join. If America had joined, the League would have had more power and authority. Other powerful countries were either excluded or chose to leave. Germany did not join until 1926. The USSR was excluded until 1934, by which time Germany had left the League.

Britain and France could not always agree
In the absence of the USA the most powerful states in the League were Britain and France. They did not trust each other and often disagreed about how the League should work. The rule that Council decisions had to be unanimous made it even more difficult for the League to make decisions.

The League lacked teeth
Collective security did not work. France, Britain and other members were more concerned about their own interests than the authority of the League. As a result they were reluctant to get involved in collective security. The League could not make powerful countries obey its rulings.

The Depression undermined the League
The League was weakened by the Great Depression that swept the world after 1929. At a time of economic crisis governments were less interested in what happened in faraway places. Japan and Italy were able to invade other countries without being punished effectively by the League.

From the Rhineland to the 'Anschluss'

In 1936 Hitler defied the Treaty of Versailles. He ordered German troops to march into the Rhineland. Two years later he broke the Treaty again by uniting Germany with Austria.

What can we learn about Hitler from the crises over the Rhineland and Austria?

SOURCE A

German troops march into the Rhineland in 1936. This action was a clear breach of the Treaty of Versailles.

The risk of war

Hitler took considerable risks in moving into the Rhineland. There was a good chance that France would send troops to resist the German forces and this would mean war. The German army was not ready for war. No one in Germany knew how the French would react. Many German generals were unhappy at Hitler's plan. If the French had sent an army into the Rhineland they could easily have outnumbered the German forces. The first troops into the Rhineland were ordered to retreat if they met with French resistance. In the days immediately after the invasion the German generals called upon Hitler to retreat. He refused.

Hitler the peacemaker?

Instead of giving way, Hitler tried to show the world that the action in the Rhineland was reasonable. The ambassadors of Britain, Italy and France were told that Hitler had important new plans for long-term peace in Europe. He proposed a 25-year agreement between Germany and France and Belgium: Germany promised not to attack its western neighbours. Hitler also suggested that there should be a demilitarised zone on either side of the French–German borders. He talked about Germany returning to the League of Nations. These were not serious proposals, but they made Hitler seem reasonable. Many people were taken in by his proposals. In Britain, for example, the Labour politician Arthur Henderson said that Hitler's offer of the 'olive branch...ought to be taken at face value'.

SOURCE B

François Poncet was the French ambassador to Germany in 1936. In 1949 he looked back at Hitler's policy of military action and skilful politics.

Hitler smacked his enemy in the face, and as he did so he declared: 'I bring you proposals for peace!'

On the day of the reoccupation Hitler spoke to the Reichstag. Again, his intention was to convince the world that the action in the Rhineland was not worth fighting for. He suggested that he was actually trying to build a new peaceful Europe.

SOURCE C

I have never forgotten my duty to uphold European civilisation. It should be possible to end this useless conflict between France and Germany which has lasted for centuries. Why not replace it with the rule of reason? The German people have no interest in seeing the French people suffer.

Hitler speaking to the Reichstag, 7 March 1935

The reaction of the French and the British

French ministers and generals met in emergency session on the day of the occupation. They thought about sending the French army to fight. In the end the French decided to protest but not to fight.

In Britain hardly anyone wanted to go to war over the Rhineland. Many British people approved of what Hitler had done; this was German territory, and they thought the German army had a right to be there. One politician said that the British did not care 'two hoots' about the Rhineland. The British government sympathised with this view. They took no action.

The Rhineland crisis showed that Hitler could seize an opportunity on the spur of the moment. He had been planning to wait until 1937, by which time the German army would have been stronger due to rearmament. However, he recognised that the Abyssinian crisis provided an unusual opportunity. Britain, France and the League of Nations were overwhelmed by the crisis in Abyssinia and there was a reluctance to get involved in any more conflicts.

SOURCE D

Years later Hitler looked back with pride to the Rhineland crisis.

The forty-eight hours after the march into the Rhineland were the most nerve-racking in my life. If the French had then marched into the Rhineland we would have had to withdraw with our tails between our legs, for the military resources at our disposal would have been wholly inadequate for even a moderate resistance.

What would have happened in March 1936 if anyone other than myself had been in charge of Germany! Anyone else would have lost his nerve. I had to lie. We were saved by my unshakeable obstinacy and my remarkable daring. I threatened, unless the situation ceased in twenty-four hours, to send six extra divisions into the Rhineland. In fact, I only had four brigades.

The 'Anschluss': the German take-over of Austria

In early 1938 Austria was in a state of crisis. Local Nazis were making life difficult for the government of Chancellor Kurt Schuschnigg. Hitler did not have complete control over these Austrian Nazis, and they sometimes acted without waiting for orders from Berlin. In January 1938 it was discovered by the Austrian authorities that there was a plot by Austrian Nazis to create chaos in Austria by killing the German ambassador. Austrian Nazis hoped that in the turmoil the German government would take over Austria.

The Austrian leader, Schuschnigg, visited Hitler for crisis talks in Germany in February 1938. Schuschnigg was badly treated at this meeting. Hitler raved and shouted at him for two hours. He demanded that Nazis be allowed to join the Austrian government and be given control of law and order. Schuschnigg felt that he had no option and agreed to Hitler's terms.

When Schuschnigg got back to Austria he was in a difficult situation. He took very seriously Hitler's threat of force unless Nazis were given more power in Austria. There was no chance of help from abroad. The British had made it clear that they would not stop a German take-over.

SOURCE E

On 12 February 1938 Hitler ranted at Schuschnigg.

The whole history of Austria is just one uninterrupted act of treason. This must come to an end. I can tell you, here and now, Herr Schuschnigg, that I am absolutely determined to end this. Germany is one of the Great Powers and no other state will raise its voice if Germany settles its border problems. I have achieved everything I set out to do, and have become perhaps the greatest German in history. Listen. You don't really think that you can move a single stone in Austria without my hearing about it the very next day, do you? You don't seriously believe that you can stop me, or even delay me for half an hour, do you?

The plebiscite

On 9 March Schuschnigg made one last desperate attempt to keep Austria independent. He announced that there would be a plebiscite, or referendum, in Austria to decide whether Austrians wanted their country to remain independent. He fixed the lowest age of voting at twenty-four, so that young Nazis would not be able to vote. Hitler was enraged when he heard about the plebiscite plan. He feared that Schuschnigg would win the plebiscite and he ordered the army to invade before the plebiscite. On 11 March 1938 the German army invaded Austria. Arrests began immediately of enemies of the Nazis. In the city of Vienna alone 76,000 people were arrested in the aftermath of the invasion. On 12 March Hitler himself crossed into Austria. He went to his own home town of Linz where he was greeted by cheering crowds.

SOURCE F

Schuschnigg made a radio broadcast on 11 March.

Men and women of Austria. Today we have been faced with a difficult situation. The German government gave us an ultimatum: appoint as Chancellor a candidate nominated by Germany, otherwise German troops will march into Austria. There is no truth in the stories that there has been unrest, that streams of blood have flowed and that the government could not maintain order.

The Austrian government has decided to yield to force. Because we do not want to shed German blood, we have ordered our armed force to offer no resistance if the invasion is carried out.

SOURCE G

An extract from Hitler's speech to the people of Linz, 12 March 1938:

I left this town years ago with precisely the same beliefs as I have today. Imagine how deeply I feel now that I have brought my beliefs to fulfilment. Providence gave me a mission to restore my dear homeland to the German Reich. I believed in that mission, I have lived and fought for it, and I believe I have now fulfilled it.

SOURCE H

Austria, 12 March 1938: cheering crowds greet the arrival of the German army.

>> **Activity**

Look back at pages 64–67.

1 Using information from this unit explain how Hitler sent troops into the Rhineland and Austria.

2 What evidence can you find to support the following statements about Hitler:

    a He was prepared to gamble and take great risks.

    b He was skilled at propaganda.

    c Sometimes he acted like a madman.

    d He did not believe that France or Britain would take action to stop his aggression.

    e He had no respect for plebiscites or democratic votes.

3 What else can you learn about Hitler from his actions over the Rhineland and Austria?

Munich and the destruction of

The peace treaties at the end of the First World War had created a new country called Czechoslovakia. In 1938 Britain and France signed the Munich Agreement that broke up Czechoslovakia and gave much of it to Germany.

What happened at Munich?

The Sudeten Germans

There were about 3 million German speakers in Czechoslovakia. They were a large minority in a country dominated by Czechs and Slovaks. They were known as Sudeten Germans and were concentrated in the border areas. Nazis were active among the Sudeten Germans. The local Nazi leader, Konrad Henlein, led a political party called the Sudeten German Party that received money from Hitler. Henlein claimed that the Sudeten Germans were not treated fairly. He took part in negotiations with the Czechoslovak government but these got nowhere.

Hitler met Henlein on 28 March 1938 to give him instructions. He told the Sudeten leader to keep making demands that the Czechoslovak government could not possibly accept. By dragging out the negotiations, Hitler hoped to create a crisis over Czechoslovakia.

SOURCE A

A tearful woman gives the Nazi salute to the German forces as they cross into Czechoslovakia during the German takeover of the Sudetenland.

Support from Britain and France?

The government of Czechoslovakia looked to Britain and France for help. British leaders had no treaty with Czechoslovakia. The leaders of the British armed services could not see any way that Britain could help. By March 1938 Chamberlain was saying in private that Czechoslovakia could not be saved.

France had signed a treaty with Czechoslovakia in 1925. This said that France would give Czechoslovakia military help if it was attacked by Germany. In April 1938 there was a change of government in France. The new Prime Minister, Daladier, was not keen on the idea of going to war with Germany over Czechoslovakia. His Foreign Minister, Bonnet, tried to find a way of avoiding war without clearly going back on the promise to Czechoslovakia.

Hitler prepares to act

Hitler was sure that neither Britain nor France would intervene if he attacked Czechoslovakia. In April he visited Rome and was told by Mussolini that Italy would support Germany. On 30 May Hitler let his generals know that he had decided to 'smash Czechoslovakia by military action in the near future'.

The British and the French governments reacted to the crisis by putting pressure on the Czechoslovaks to make concessions. The British government sent a politician called Lord Runciman to Czechoslovakia in July to try to work out a settlement between the two sides. Runciman was biased in favour of the Sudeten Germans. He recommended to the British government that the Sudetenland should be separated from Czechoslovakia.

Czechoslovakia

SOURCE B

The mood of some French people was described by the novelist Jean-Paul Sartre. Sartre was a left-wing intellectual who lived in this period. A character in one of his novels, set in 1938, explained why it was wrong for France to think about going to war over Czechoslovakia.

I know what the Czech government is like. I know what tyrants they can be. Is it right that France – the land of liberty – should allow Frenchmen to be killed so that the Czech government should continue to torment the Sudeten Germans? Is that a good enough reason why an educated young Frenchman should end up ten feet underground? We ought to say to our Government, 'If the Sudeten Germans want to join Germany, that's fine, its none of our business.'

J-P. Sartre, The Reprieve

>> Activity

Look at the sources on this page. They shed light on Western attitudes to Czechoslovakia. What can we learn from these sources about why some people in France and Britain were not ready to stand by Czechoslovakia?

SOURCE D

An extract from the Runciman Report on the Sudetenland:

I have much sympathy with the Sudeten case. It is a hard thing to be ruled by an alien race. Czechoslovak rule in the Sudeten areas for the last twenty years has been marked by discrimination, to a point where the German population was inevitably moving in the direction of revolt. The Sudeten Germans felt that in the past they had been given many promises by the Czechoslovak Government, but that little or no action had followed. Czech officials and Czech police, speaking little or no German, were appointed to purely German districts; Czechs were encouraged to settle on land in the middle of German populations. Czech firms were favoured against German firms. The State provided work and relief for Czechs more readily than for Germans.

The feeling of the Sudeten Germans until about three or four years ago was one of hopelessness. But the rise of Nazi Germany gave them new hope. I regard their turning for help to their kinsmen and their desire to join the Reich as a natural development.

SOURCE C

INCREASING PRESSURE.

A British cartoon of the time criticising British and French attitudes to German aggression.

The Munich crisis

Hitler was ready to go to war against Czechoslovakia in the summer of 1938. Many of his leading generals disagreed. They were afraid that Britain and France would fight and they did not feel that Germany was ready for a large-scale war. Hitler refused to listen to the generals. He was sure that Britain and France would do nothing.

Tension rose in early September. Henlein ordered local Nazis to attack Czech and Jewish targets. As a result of this violence, negotiations between the Sudeten Germans and Prague were broken off. Henlein left Czechoslovakia on 15 September. In Germany much publicity was given to his stories of the mistreatment of Sudeten Germans.

SOURCE E

Mussolini, Hitler and Chamberlain meet at Munich. (Hitler's interpreter, Schmidt, is sitting on his left.)

Chamberlain flies to Germany

Chamberlain met Hitler in Germany at Berchtesgaden on 15 September. Hitler complained to Chamberlain about the treatment of the Sudeten Germans. Chamberlain gave in to Hitler. He agreed with him that the Sudetenland should be annexed by Germany. In return he asked Hitler not to use force to take control. Chamberlain returned to London and got Cabinet support for a peaceful German take-over. The French leaders Daladier and Bonnet came to London on 18 September and agreed to support the partition of Czechoslovakia in return for a British promise to defend what was left of the Czechoslovak state. A day later the Czech President, Beneš, was told that he must hand over the Sudetenland. Beneš was extremely unhappy about this, and at first he refused to co-operate. By 21 September he realised that he was powerless to resist without Allied support so he reluctantly agreed to the take-over.

Hitler did not want a peaceful settlement. He wanted to destroy Czechoslovakia by force. He was annoyed when Chamberlain came to see him for a second time on 22 September at Bad Godesberg with news that Britain, France and Czechoslovakia had agreed to his proposals. To Chamberlain's horror, Hitler then refused to accept the deal he had suggested a week earlier. Hitler made new demands: that the German take-over should be immediate, that there should be votes on whether to stay in Czechoslovakia in additional areas, that the claims of Hungary and Poland to other parts of Czechoslovakia needed consideration. Chamberlain tried to get him to compromise, but he refused. Chamberlain returned to London disappointed.

War?

At this point a war between Britain and Germany seemed a real possibility. The British government prepared to issue 38 million gas masks and anti-aircraft guns were put in place. Chamberlain tried once again to get Hitler to find a peaceful solution. He sent Sir Horace Wilson to talk to Hitler on 26 and 27 September. Hitler was not in a mood for negotiation. He told Wilson several times that he was going to 'smash the Czechs'.

SOURCE G

Sudeten Germans greet the German invasion in October 1938. The banner offers thanks to Hitler.

SOURCE F

When Horace Wilson suggested that an attack on Czechoslovakia could lead to war with France and Britain Hitler replied:

If France and England strike, let them do so. It is a matter of complete indifference to me. I am prepared for every eventuality. It is Tuesday today, and by next Monday we shall be at war.

An invitation to Munich

On 28 September Chamberlain was in the middle of a speech to parliament describing the negotiations when he was passed an important note. The note told him that Hitler had agreed to a conference at Munich with representatives of Britain, France and Italy. The conference would try to explore a peaceful solution to the crisis over Czechoslovakia. There was wild cheering among MPs, who were relieved to hear that war might be avoided.

The Munich Conference began on 29 September. A day later the British and French Prime Ministers agreed with Hitler on the terms of the annexation of the Sudetenland. Czechoslovakia was not represented at the conference. The conference did not involve any real negotiations. Britain and France simply agreed to give Hitler what he wanted. On 1 October German troops marched unopposed into the Sudetenland. The Czech President, Beneš, was forced to go into exile.

SOURCE H

On 30 September the German general, Jodl, wrote about the Munich Agreement in his diary.

The Pact of Munich is signed. Czechoslovakia as a power is out. The genius of the Führer and his determination not to avoid the risk of world war have again won us victory without the use of force.

>> Activity

1 Who was Konrad Henlein? What part did he play in the Czechoslovak crisis?

2 What happened when Chamberlain met Hitler on 15 and 22 September 1938?

3 What was agreed at the Munich Conference?

4 What clues can you find as to why Chamberlain and Daladier decided to give way to Hitler over Czechoslovakia?

5 What can we learn from the Munich crisis about the personality of Hitler?

Different views of appeasement

Since 1945 historians have disagreed passionately about Chamberlain's policy of trying to satisfy Hitler's demands, known as 'appeasement'. There have been two conflicting views: some historians say appeasement was cowardly and stupid because it encouraged Hitler to demand more and more; other historians are much more sympathetic and say that Chamberlain's decisions made a lot of sense at the time.

Was the British policy of appeasement justified?

TWO INTERPRETATIONS OF CHAMBERLAIN'S RESPONSE TO HITLER

Interpretation A

Chamberlain was foolish. He misunderstood Hitler. Chamberlain thought that Hitler was a reasonable man. He was wrong.

Interpretation B

Chamberlain was no fool! It's easy to look back and criticise Chamberlain but he was in a difficult position. Appeasement seemed sensible at the time.

>> Activity

1 Look back to the story of how Hitler took over Austria and the Sudetenland (pages 68-71). Do you think that Chamberlain took the right approach to Hitler?

2 Consider the following four factors that led Chamberlain to believe in appeasement. For each factor work out whether it fits in with Interpretation A or Interpretaton B.

SOURCE A

Neville Chamberlain.

FACTOR 1
THE PERSONALITY OF CHAMBERLAIN

Like many people who had lived through the First World War, Chamberlain was horrified at the idea of another war. He believed passionately in the importance of peace.

SOURCE B

Writing before he became Prime Minister Chamberlain said:

War wins nothing, cures nothing, ends nothing. When I think of the 7 million young men who were cut off in their prime, the 13 million who were maimed or mutilated, the misery and suffering of the mothers and the fathers...in war there are no winners, but all are losers.

Chamberlain was not used to dealing with fanatics like Hitler. He was a great believer in the power of talk and negotiations. In 1937 he said to the Soviet ambassador to London: 'If only we could sit down at a table with the Germans and run through all their complaints and claims. That would greatly reduce the tension.' Chamberlain was an honest man and assumed that other leaders were also honest. He believed Hitler when the German leader said that after Czechoslovakia there would be no more threats to peace in Europe. Hitler was, in fact, lying. On his return from Munich Chamberlain told his colleagues that Hitler now respected him. This was not true. In private Hitler described Chamberlain as a worm and said that he would like to kick him down a flight of stairs.

SOURCE C

Chamberlain's comments to the Cabinet at the time of the Munich crisis were summarised in the Cabinet records:

He [Chamberlain] also had in mind that you could say more to a man face to face than you could put in a letter. He thought that doubts as to the British attitude would be better removed by discussion than by any other means.

In his view, Herr Hitler had certain standards. He had a narrow mind and was violently prejudiced on certain subjects; but he would not deliberately deceive a man whom he respected. He was sure that Herr Hitler now felt some respect for him. When Herr Hitler announced that he meant to do something, it was certain that he would do it. Hitler had said that once the present situation had been settled he had no more territorial ambitions in Europe. To miss all this would be a great tragedy. A peaceful settlement of Europe depended upon an Anglo–German understanding.

FACTOR 2
CONCERN FOR THE EMPIRE

The British Empire mattered a great deal to British politicians in the 1930s. The most powerful voices in the Empire were those of the self-governing countries, known as the dominions – Canada, Australia, New Zealand and South Africa. The dominions were great supporters of appeasement and made it very clear at the time of Munich that they would not back Britain if it came to a war over Czechoslovakia.

On 1 September 1938 Chamberlain was told that the South African and Australian governments would not give military support if war broke out. On 24 September the South African parliament voted in favour of neutrality if war broke out between Germany and Britain. It was clear to Chamberlain that an aggressive policy towards Germany would split the British Empire.

The Empire influenced Chamberlain in another way. Much of the Empire was in Asia where Britain faced another threat in the form of the rise of Japan. British military leaders were terrified at the idea of a war with both Germany and Japan. The generals and admirals did not believe that Britain was strong enough to fight both countries at the same time. The military leaders supported the idea of appeasement of Germany.

SOURCE D

The Defence Requirements Committee 1936 stated:

It is a cardinal requirement of our national and Imperial security that our foreign policy should be so conducted as to avoid a possible development of a situation in which we might be confronted simultaneously with the hostility of Japan in the Far East, Germany in the West and any power on the main line of communication between the two.

SOURCE XX

"EUROPE CAN LOOK FORWARD TO A CHRISTMAS OF PEACE", SAYS HITLER

A criticism of appeasement. This David Low cartoon of the time suggests that Hitler was effortlessly destroying small countries who had put their trust in Britain and France.

FACTOR 3
THE SLEEPING SUPERPOWERS

If Britain had been given effective support by the USA or the USSR its leaders could have taken a harder line towards Germany. This was not possible because the USA maintained its 'isolationist' policy and the British leaders did not trust the communist USSR.

Until the late 1930s American spending on defence was very limited. As a result, the Americans did not have the military strength to match their economic strength. Although the USA was a very rich country, in 1937 it spent only 1.5 per cent of its national income on defence. By contrast, Germany was spending 23.5 per cent of its total income on defence in the same year. The USA was rightly described as a 'sleeping giant'. As a result of the long-standing policy of isolation, the American armed forces were in no position to fight. In 1937 the USA had a small standing army, largely equipped with inefficient, old-fashioned weapons. The American air force was considerably outnumbered by the German and Japanese air forces.

The American President, F. D. Roosevelt, hated war. He was also a realistic politician who tried to respond to the mood of the American people. America had been devastated by the Depression and the American people were concerned with the need to rebuild their own country. Many Americans were not interested in what happened in Europe. Other Americans did care about the wider world but felt that the USA should try to stamp out war and the arms trade. A temporary Neutrality Act was passed in 1935 and this was made permanent in 1937. As result, Chamberlain could expect no help from America in any struggle with Germany.

SOURCE E

Roosevelt in 1936:

We shun political commitments which might entangle us in foreign wars. We are not isolationists except insofar as we seek to isolate ourselves from war.

The Soviet Union was another source of potential support against Hitler. The Soviet Red Army was large but the British authorities did not have a very high opinion of its ability. The British leaders hated communism. The unreliability of the USSR was heightened by the purges that Stalin carried out in the late 1930s. The Soviet leader accused many leading communists of treachery and many of them were killed. In 1937 the purges reached the Red Army. Stalin destroyed almost his entire military leadership: 35,000 leading officers were executed, including nearly all his top military experts. Of the 80 members of the Supreme Military Council, 75 were executed. This greatly weakened the fighting capacity of the Soviets. It also convinced British leaders that Soviet military help against Germany was of little use.

Chamberlain knew that without support from other powerful countries, war with Germany was risky. In the First World War, Britain and France fought Germany with allies in Russia, Italy and Japan. Even with these allies Britain and France were only able to defeat Germany when the USA entered the war. In the late 1930s Britain and France had no powerful allies. If it came to war they could not be sure of winning.

SOURCE F

A German cartoon of 1937 shows Russia at war with itself. A two-headed creature (with the face of Stalin) attacks itself. At this time Stalin's purges were greatly weakening the strength of the Soviet army.

FACTOR 4
PLAYING FOR TIME

Appeasement was a complex policy. It was not just a question of giving in to Hitler. The negotiations were accompanied by a policy of rearmament so that, if necessary, aggression could be resisted by force.

Between 1934 and 1938 Britain increased four-fold the amount of money spent on defence. One view of appeasement is that it gave Britain time to rearm so that when the crisis with Germany finally came to a head in 1939 Britain was better prepared. At the time of Munich in 1938 Chamberlain felt that rearmament had not gone quite far enough for Britain to risk a war. His military advisers urged him to play for time.

SOURCE G

Advice from the British military leader, General Ismay, to Chamberlain at the time of Munich:

From the military point of view time is in our favour. If war has to come, it would be better to fight her in say 6–12 months than to accept the present challenge.

At the end of the war Hitler himself looked back to Munich and wondered if he had not made a mistake. He felt cheated by the Munich deal. He told his assistant, Bormann, that Germany should have gone to war in 1938 over Czechoslovakia.

SOURCE H

We ought to have gone to war in 1938. Although we were ourselves not fully prepared, we were better prepared than the enemy. September 1938 would have been the favourable date.

Adolf Hitler, February 1945

>> Activity

Why did a policy of appeasement make sense to Chamberlain?

In your answer you could mention the following factors:

> Chamberlain's own character
> The needs of the British Empire
> A lack of support from the USA and the USSR
> Plans for rearmament

SOURCE I

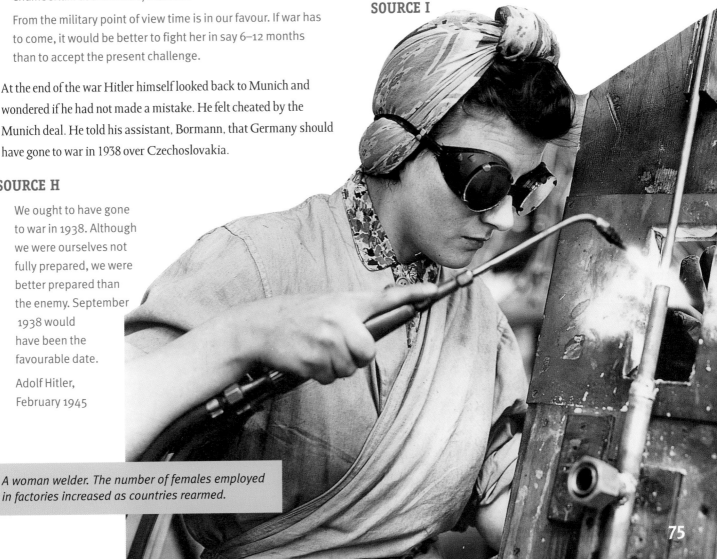

A woman welder. The number of females employed in factories increased as countries rearmed.

75

The Nazi–Soviet Pact

In 1939 Stalin amazed the world by doing a deal with his deadly enemy, Hitler.
Within a few days of the signing of the Nazi–Soviet Pact the Second World War broke out.

Why did Stalin agree to the Nazi–Soviet Pact?

Communist beliefs

As a communist Stalin believed that there was little difference between the fascist dictatorships and the Western democracies. Germany, Italy, Britain and France were all, to him, capitalist states and potential enemies of the Soviet Union. The most important task for him was to ensure that they did not unite to fight against the USSR. He was perfectly happy to do a deal with either.

Communist writers taught that capitalist powers were naturally aggressive. Countries attacked each other to get more markets or raw materials. Stalin believed this and expected that sooner or later there would be another war like the First World War. His concern was that capitalist countries did not gang up together against the Soviet Union. He tried to make sure that the USSR was on the winning side in any war among capitalist countries.

SOURCE A

In 1925 Stalin stated that sooner or later there would be another world war.

Should such a war begin we will not be able to stand idly by. We will have to take part, but we will be the last to take part so that we may throw the decisive weight onto the scales, a weight that should prove the determining factor.

Reacting to Hitler

The rise of Hitler posed a problem for Stalin. As early as January 1934 Stalin made it clear that he was prepared to do business with Hitler. In that month he made a speech stating that the USSR could work with any country that did not threaten it. At this stage Hitler had no interest in good relations with Stalin and this early attempt by Stalin to do a deal with Nazi Germany was not successful.

SOURCE B

Hitler had always hated Soviet communism. This Nazi election poster of 1932 shows Bolshevism as an armed monster.

Support for the League and collective security

Having failed to establish a relationship with Hitler, Stalin turned instead to the Western powers. In September 1934 the Soviet Union suddenly joined the League of Nations. Before that the Soviet government had referred to the League as 'a gang of robbers'. In 1935 communist parties across the world were ordered to stop trying to organise revolution. Instead they co-operated with any anti-fascist forces.

The Soviet Foreign Minister was Maxim Litvinov. Between 1934 and 1938 he tried to build links with Britain and France, in order to counter the threat from Germany. He was a great believer in the idea of collective security: by standing together, the countries of Europe could stop German aggression.

Appeasement and the Soviets

The policy of appeasement disappointed Litvinov and Stalin and forced them to think again about the value of a link with Britain and France. With regards to the Rhineland, Austria and at Munich the Western Allies seemed too ready to ignore Hitler or do a deal with him. Stalin had never really trusted the British and the French. He suspected that their secret aim was to encourage a war between Nazi Germany and the Soviet Union in the hope that the two sides would destroy each other.

SOURCE C

Maxim Litvinov, Soviet Foreign Minister 1934–9. He tried to link up with Britain and France to build an anti-German alliance. The Western powers did not trust the Soviets and the alliance came to nothing.

SOURCE D

In June 1938 the Soviet Foreign Minister, Litvinov, reflected on the crisis over Czechoslovakia.

The entire diplomacy of the Western powers over the last five years has been an attempt to avoid any resistance to German aggression and to agree to every demand for fear of arousing German disapproval. The Soviet Government takes no responsibility for future developments.

SOURCE E

At the height of appeasement the government of the USSR began to show its annoyance with both Germany and the Western powers of Britain and France. This view is seen in an extract from the official party newspaper, Pravda, in September 1938.

The Soviet Union is indifferent to the question which imperialist brigand falls upon this or that country, this or that independent state.

SOURCE F

Stalin made this speech on 10 March 1939:

Britain and France have rejected the policy of collective security and have taken up a policy of non-intervention and neutrality. The policy of non-aggression is a way of encouraging aggression. Britain and France are encouraging the Germans to march east. They are saying to Germany, 'Just start war on the Bolsheviks and everything will be all right.'

>> Activity

What can we learn from these sources about how appeasement affected the way the Soviet Union viewed Britain and France?

A Soviet offer to the West

By the spring of 1939 there was a real possibility of Britain and France going to war with Germany. What was not clear was the position of the Soviet Union. Both sides wanted a deal with the Soviet Union. For a while it still seemed that the Western powers would succeed in winning Soviet support. On 17 April 1939 the Soviet Foreign Minister, Litvinov, outlined the basis for a treaty to France and Britain. This would have involved all three promising to defend the existing borders of the states of Eastern Europe from German attack, and each country promising to help the others in case of German attack.

A change of foreign minister

It took Britain six weeks to reply to this offer. Stalin was not impressed that it took so long. He thought it indicated that the Western allies were not serious about an alliance. He began to look towards Germany for a deal. Stalin indicated a change of approach in May. He dismissed Litvinov and appointed Molotov to be the Soviet Foreign Minister. Litvinov had been on friendly terms with some Western politicians. His dismissal was a sign that Stalin was open to offers from Nazi Germany. Exploratory talks began between the Soviets and the Germans in May. These were secret talks and the British and the French knew nothing of them. Contacts between the Germans and the Soviets continued through the summer. Germany made it clear that, if the Soviet Union stayed neutral, the Soviet government could increase its territory in Eastern Europe.

SOURCE G

Hitler explained the consistency of his foreign policy on 11 August 1939 in conversation with Carl Burckhardt, the High Commissioner of the League of Nations in Danzig.

Everything that I undertake is directed against Russia; if the West is too stupid and too blind to understand this, then I will be forced to reach an understanding with the Russians, smash the West, and then turn all my concentrated strength against the Soviet Union. I need the Ukraine so that no one can starve us out again as in the last war.

Failure in Leningrad

Public talks between the Western powers and the Soviets carried on in the early summer of 1939 but they got nowhere. On 12 August British, French and Soviet military leaders met for talks in Leningrad. The Soviet delegates asked the British and the French if they could ensure a right of passage for Soviet troops through Polish and Romanian territory. The British and the French said 'no'. The Polish and Romanian governments did not want Soviet troops entering their territory on the way to fight the Germans. The Soviet generals were exasperated by this. Voroshilov, the leader of the Soviet delegates, said, 'Are we supposed to beg for the right to fight our common enemy?' The talks ended in failure on 21 August.

SOURCE H

Soviet troops in 1938. At this time, Stalin was unsure whether to use these forces against Germany.

Hitler sends a letter

The Soviets were further annoyed that the British and French delegates did not include senior ministers or top generals. As a result they did not have the power to sign a treaty. The Germans did things differently. On 20 August Hitler took the unusual step of writing a personal letter to Stalin offering high level talks in Moscow. Stalin was impressed by this.

SOURCE I

Hitler sent this personal letter to Stalin on 20 August:

The tension between Germany and Poland has become intolerable. A crisis may develop any day. In my opinion it is desirable for our two states to enter into a new relationship, without losing any time. I propose that you receive my foreign minister in Moscow. He will have the fullest power to sign the pact. I should be glad to receive your early answer.

SOURCE J

Stalin replied to Hitler the next day.

I thank you for your letter. I hope that the German–Soviet Non-Aggression Pact will mark a decided turn for the better in the political relations between our two countries.

Ribbentrop calls on Stalin

On 23 August, two days after the talks with Britain and France had broken down, Hitler sent Ribbentrop, his Foreign Minister, to Moscow. Ribbentrop, unlike the British and the French delegates, was a senior figure and he had full power to negotiate and sign a non-aggression treaty.

In Moscow, Ribbentrop met Stalin and began bargaining. Stalin was particularly interested in a secret section of the proposed treaty. In the so-called 'secret protocol', Germany and the Soviet Union agreed to carve up most of the territory that lay between their two countries. The Soviet Union was offered control of vast areas of territory, including Finland, Latvia, Estonia, Lithuania, and parts of Belarus and the Ukraine that were ruled by Poland. The pact was soon signed. Stalin celebrated by drinking champagne with Ribbentrop and proposing a toast to Hitler: 'I know how much the German people loves its Führer; I should therefore like to drink his health'.

SOURCE K

Molotov signs the Non-Aggression Pact with Germany. Ribbentrop, Stalin and others look on.

The two choices

Focus

By the middle of August 1939 Stalin was faced with two clear choices. He opted for the German offer. Look at the following details of the two offers. Can you work out why Stalin found the German offer more attractive?

The British and French offer

The British and French offered a military agreement with the Soviet Union. If Germany attacked Poland, the Soviet Union would join Britain and France and go to war against Germany. The theory was that the threat of war from Britain, France and the Soviet Union would be enough to stop Hitler from sending his troops into Poland. It was not at all clear how this military agreement would work in practice. The Polish government disliked the Soviet leaders and refused to accept that Soviet troops could enter Poland. By signing, the Soviet Union risked getting involved in a war. In return, the Soviet Union would receive support from Britain and France if German troops attacked Soviet territory. The Soviet Union would not gain any additional land by signing.

The German offer

The Germans offered a non-aggression pact with the USSR. This meant that each side promised not to attack the other. In addition there was a secret offer to divide up much of Eastern Europe between Germany and the USSR. In return for allowing the Germans to conquer most of Poland, the USSR would be given control of the Baltic states and parts of Belarus, the Ukraine and the remainder of Poland. These were territories that Russia had controlled before the 1917 Revolution. By signing the Soviet Union avoided, at least for a while, involvement in a war. In return the Soviet Union would be given control of huge areas in Eastern Europe.

>> Activity

Look at these interpretations of the negotiations in 1939. Do they help us to understand why Stalin agreed to a deal with Germany?

SOURCE L

A modern British historian has tried to explain Stalin's decision.

Stalin was presented with a choice, an agreement with France and Great Britain or one with Germany. On 23 August 1939 von Ribbentrop and Molotov signed the German–Soviet non-aggression pact in Moscow. This pact made war in Europe inevitable. Why did Stalin not opt for an agreement with France and Great Britain? Stalin decided that war was inevitable, with Germany the aggressor, so he set out to make sure that the Soviet Union came out on top.

M. McAuley, *The Soviet Union since 1917*, 1981

SOURCE M

In November 1958 Khrushchev, the Soviet leader, explained his view of how the Second World War could have been avoided.

Given a more far-sighted policy on the part of the Western Powers, co-operation between the Soviet Union, the United States and France could have been established much earlier, in the first years after Hitler seized power in Germany. Then there would have been no occupation of France, no Dunkirk and no Pearl Harbor. It would have been possible to save millions of human lives.

SOURCE N

In his memoirs Churchill, the former British Prime Minister, said that the Western powers had missed a big opportunity in 1939.

There can be no doubt that Britain and France should have accepted the Russian offer. The alliance of Britain, France and Russia would have struck deep alarm into the heart of Germany in 1939 and war might have been averted. If Mr Chamberlain on receipt of the Russian offer had replied: 'Yes. Let us three band together and break Hitler's neck', history might have taken a different course.

W. Churchill, 1948

SOURCE O

The official Soviet view of the pact was expressed in 1985 by a communist historian called Vasili Ryabov.

The Soviet government knew that it would be a short-lived agreement. Yet it was the right step to take in the situation. History proved the Soviet Union right. Almost two years of peace followed and this showed that the right step had been taken. From 1939 to June 1941 the total strength of the Soviet armed forces rose 2.8 times to well over five million. The strengthening of Soviet air defences also received considerable attention.

SOURCE P

A cartoon of the time from a Turkish newspaper ridiculing the unlikely alliance of Hitler and Stalin.

>> Activity

Explain in your own words why you think Stalin agreed to do a deal with Hitler. In your answer you could mention:

> Stalin's beliefs as a communist;

> the failure of appeasement;

> the weakness of the British and French offer in 1939;

> the strength of the German offer in 1939.

Hitler's war

German forces entered Polish territory on 1 September.
Two days later, on 3 September 1939, the British and the
French governments declared war on Germany.
The Second World War had begun.

Why did the Second World War break out?

SOURCE A

In March 1939 Germany invaded what was left of Czechoslovakia. Britain and France took no action. Hitler then turned to Poland. Having taken Czechoslovakia without any resistance, he thought that Britain and France would not try to stop him over Poland. Hitler said that the city of Danzig must be returned to Germany and Germany must have access to Danzig through Polish territory. The Treaty of Versailles had taken Danzig from Germany and put it under League of Nations control.

The fall of Czechoslovakia, however, had convinced the British and the French that appeasement had failed. Chamberlain's

An angry and bewildered crowd of people look on as German forces take control of the remnants of Czechoslovakia, March 1939.

reaction when he heard the news from Czechoslovakia was to say, 'After this I cannot trust the Nazi leaders again.' On 31 March the British government stated that Britain would stand by Poland in case of war. British politicians had concluded that Hitler had to be stopped otherwise he would eventually challenge the existence of the British Empire. Similarly, the French Prime Minister, Daladier decided that only war would stop Hitler from dominating Europe and controlling France. Hitler thought that Chamberlain and Daladier were bluffing.

On 23 August 1939 the Nazi–Soviet Non-Aggression Pact was signed. This was part of Hitler's plan for the conquest of Poland. He thought that without Soviet support Britain and France would not feel strong enough to risk a war with Germany. The pact led

Hitler to make an enormous mistake. He did not realise that by this stage Britain and France were prepared for war.

The governments of Britain and France were not as frightened by the German–Soviet Pact as Hitler had hoped. They did not think much of the Soviet army so they were not too worried by Soviet neutrality. Italy and Japan were annoyed by the news of the pact and they refused to help Hitler. The loss of Italy and Japan was good news for leaders in Britain and France. The British government was also heartened to know that the dominions of Canada, Australia and New Zealand supported a new tough line and had abandoned appeasement. To Hitler's surprise, Britain and France responded to his attack on Poland by declaring war.

Hitler's mistake

>> Activity

A number of factors encouraged Hitler to believe that an attack on Poland would not lead to war with Britain and France:

> His experience of appeasement led him to think that British and French politicians were not prepared to fight.
> His key advisers told him that the British and the French would not go to war.
> He overestimated the impact of the Nazi–Soviet Pact on Britain and France.
> Hitler did not understand the motives of the Western leaders.

Look at the sources opposite. Can you see any links between them and the factors which led Hitler to misjudge the attitude of Britain and France?

SOURCE B

A London newspaper vendor with the headline that war is declared, 3 September 1939.

SOURCE C

This was the view of Ribbentrop, the German Foreign Minister, in May 1939.

It is certain that within a few months not one Frenchman nor a single Englishman will go to war for Poland.

SOURCE D

Hitler in August 1939:

Our enemies have men who are below average. No personalities. No masters. No men of action. Our enemies are little worms. I saw them at Munich. They will be too cowardly to attack. They won't go beyond a blockade. My only worry is that Chamberlain or some other such pig of a fellow will come at the last moment with proposals.

SOURCE E

Albert Speer was Hitler's Minister of Armaments. He later recalled Hitler's reaction when he heard the news that the German–Soviet Pact had been signed:

He stared into space for a moment, flushed deeply then banged on the table so that the glasses rattled and exclaimed in a voice breaking with excitement. 'I have them! I have them!'

SOURCE F

Hitler's reaction to the news that Britain intended to declare war:

When I finished [reading out the British ultimatum] there was complete silence. Hitler sat immobile, gazing before him. After an interval, which seemed like an age he turned to Ribbentrop. 'What now?' asked Hitler with a savage look, as though implying that his foreign minister had misled him about England's probable reaction.

P. Schmidt, *Hitler's Interpreter*, 1951

SOURCE G

In October 1939, after the war had started, Hitler was puzzled by the British attitude.

Why do they fight, they have nothing to gain? They have no definite objectives. We want nothing from Great Britain or France. I have not a single aspiration in the West. I want England to retain her Empire and her command of the seas unimpaired.

Complex causes?

During and immediately after the Second World War the cause of the conflict seemed very simple: the war was caused by the aggression of Hitler. More recently, historians have argued about the part played by Hitler. Some of them have put more emphasis on other causes. Several of these causes have been explored in earlier sections of this book.

ONE WAR: MANY CAUSES

The Treaty of Versailles, 1919

Most Germans disliked the terms of the Treaty of Versailles. They were unhappy at the way land was taken from Germany.

The failure of the League of Nations

After the First World War people hoped that the League of Nations would sort out arguments between states. The League and its policy of collective security did not work well. It was unable to stop aggression in Manchuria and Abyssinia.

The Depression of the early 1930s

The political results of the Depression made the world a more dangerous place – there was an increase in:

> isolationism in the USA;

> support for the Nazi Party in Germany;

> disarmament and a sense of weakness in France and Britain.

The Policy of Appeasement

Britain and France were reluctant to take a firm line against Germany 1936–1938.

Stalin's decision in August 1939

The Soviet leader rejected an alliance with Britain and France. Instead he signed an agreement with Nazi Germany.

An argument among historians

Debate about the start of the war has centred on a number of questions:

> How far was Hitler to blame for the war?

> Did Hitler have a plan to get Germany involved in a world war?

> Were Hitler's policies before 1939 any different from those of earlier German leaders, such as Wilhelm II and Stresemann?

SOURCE H

Great controversy was caused in 1961 when A. J. P. Taylor wrote a book called The Origins of the Second World War. *He argued that:*

The British government, not Hitler, took the lead in dismembering Czechoslovakia. The British government in 1939 gave Hitler to believe that they were more concerned to impose concessions on the Poles than to resist Hitler.

Taylor asserted that:

> Hitler did not stick to a grand plan. He made his policies up as he went along.

> He hoped to make gains through threatening war but wanted to avoid war.

> Hitler's views were similar to those of many other Germans.

> Other factors, besides the personality of Hitler, played a crucial role in the outbreak of war. These factors include the appeasement policy of Britain and France.

>> Activity

Look at the table 'One war: many causes'. Can you explain any links between the causes and the outbreak of war between Britain and France on one side and Germany on the other side?

SOURCE I

Followers of Hitler marching at a Nazi rally at Nuremberg.

> How far was there a long-term plan behind Nazi acts of aggression?

SOURCE J

Alan Bullock is a leading modern British biographer of Hitler. He wrote an important book about Hitler in 1991. Bullock disagrees with Taylor, arguing that:

> there was a consistency in Hitler's thinking from 1924 when he wrote *Mein Kampf* until his death in 1945 – he wanted to set up a German empire in Eastern Europe;

> Hitler knew that sooner or later a great war would be necessary to achieve a German empire in Eastern Europe.

> no other German leader would have dared to carry out foreign policy in the way that Hitler did;

> a major responsibility for causing the Second World War lies with Hitler.

>> Activity

Look at these quotations. Which do you think come from Bullock and which from Taylor?

a I find it difficult to imagine under any other German leader the extraordinary successes of the Nazis between 1930 and 1933 and the foreign policy and military successes of 1936–1941.

b In one sphere Hitler changed nothing. His foreign policy was the same as that of his predecessors and indeed of virtually all Germans. Like them Hitler, too, wanted to free Germany from the restrictions of the peace treaty; to restore a great German army; and then to make Germany the greatest power in Europe.

c Hitler never doubted that the racist empire in the east would have to be won by force.

d The vital question concerns Great Britain and France. They were the victors of the First World War. They had the decision in their hands. It was perfectly obvious that Germany would seek to become a great power again. Why did the victors not resist her?

The 1930s: the road to war

THE IMPACT OF THE DEPRESSION

After Locarno in 1925 it seemed that the world was entering a new period of peace. The years of optimism ended with the Wall Street Crash in October 1929. Many American investors were ruined when millions of dollars were wiped off the value of shares. This led to a great economic crisis that swept the whole world. Most governments made matters worse by 'protectionism': putting up taxes on imports.

The Depression had serious political consequences that made war more likely:

> The USA became more isolationist. Roosevelt was elected as US President in 1932. He was more concerned with rebuilding the American economy than foreign affairs.

> The Depression encouraged extreme politics in Germany. The fanatical nationalist, Hitler, became Chancellor in 1933.

> In Italy and Japan, leaders were keen to win new territory to offset the effect of the economic crisis.

> Both Britain and France went through political turmoil and felt less able to take a firm line against aggressive nationalism.

A crowd of unemployed men in the USA – the economic crisis soon spread to much of the rest of the world.

A CATALOGUE OF AGGRESSION

Japan, Italy and Germany went on the offensive in the 1930s. In each country the leaders believed in aggressive nationalism. They challenged the peace by seizing land from other countries. At first, other powerful countries did virtually nothing to stop them.

1931: Japan seized the Chinese province of Manchuria. Japan was criticised by the League of Nations but no action was taken to stop Japanese aggression.

1932–3: A major disarmament conference ended in failure. The new leader of Germany, Adolf Hitler, took Germany out of the conference. Germany also left the League of Nations.

1935–6: Italy conquered the African state of Abyssinia (modern Ethiopia). The League of Nations imposed a ban on trade with Italy but this did not include restrictions on the sale of petrol. The trade ban did not stop Italy from conquering Abyssinia.

1936: Hitler marched German troops into the Rhineland. The positioning of German forces in this border area was forbidden by the Treaty of Versailles. The government of France considered sending troops to stop the Germans but they decided to take no action.

1938: In March Germany annexed Austria. The unification of Germany and Austria was called the 'Anschluss'. In September Germany annexed the Sudetenland area of Czechoslovakia. Britain and France agreed to the takeover of the Sudetenland.

1939: Germany invaded the remaining part of Czechoslovakia in March. Hitler then threatened Poland and demanded control of the city of Danzig.

THE COLLAPSE OF THE LOCARNO SETTLEMENT

> In 1925 Britain, France, Italy and Germany accepted the borders in Western Europe established in the Treaty of Versailles. Agreement between these powerful countries ended in the 1930s.

> Germany left the League of Nations in 1933.

> In 1935 an anti-German grouping of Britain, France and Italy was established called the Stresa Front.

> In 1936, after Abyssinia, the Stresa Front fell apart.

> Italy, Germany and Japan signed the Anti-Comintern Pact in 1936; they pledged to fight against communism.

APPEASEMENT

In every international crisis between 1931 and 1938 Britain and France refused to use force to stop aggression. Often they tried to negotiate a deal and to give way to the aggressor states. This was called 'appeasement'. It was the policy of the British Prime Minister, Neville Chamberlain. The climax of appeasement came at the Munich Conference in September 1938. Here Britain and France agreed to the carving-up of Czechoslovakia: the Sudetenland area was handed over to Hitler.

Appeasement has been widely criticised as a weak response to aggression. Some critics say that appeasement encouraged more aggression. Recently historians have been more sympathetic and have tried to understand why Chamberlain believed in appeasement.

> Appeasement was based on the idea that Mussolini and Hitler were reasonable men who had just grievances.

> The richest country in the world was the USA. Its policy was 'isolationist' – Americans wanted nothing to do with foreign problems. Without American support it was hard for Britain and France to take action against aggression.

> British leaders were very worried about the defence of the British Empire. They avoided conflict in Europe in order to protect the Empire.

> Under Chamberlain, appeasement went hand in hand with rearmament. He wanted to make sure that Britain was properly armed before risking war in Europe.

THE END OF APPEASEMENT

Having been successful in the Rhineland, Austria and the Sudetenland, Hitler continued his aggressive foreign policy. In March 1939 he seized the remaining parts of Czechoslovakia.

In the early summer of 1939 Hitler prepared for a war against Poland. He created a crisis over the city of Danzig. He did not believe that Britain or France would help Poland.

The complete take-over of Czechoslovakia led to an abandonment of appeasement in Britain and France. They got ready for war with Germany. Hitler thought they were bluffing.

Both sides tried to win the support of Stalin, the Soviet leader. Hitler was successful. A German–Soviet Pact was signed in August 1939. Hitler felt that without Soviet support Britain and France would not risk war.

On 1 September 1939 Hitler invaded Poland. To his surprise Britain and France responded by declaring war on 3 September 1939. The Second World War had begun.

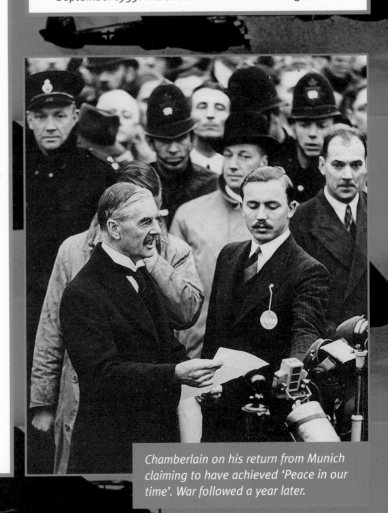

Chamberlain on his return from Munich claiming to have achieved 'Peace in our time'. War followed a year later.

The Second World War

Blitzkrieg in Poland

The Second World War began when Germany invaded Poland on 1 September 1939. Britain and France had pledged to defend Poland. On 3 September the French and the British governments declared war on Germany. The French and the British could do very little to stop a German victory in Poland. By the end of the month, Polish resistance had collapsed. On 17 September Soviet forces crossed the Polish frontier and took control of part of eastern Poland. This was part of the deal Hitler had struck with Stalin before the war in the Nazi–Soviet Pact. Stalin also moved his troops into the Baltic states of Latvia, Lithuania and Estonia.

In Poland and each of the following campaigns Hitler's methods became known as a 'Blitzkrieg' or lightning war. Blitzkrieg involved the use of overwhelming force, in as short a time as possible, in order to crush the enemy. Extensive use was made of tanks and other armoured vehicles. The Germans had much success with this technique.

The phoney war

Having succeeded in the east, Hitler's thoughts turned west. He began to make plans for an attack on France. Meanwhile the British and the French tried to weaken Germany by stopping German trade by sea. In particular they tried to cut off the supply of iron ore from Scandinavia. From October 1939 to April 1940 there was little fighting between Britain, France and Germany. This period became known as the 'phoney war'.

Fighting did take place in the winter of 1939–40 between the USSR and the small Baltic state of Finland. The Finnish army fought with great skill and ferocity and it took from October 1939 to March 1940 for the USSR to defeat her small neighbour. Eventually Finland was defeated and forced to give territory and a naval base to the USSR. The Soviet struggle to defeat Finland convinced Hitler that the

Hitler visiting Paris in 1940 after the defeat of France.

Red Army could easily be beaten by Germany. His secret long-term plan was to turn against the Soviet Union and set up a new German empire in the east.

In April 1940 the French and the British started mining Norwegian waters to stop the trade in iron ore. Germany responded by invading Norway and Denmark. The fall of Finland, Norway and Denmark led to a political crisis in Britain and France. Both prime ministers were forced to resign. In Britain Winston Churchill came to power in May 1940.

The fall of France

After months of waiting Hitler struck west in May 1940. The Netherlands, Belgium and France were invaded and rapidly defeated by German forces. A British army was forced to flee from the continent back to Britain from the port of Dunkirk. Germany took direct control of much of France, leaving part of the south and and south-east of the country under a puppet French government, with its capital in the town of Vichy. At this point it seemed that Hitler had virtually won the war. France was beaten and much of Europe was occupied. Only Britain remained to fight Germany. Sensing that the war was nearly over Mussolini joined forces with Germany in June 1940. He wanted Italy to get some of the rewards of victory.

Having defeated France, Hitler prepared for a German invasion of Britain. The German airforce, the Luftwaffe, set out to win control of the air over Britain. This was the first stage of the invasion plan. German planes bombed military sites, factories and the capital city, London, in August and September 1940. The British airforce, the RAF, fought back and the clash of the two airforces became known as the Battle of Britain. Although there were heavy losses on both sides, the RAF got the upper hand in the Battle of Britain and as a result Hitler was forced to put off his plans for an invasion of Britain.

The Italian attempt to share in Hitler's victory went disastrously wrong. An Italian army was defeated by Britain in North Africa, and Greece successfully stopped an Italian attempt to invade. Hitler was obliged to send German forces to north Africa and to Greece in order to help his ally.

German forces in the Soviet Ukraine, July 1941. Hitler's decision to attack the Soviet Union was one of the key turning-points in the war.

Hitler turns east

One of the great turning points of the war took place on 22 June 1941 when Germany invaded the Soviet Union in an operation known to the German leaders as Barbarossa. At first the blitzkrieg approach was successful for Germany. An army of over 3 million men stormed into the USSR, armed with over 3,000 tanks and 5,000 aircraft. Stalin was taken completely by surprise. German forces penetrated deep inside the Soviet Union capturing key cities such as Smolensk and Kiev. By mid-October over 3 million Soviet troops had been captured and the Germans were moving in on Moscow. At this point the campaign began to go wrong for Hitler. The German army reached the suburbs of the Soviet capital but met with fierce resistance and failed to capture the city. German troops were not equipped for the freezing Russian winter because Hitler thought that the war would be over in three months.

America joins the war: the attack on Pearl Harbor

While the battle for Moscow raged, the most powerful country in the world, the USA, became involved in the war. On 7 December 1941 the Japanese went to war against the USA with a surprise attack on the US naval base of Pearl Harbor. The result of this was that the USA joined forces with Britain and the USSR to fight Germany, Japan and Italy. In the end this was to swing the balance of the war decisively against Germany. At first Japan was all-conquering and in the early months of 1942 Japanese forces seized control of much of Eastern Asia and the islands of the Pacific.

The Japanese attack on the American fleet at Pearl Harbor. This led to American involvement in the war.

The tide turns

In the summer of 1942 the Germans renewed their attack on the USSR. They concentrated their forces in the south and tried to capture the southern city of Stalingrad. A fierce battle for the control of the city was fought in the autumn of 1942. The Soviet forces launched a counter-attack in November and the German army was eventually surrounded. At the end of January 1943 the German army at Stalingrad surrendered. The battle for Stalingrad was a crucial event. It proved that the Red Army could beat the German army. After Stalingrad Germany was on the defensive and the war began to go against Hitler.

There were further decisive battles in 1942. In June the USA stopped the tide of Japanese conquest at the Battle of Midway Island. After Midway, American forces began a slow process of capturing the islands of the Pacific from the Japanese. In October 1942 the German army in north Africa was defeated by British forces at the Battle of El Alamein. By May 1943 the Germans and Italians had been completely driven out of north Africa.

The Holocaust

Both the Germans and the Japanese treated many of their prisoners with extreme brutality. The most horrific atrocity of the war was the way millions of Jewish civilians were systematically murdered in Europe. This act is now known as the Holocaust. As German forces captured territory in Eastern Europe special army units massacred local Jews and other groups disliked by the Nazi Germans. In July 1941 the German leadership decided on a 'Final Solution' to the question of how Jewish people should be treated by the Nazi authorities. Death camps were set up to exterminate the Jewish population. Many were gassed to death; others were used as slave labour until they died. There can be no doubt that Hitler personally approved the decision.

The end game

After the decisive battles of 1942 the war went against Hitler and his allies. However, progress was slow:

> British and American forces landed in Italy in 1943. The Germans put up stiff resistance to the liberation of Italy. Rome was taken in June 1944 but it was not until 1945 that the whole of Italy was under British and American control.

> In January 1944 the Germans abandoned the siege of Leningrad, which had been going on for over two years. By the summer of 1944 the Germans were in retreat across the Soviet Union.

> France was invaded on 6 June 1944. This was known as 'D Day'. By 25 August the British and American forces had reached Paris. The Germans launched a counter-attack in December 1944 in the Ardennes area of Belgium. After some early success the German attack was turned back.

> The USA liberated territories in the Pacific taken by Japan. The Japanese forces put up ferocious resistance at every stage. In October 1944 the Americans invaded the Philippines. Over 170,000 Japanese soldiers were killed before the capital, Manila, was taken.

German power in Europe finally collapsed in April 1945. Soviet forces captured Berlin and Hitler committed suicide. The German forces finally surrendered on 8 May 1945 but the war continued against Japan. The American government was very worried at the level of Japanese resistance. The Americans expected a huge loss of life if they invaded and tried to conquer the islands of Japan. American scientists had been working for some years on the development of a new kind of weapon – the immensely powerful atomic bomb. In August 1945 two atomic bombs were dropped on the Japanese cities of Hiroshima and Nagasaki. The devastation caused by these bombs forced the Japanese government to surrender on 14 August 1945. The Second World War was over.

Discussion points

> In what ways was Germany successful between 1939 and 1941?

> Why was the attack on Pearl Harbor important?

> What happened in the Holocaust?

> How did the Second World War end?

The Holocaust. The greatest atrocity of the war was the systematic murder of millions of Jewish people.

The fall of the European empires

In the early twentieth century much of Africa, Asia and the Caribbean was controlled by European countries. These European empires all collapsed in the years after 1945.

THE CAUSES OF THE COLLAPSE OF EMPIRE

> The colonies suffered badly during the Depression of the 1930s. The imperialist European countries had encouraged their colonies to produce raw materials for European factories. The price of raw materials fell catastrophically during the Depression. The result was poverty and great unrest in the colonies.

> During the war much of the Asian territory held by the Europeans was conquered by the Japanese forces. Eventually the Japanese were defeated but the war had

fatally weakened the control of the Europeans. It was now clear to the local people that the Europeans could be beaten.

> After the war Britain, France and other European states faced many economic problems. They could no longer afford the cost of keeping their empires.

> After the war there was a rising tide of nationalism in the colonies. At the same time there was a decline in imperialist feeling in the European countries.

THE MAJOR EUROPEAN EMPIRES IN AFRICA AND ASIA

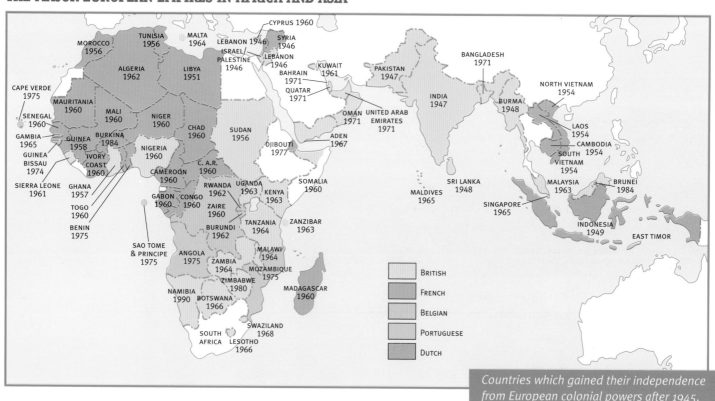

Countries which gained their independence from European colonial powers after 1945.

Handing over power

In the late 1940s there was a wave of de-colonisation in Asia and the Middle East. French forces left Syria and the Lebanon in 1946. The Philippines was given independence from the USA in 1946. At first the Dutch tried to fight nationalists in the Dutch East Indies but by 1948 the Dutch admitted defeat and granted independence to a new state known as Indonesia. Britain gave up control of the Indian sub-continent in 1947: two new states were created called India and Pakistan. A year later the British colonies of Burma and Ceylon (Sri Lanka) became free.

Independence came a little later for African and Caribbean countries. Most French and British colonies were given independence in the early 1960s. The sudden decision of the Belgian government to pull out of the Congo (modern Zaire) in 1960 led to a civil war. The end of European colonialism was complicated in those countries where a large number of European people had settled permanently. A bitter war was fought in Algeria from 1954 to 1962 between French forces and Algerian nationalists. The white minority in Rhodesia (modern Zimbabwe) refused to share power with the black majority until 1980. In South Africa there was a large minority of white people, largely descended from Dutch and British settlers. Britain had given independence to South Africa in 1910 but this white minority held on to power. It was not until 1994 that the black majority of South Africans were allowed to vote, and the black nationalist, Nelson Mandela, came to power.

The French tried to keep their old colonies in Indo-China, which included the modern countries of Vietnam, Laos and Cambodia. Local communists fought a war against the French. The Vietnamese communists defeated French forces in 1954 and won control of northern Vietnam. At this point the USA intervened and propped up a pro-western government in South Vietnam until 1975. The government of Portugal was extremely reluctant to grant independence to its African colonies of Angola and Mozambique. There was fierce fighting between nationalists and the Portuguese before independence was granted in 1975.

AFTER EMPIRE

> The history of the newly independent states was often troubled. The European states had imposed artificial boundaries, which sometimes led to ethnic unrest. The economies of most former colonies were undeveloped and relied too heavily on the sale of raw materials to the former colonial powers.

> The passing of their empires caused a sense of crisis in many European countries. There was a marked decline in power and status for those countries like Britain and France that had lost large world empires. Arguments over empire led to political turmoil and the fall of governments in France in 1958 and Portugal in 1975. Eventually most of the former colonial powers found a new identity as part of the European Community.

> The end of empire led to a large number of newly independent countries. Some of the leaders in these countries were unhappy that world politics was dominated by the conflict between the USA and the Soviet Union. A new 'non-aligned' movement began in 1955, when representatives from 29 countries met in Indonesia for the Bandung Conference setting up a loose organisation of states that were not allied to the superpowers.

Discussion points

> Why did the age of European empire come to an end?

> How did the transfer of power sometimes lead to violence?

> What have been the consequences of the end of empire?

93

The roots of the Cold War

Almost as soon as the Second World War ended, the winners started to argue with each other. In particular, a bitter conflict developed between the USA and the USSR. This struggle continued until the late 1980s. Walter Lippmann, an American journalist writing in the 1940s, called it a 'cold war' and the phrase has been widely used since.

Historians have produced three conflicting explanations for the start of the Cold War:

1 The USSR was to blame. Stalin planned for a communist take-over of the world. The take-over of Eastern Europe was the first step towards world control.

2 The USA was to blame. Soviet actions were defensive. The USA wanted to control its area of influence but refused to allow the USSR to do the same.

3 Neither side was to blame. The Cold War was based on misunderstanding and forces beyond the control of both sides.

Focus

As you find out more about the Cold War, try to work out which of these three explanations you find most convincing.

The long-term causes of the Cold War

The roots of the Cold War are to be found in earlier history. One historian said that the Cold War started, not in the 1940s, but in 1917, when the Russian Revolution took place and Soviet communism was born. By 1917 the USA was the richest country in the world. The two countries were both enormous and both had great natural resources. However, there was no chance of real friendship between them because the leaders of the new Soviet Union had extremely different beliefs from those of American politicians.

AMERICAN CAPITALISM

1 People should be free to make as much money as they can.

2 Factories and other property should be owned by individuals and companies.

3 The government should interfere as little as possible in the lives of ordinary people.

4 At elections people should be allowed to choose anyone they want for the government.

5 The Press should be able to criticise the government.

6 The government should not interfere in religion.

SOVIET COMMUNISM

1 Rich people are wicked and selfish. They should be forced to share their wealth.

2 Factories and other property should be owned by the state on behalf of all the people.

3 A communist government should get involved in every aspect of life.

4 At elections people should only be allowed to choose communists for the government.

5 The Press should never criticise a communist government.

6 Religious belief is nonsense and should be wiped out by the government.

Not only did American and Soviet leaders disagree totally. Each side was completely convinced that it was right and that other countries around the world should follow their lead. Americans believed that the answer to world problems was for other people to learn to live in an American way. The Soviet leaders were sure that their communist ideas would eventually spread to every country in the world. As a result the USA and the Soviet Union were very hostile towards each other after 1917. In 1919 the USA joined Britain, France and other countries in an attempt to destroy Soviet communism by force. They invaded the Soviet Union in support of the White Russians who were engaged in a civil war with the Bolshevik revolutionaries. This use of force failed but the hostility remained.

A female Soviet soldier meets American troops near the River Elbe, 1945. The smiles soon disappeared as the wartime allies became Cold War enemies.

The common enemy

The hostility between the the USA and the Soviet Union was suspended in 1941. They were linked by their common wish to destroy Hitler. As soon as it looked as though Hitler was going to be defeated the old tension began to re-emerge. Hitler predicted that once the war was over the two wartime allies would no longer have anything in common and would become hostile towards each other once again. The end of the war produced a difficult situation. Nazi power over Europe had been destroyed but what should replace it? In many countries there was no proper government. Decisions had to be made about the future of these countries. Inevitably, American and Soviet leaders had very different views on the best type of government for the countries of the new Europe. Shortly before his death, Hitler predicted the start of the Cold War.

'After the collapse of the German Reich, and until there is a rise in nationalism in Asia, Africa or Latin America, there will only be two powers in the world: The United States and Soviet Russia. Through the laws of history and geographical position these giants are destined to struggle with each other either through war, or through rivalry in economics and political ideas.'
Hitler's Political Testament, April 1945

Discussion points

> Explain in your own words the difference between American and Soviet ideas.

> Why did the destruction of Germany make a conflict likely between the USA and the USSR?

1945: the breakdown of the wartime alliance

The victory over Hitler created new worries for the winners. They had different views as to the future of Europe after the war. Before the end of 1945 deep divisions were emerging between the leaders of the USA and the Soviet Union.

Why did the wartime alliance fall apart in 1945?

Yalta and the argument over Poland

In February 1945 the leaders of Britain, the USA and the Soviet Union met at a place called Yalta. The three leaders were Churchill, Roosevelt and Stalin. The end of the war was in sight and they met to decide on the shape of the post-war world. Much of their time was spent discussing the future of Poland. They disagreed about how Poland should be governed.

YALTA: THE ATTITUDES OF THE LEADERS

> Roosevelt was already very ill – two months later he would be dead. Roosevelt was keen that democracy should be introduced into Eastern Europe. However, he trusted Stalin and wanted to make sure that the USA and the USSR remained on good terms after the war.

> Churchill was very concerned about the future of Poland and Eastern Europe. He did not trust Stalin. He wanted to stop Stalin from imposing communism on the territory taken by the Red Army. Britain had gone to war in 1939 to help Poland and Churchill did not want to abandon Poland to Soviet control.

> Stalin was obsessed with the security of the USSR. He wanted the Soviet Union to retain the Polish territory he had taken in 1939 as part of the Nazi–Soviet Pact. He also wanted to make sure that the new government of Poland would be friendly towards the Soviet Union.

Why was Poland the centre of attention at Yalta?

Poland was the largest country in Eastern Europe. Its post-war settlement was likely to set a pattern for the rest of Eastern Europe but the wartime allies had disagreed strongly about that settlement before Yalta.

Two different groups wanted to form the new government for Poland. Each group had a very different relationship with Stalin:

The London Poles

When the war broke out, some members of the Polish government fled to London and set up a 'government-in-exile'. They were strongly anti-Soviet. Much of Poland had been in the Russian Empire before 1917. The London Poles were Catholics and many were landowners: they hated both the idea of communism and Stalin because he had carved up their country through the German–Soviet Pact in 1939. In 1943 they were horrified to learn that the Soviet army had executed about 15,000 Polish officers and buried their bodies at a place called Katyn. Stalin knew that if the London Poles formed a Polish government, it would be hostile to the USSR.

The Lublin Poles

In July 1944 the USSR set up its own future government for Poland. This first met at the town of Lublin, and they became known as the Lublin Poles. They were mostly communists and Stalin felt that they could be trusted.

The Warsaw Uprising

The London Poles decided that their only chance of frustrating Stalin was to seize control of part of Poland before the Red Army did. In August 1944 Polish resistance fighters, loyal to the London Poles, attacked the German forces occupying Warsaw, the capital of Poland. The Soviet army was nearby but did nothing to help the Poles. Stalin did not want them to defeat the Germans. He wanted the Lublin Poles to take over after the war. The British and the Americans were appalled by the Soviet attitude. Without Soviet help, the Rising was ruthlessly smashed by the Germans and nearly 300,000 Poles were killed. The Germans sent the surviving people of Warsaw to concentration camps and when the Red Army finally took the city it was completely deserted. The Red Army went on to take control of the whole of Poland. By January 1945 the USSR announced that Poland had been liberated and the Lublin group was now in charge of Poland.

>> Activity

1 Explain in your own words the different attitudes of the leaders who met at Yalta towards Poland.

2 Who were the Lublin Poles and the London Poles?

3 What was the Warsaw Uprising?

4 Why do you think that Stalin refused to help the Warsaw rebels?

SOURCE A

German troops patrol the devastated streets of Warsaw after the abortive uprising.
> Why did Stalin fail to help the Warsaw Rising?

The meeting at Yalta

The three leaders had met before — at the Tehran summit in late 1943. The meeting at Yalta, in the Soviet Union, took place between 4 and 11 February 1945. Stalin had refused to leave the USSR so the two Western leaders had to go to him. The three men were pleased at the way the war was going. President Roosevelt talked about the friendly, 'family' atmosphere of the meeting but beneath the surface, serious disagreements existed.

The discussions at Yalta were very wide-ranging but the future of Poland dominated. The three leaders had previously agreed that the Soviet Union would take land from Poland and Poland would, in turn, be given German land. At Yalta they argued about the details and Churchill tried to limit the changes. He was worried about taking too much land from Germany and said: 'I do not want to stuff the Polish goose until it dies of German indigestion'. There was even greater disagreement about who should govern Poland.

Eventually, Truman and Churchill thought that they had won a major concession from Stalin: the Soviet leader agreed that the Lublin government should be expanded to include some of the London Poles and he accepted that free elections should be held as soon as possible in Poland. When asked how soon these elections could be held, Stalin replied: 'It should be possible within a month.'

> > **Activity**

Look at the Sources B and D. Summarise in your own words the details of the Yalta Agreement on Poland and Eastern Europe.

SOURCE B

The Yalta Agreement made the following statement about the future of Eastern Europe. This became known as the Declaration on Liberated Europe:

The three governments [USA, USSR, Britain] will assist the people in any European liberated state to form interim governments broadly representative of all democratic elements in the population and pledged to the earliest possible establishment through free elections of governments responsive to the will of the people.

SOURCE C

Churchill, Roosevelt and Stalin at Yalta, February 1945. Their discussions centred on the future of Poland.

SOURCE D

The Yalta Agreement included specific plans for the future of Poland.

A new situation has been created in Poland as a result of her complete liberation by the Red Army. This calls for the establishment of a Polish government which can be more broadly based than was possible before the recent liberation of the Western part of Poland. The Provisional Government should therefore be re-organised on a more democratic basis with the inclusion of democratic leaders from Poland itself and from Poles abroad. This Polish government shall be pledged to the holding of free elections as soon as possible. In these elections all democratic and anti-Nazi parties shall have the right to take part and to put forward candidates.

THE TERMS OF THE YALTA AGREEMENT

The final Agreement included a Declaration on Liberated Europe. This stated that each liberated country would be given an emergency government with representatives from any important non-fascist groups and that free elections would be held as soon as possible to set up a democratic government.

The borders of Poland were to be altered so that the USSR gained a huge amount of territory from eastern Poland. In return Poland was promised land taken from the eastern part of Germany.

The Lublin government in Poland was to be expanded so that it also included some of the London Poles. Free elections would be held in Poland as soon as possible.

The British and the Americans held many prisoners of war from Soviet territory. These were men from German-occupied lands who had chosen or been forced to join the German army. At Yalta it was agreed that they would be sent back to the USSR. About 10,000 of these men were executed on their return and many more were imprisoned.

The leaders agreed that Germany should be divided into occupied zones. Churchill argued that there should be a French zone, as well as a British, American and Soviet zone. This was because Churchill was keen to restore the power of France. Stalin and Roosevelt accepted this suggestion.

The USSR agreed to help in the war against Japan. In return the USSR gained control of island territories north of Japan. This turned out to be a very good deal for the USSR because Soviet troops did not have to do very much fighting before the Japanese surrender.

The leaders agreed to the setting up of the United Nations. Stalin successfully argued that each country should have a veto on the decisions of the powerful Security Council.

SOURCE E

One of the achievements of the Yalta conference was the decision to establish the United Nations.

>> Activity

The Yalta Conference covered many important topics and the table on this page gives a summary of the areas of agreement. Using the table and your knowledge of the background make a list of what Stalin gained from the Yalta Conference.

The weakness of the Yalta Agreement

Yalta was the high-point of the wartime alliance. To Roosevelt and many Americans it seemed like the beginning of a post-war period of co-operation. There was enthusiastic cheering in the American Senate when the Agreement was read out. In fact, the Yalta Agreement was flawed in a number of important ways:

> ### YALTA: THE PROBLEMS
>
> > The Soviets and the Americans interpreted it differently. The Agreement talked about the need for 'democracy' and 'free elections'. For Roosevelt democracy was the American system of free speech. Stalin's idea of democracy was a communist one, in which the communist party represented the people and no opposition was allowed.
>
> > Yalta raised false expectations in the USA. People expected that Stalin would now allow western-style governments to be set up in Eastern Europe. They were bitterly disappointed when this did not happen.
>
> > The Agreement tried to achieve compromise over the future of Poland. In fact, compromise was not possible. Either Poland was democratic or it was friendly towards the USSR. Leading figures in Polish society were anti-Russian. Stalin knew that he could only make sure that Poland was friendly by destroying free speech.

Yalta in practice

Roosevelt was proud of the Yalta Agreement. He was disappointed to see how Stalin put it into practice. Stalin paid only lip service to the idea of bringing non-communists into the government of Poland. At Yalta it was agreed that the Soviet Foreign Minister, Molotov, would negotiate the details of the new Polish government with the British and American ambassadors to Moscow. These talks were not successful. Molotov refused to let the London Poles play a significant part in the government. Harriman, the American ambassador, later said: 'We began to realise that Stalin's language was somewhat different from ours.' By the beginning of April Harriman was reporting to Truman that the talks had achieved nothing. At the same time Polish opponents of communism were dealt with ruthlessly. In March, 16 leaders of the Polish Resistance went, at the invitation of Stalin, to have talks with the Soviet authorities near Warsaw. They were promised their own personal safety. They were arrested and were never seen again.

SOURCE F

Roosevelt was now dying, but he managed to write a letter of criticism to Stalin:

I cannot conceal from you the concern with which I view the development of events since our fruitful meeting at Yalta. So far there has been a discouraging lack of progress made in the carrying out of the decisions we made at the Conference, particularly those relating to the Polish question. I am frankly puzzled as to why this should be and must tell you that I do not fully understand the attitude of your government.
F. D. Roosevelt, 1 April 1945

SOURCE G

Churchill was not pleased by the news from Poland. He wrote to Stalin on 29 April 1945.

The British went to war on account of Poland. They can never feel this war will have ended rightly unless Poland has a fair deal in the sense of independence and freedom, on the basis of friendship with Russia. It was on this that I thought we agreed at Yalta.

SOURCE H

Stalin refused to give any ground. In May, Stalin said the Americans were to blame for any bad feeling.

At Yalta it had been agreed that the existing government of Poland was to be reconstructed. Anyone with common sense could see that this means that the present [Lublin] government was to form the basis of the new government. No other understanding of the Yalta Agreement is possible. The Russians should not be treated as fools.

A new face at the White House

A key figure in the early stages of the Cold War was the American President, Harry Truman. It was only through chance that he became President. As Vice President he took over when Roosevelt died in April 1945. Truman was a Democrat politician from Missouri. He had made his reputation in domestic politics. He had only been Vice President for a few weeks and he had almost no experience of international politics. He was very different from Roosevelt and his personality played a part in the development of a tougher American policy. Roosevelt was much more diplomatic than Truman. Roosevelt was sure that the USA and the Soviet Union could remain friendly after the war. Just a few hours before he died Roosevelt sent a message to Churchill. The British leader had been trying to get Roosevelt to take a tough line on communist control in Poland. Roosevelt replied: 'I would minimize the general Soviet problem as much as possible.' To the last, Roosevelt remained convinced that the USA would stay on good terms with the Soviet Union. Truman was less certain about Soviet intentions.

SOURCE I

Harry Truman, the new American President, took a tougher line towards the Soviet Union than his predecessor, F. D. Roosevelt.

>> **Activity**

1 Explain in your own words why Roosevelt and Churchill were disappointed at the way Stalin put the Yalta Agreement into practice.

2 What evidence is there from Sources F–H, that the leaders had different interpretations of the Yalta Agreement?

Truman takes a tough line

Truman showed his different style as soon as he came to power. In April 1945 Truman spoke angrily to the Soviet Foreign Minister, Molotov. He insisted that the Soviets must carry out the Yalta Agreement and allow free elections in Poland. He would not listen to Molotov's explanations. As Molotov left he said: 'I have never been talked to like that before in my life.' To which Truman said: 'Carry out your agreements and you won't get talked to like that.'

SOURCE J

An American historian saw Truman's angry meeting with Molotov as a major step towards the start of the Cold War.

After only eleven days in power Harry Truman made his decision to lay down the law to an ally which had contributed more in blood and agony than we had – and about Poland, an area through which Russia had been invaded three times since 1914. The basis for the Cold War was laid on 23 April in the scourging which Truman administered to Molotov, giving notice that in areas of the most crucial concern to Russia our wishes must be obeyed.

D. F. Fleming, The Cold War and its Origins 1917–1960, 1961

SOURCE L

Truman described his new approach to the Soviet Union in May 1945.

We have to get tough with the Russians. They don't know how to behave. They are like bulls in a china shop. They are only twenty-five years old. We are over a hundred and the British are centuries older. We have got to teach the Russians how to behave.

The Potsdam Conference

The leaders of the USA, USSR and Britain met at Potsdam, near Berlin, between 17 July and 2 August 1945. This was the last of the great wartime summit meetings. The membership of the Conference showed that the wartime alliance was changing. At previous conferences the American leader had been Roosevelt; now it was Truman. Churchill was replaced halfway through by the Labour leader, Clement Attlee.

At Potsdam, Truman told Stalin that America had the atomic bomb. Churchill noticed the sense of power that Truman seemed to feel now that he had this powerful weapon. Later Churchill wrote: 'Truman was a changed man. He told the Russians where they got on and off and generally bossed this whole meeting.' The US government thought that it might take 20 years for the Soviet Union to develop an atom bomb. Truman believed that the bomb put the USA in a strong position in any arguments with the Soviet Union.

SOURCE K

The Allied leaders at Potsdam: Attlee, Truman and Stalin. The British and American leaders were new to their posts. Truman was determined to treat Stalin with firmness.

Focus

What was agreed at Potsdam? What were the areas of disagreement from the Potsdam discussions?

POTSDAM: AREAS OF AGREEMENT AND DISAGREEMENT

> German reparations were agreed. Each country was to take reparations from its own area of occupation. The Soviet Union was to receive some additional industrial equipment from the western zones of occupation: little of this was ever handed over.

> The details of the German–Polish borders on the rivers Oder and Neisse were finally agreed. The British and Americans disliked the position of the new border but could do little about it.

> It was agreed that the Nazi Party should be stamped out in all sectors of Germany.

> The Soviet Union wanted to play a part in the running of the rich German industrial area of the Ruhr. The USA rejected this idea.

> The Soviet Union wanted to share in the occupation of Japan. Truman firmly blocked this idea.

> The USA and Britain asked for a greater say in what went on in Eastern Europe. Stalin rejected this suggestion.

SOURCE M

Winston Churchill was the former British Prime Minister. He lost power in the 1945 general election. He made the famous 'iron curtain' speech in March 1945.

From Stettin in the Baltic, to Trieste in the Adriatic, an iron curtain has descended across the continent. Behind that line lie all the capitals of the ancient states of Central and Eastern Europe: Warsaw, Berlin, Prague, Vienna, Budapest, Bucharest and Sofia. All these famous cities lie in the Soviet sphere, and all are subject to a high and increasing control from Moscow. The Russian-dominated Polish government has been encouraged to make enormous and wrongful inroads upon Germany, and mass expulsions of millions of Germans are now taking place. The Communist Parties, which were very small in all of these Eastern states, are seeking everywhere to obtain totalitarian control.

The Iron Curtain

The new hostility towards the Soviet Union was encouraged by Winston Churchill in a famous speech on 5 March 1946. The speech was made at Fulton, Missouri. President Truman was in the audience and had seen the speech before it was given. Churchill called for an American–British alliance to meet the communist menace. At first some Americans felt that he was exaggerating. Gradually most Americans came to agree with him.

>> Activity

Look back at this unit. Explain in your own words how each of the following factors made the Cold War more likely:

a long-term hostility between the USA and the Soviet Union;

b arguments over the Yalta Agreements;

c the personality of Truman.

The Soviet take-over of Eastern Europe

After 1945 the Soviet Union took control of much of Eastern Europe. Historians are still debating the motives behind this take-over. Was this a defensive move or was this a step towards a take-over of the whole of Europe?

Why did Stalin take control of Eastern Europe?

Liberation?

The Soviet take-over was not complete until 1948 but it began before the end of the Second World War. As the Red Army drove the Germans westwards the Soviet leadership made sure that territory came under the control of people friendly to the Soviets. In most countries the Soviet government set up anti-fascist coalition governments, but gave local communists a leading position. These communist-dominated governments introduced nationalisation and took land away from the landlords. Opposition parties were gradually undermined. Elections were rigged. Eventually all opposition was destroyed and Soviet control was complete. The process was more rapid in some countries than in others.

THE SOVIET TAKE-OVER OF EASTERN EUROPE

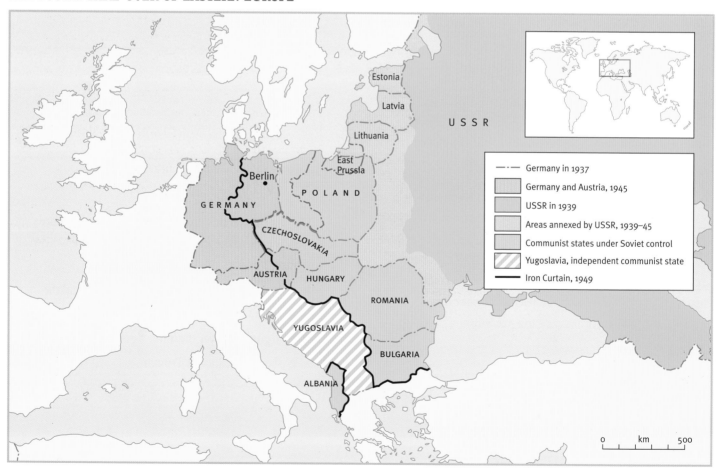

Legend:
- — · — Germany in 1937
- Germany and Austria, 1945
- USSR in 1939
- Areas annexed by USSR, 1939–45
- Communist states under Soviet control
- Yugoslavia, independent communist state
- —— Iron Curtain, 1949

STAGE 1: THE TAKE-OVER OF POLAND

As we have seen, Stalin's first priority was control of Poland. At the end of June 1945 a few London Poles were included in the Polish government. However, it remained completely dominated by the communists of the Lublin group. The Western allies admitted defeat over Poland by 'recognising' the largely communist government on 5 July 1945. This meant that Britain and the USA accepted that the communists were in charge in Warsaw. Communist power was strengthened even further in January 1947 when rigged elections were held in Poland. The leader of the London Poles, Mikolaczyk, thought his life was in danger and fled the country.

STAGE 2: THE TAKE-OVER OF ROMANIA AND BULGARIA

After Poland, Stalin's immediate priorities were the control of Romania and Bulgaria. Look at the map; can you work out why these three countries were important to Stalin? As the Red Army swept into Bulgaria and Romania in late 1944 coalition governments dominated by communists were set up. In February 1945, within days of the Yalta agreement, a top Soviet politician, Andrei Vyshinsky, ordered the King of Romania to appoint a new prime minister chosen by Stalin. When the King said that this was not in line with the Yalta agreement, Vyshinsky slammed his fist on the table and shouted at the King. Stalin got his prime minister. By the middle of 1945 communists were in firm control in Romania. Elections took place in Bulgaria in November. These elections were rigged and the communist Fatherland Front won. In September 1946 the communist government in Bulgaria abolished the monarchy. The monarchy in Romania was abolished in 1947.

STAGE 3: THE TAKE-OVER OF HUNGARY AND CZECHOSLOVAKIA

In contrast with Poland, Romania and Bulgaria Stalin did not at first have a clear view of what he wanted for Hungary and Czechoslovakia. He allowed free elections to take place in Hungary in November 1945. The non-communist Smallholders' Party was the most successful party. Fresh elections were held in August 1947. This time the elections were rigged and an exclusively communist government took power. In November all non-communist parties were banned.

The final stage in the take-over came when communists seized power in Czechoslovakia in 1948. Before that the country was ruled by a coalition of communists and non-communists. This was the one country in Eastern Europe with a strong local communist party. There were fair elections in 1946 and the communists won 38 per cent of the vote. The President, Beneš, was a non-communist while Gottwald, the Prime Minister, was a communist. The Foreign Minister, Jan Masaryk, was also a non-communist. There was an economic crisis in the country from mid-1947. The harvest was bad and industry was in trouble. Elections were due for May 1948. The communists were afraid that they would do badly. The communists used armed force to seize power. Many non-communists were arrested and Masaryk was murdered. Rigged elections were held shortly afterwards and the communists won a huge majority. The Soviet take-over was complete.

The war as a triumph for Soviet communism

The Soviet leaders felt that their country had made by far the most important contribution to the winning of the war. The British and the Americans had helped, but Stalin believed, with some justification, that the Soviet Union had cut the heart out of the German army. 10 million Germans, who represented 80 per cent of German losses, died on the Eastern Front. The Soviet leaders believed their country had largely won the war, so they had a right to shape the future of Europe.

Stalin also saw the war as proof that communism worked: in the battle to the death between communist Russia and capitalist Germany, communism had triumphed. This gave a new sense of confidence and determination to the Soviet government.

Never again: the level of the Soviet wartime sacrifice

The Soviet Union suffered much more than the other allies during the war. This made a difference to attitudes after the war. About 15 million Soviet soldiers and civilians had been killed by the Germans. In addition, many people had died because of shortages of food and the other harsh conditions of wartime. As many as 25 million Soviet citizens may have died because of the war. Stalin was determined that this should never be allowed to happen again.

Soviet strategic thinking

How could the Soviet Union ensure that the devastation of the Second World War was not repeated? In 1914 and 1941 Germany had attacked Russia through Poland. In 1945 Stalin thought that sooner or later there could be yet another attack through Poland. To stop this he was determined to control Poland and other East European states. Before the Second World War these countries had been independent. Almost all of them had been governed by right-wing, anti-communist leaders. In Moscow it seemed quite likely that if the countries of Eastern Europe were again allowed to be independent, the states would again become anti-Soviet.

US imperialism?

The USA was by far the wealthiest country in the world in 1945. The Soviet government was convinced that American business leaders were planning to spread their power and increase their profits by buying up companies in other countries and selling American goods wherever they could. In this way the USA could build up a new kind of world empire. American troops would not need to conquer new lands: American capitalism would do it instead. As good communists it was the job of the Soviet leaders to try to stop American businesses from dominating the world. The setting up of a group of friendly communist countries was one way of doing this.

SOURCE A

The devastated landscape of Stalingrad at the end of the war. The Soviet Union suffered far greater damage than any other country.

Stalin's motives

Look at Sources B–F. What can we learn from them about the Stalin's motives at the end of the Second World War? Can you find evidence that:

a Stalin wanted a barrier to stop the Soviet Union from being invaded in the future;

b Stalin did not trust the Americans;

c Stalin believed in communism and thought that every country should be communist.

SOURCE E

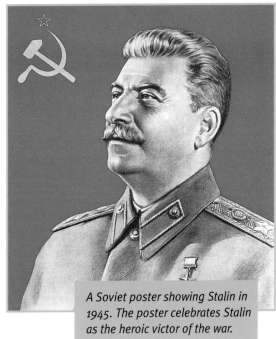

A Soviet poster showing Stalin in 1945. The poster celebrates Stalin as the heroic victor of the war.

SOURCE B

Stalin speaking on 9 February 1945:

Victory means, first of all, that our Soviet social system has won. The Soviet social system has successfuly stood the test in the fire of war and it has proved its complete vitality. The Soviet social system has proved to be more capable and more stable than a non-Soviet social system. The Soviet social system is a better form of society than any non-Soviet social system.

SOURCE C

At Yalta, in February 1945, Stalin tried to explain to Churchill and Roosevelt why Poland was so important to the Soviet Union.

Mr Churchill has said that for Great Britain the Polish question is one of honour. But for the Russians it is a question both of honour and security. Throughout history Poland has been the corridor for attack on Russia. It is not merely a question of honour for Russia, but one of life and death.

SOURCE D

In May 1945 Stalin was worried at the end of the war in Europe and felt unhappy at the approach of the new US president, Harry Truman.

The Soviet government is alarmed by the attitude of the US government. The American attitude cooled once it became clear that Germany was defeated. It was as though the Americans were saying that the Russians were no longer needed.

SOURCE F

In March 1946, Stalin replied to Churchill's famous speech about the 'iron curtain':

It should not be forgotten that the Germans invaded the USSR through Finland, Poland, Rumania, Bulgaria and Hungary. The Germans were able to invade because governments hostile to the Soviet Union existed in these countries. As a result the Soviet Union had a loss of life several times greater than that of Britain and the United States put together. Some people may be able to forget the huge sacrifices of the Soviet people but the Soviet Union cannot forget them. And so what is surprising about the fact that the Soviet Union, anxious for its future safety, is trying to see that governments loyal to the Soviet Union should exist in these countries? How can anyone who has not taken total leave of his senses describe these peaceful wishes of the Soviet Union as expansionist tendencies on the part of the Soviet Union?

>> Activity

It has been argued that Stalin took over Eastern Europe as the first stage towards a communist take-over of the world. Does the information in this unit support this explanation? Explain your answer in detail.

The Truman Doctrine and the Marshall Plan

The government of the USA was deeply unhappy at the spread of communism to Eastern Europe. Traditionally American foreign policy was based on isolationism: having as little to do as possible with international politics. The Soviet take-over forced American politicians to think again and to reject traditional thinking.

How did the USA react to the Soviet take-over of Eastern Europe?

After 1945 the USA moved away from isolationism and became active throughout the world. Eventually the USA built up its own 'sphere of interest': a group of pro-American states that included all of the world's richest industrialised countries.

1946: Cold War attitudes develop

Relations between the USA and the Soviet Union deteriorated throughout 1946:

> The Americans were very critical of Soviet policy in Iran. Soviet troops were in the north of Persia, now Iran, at the end of the war. Under wartime agreements they were supposed to withdraw in March 1946. The US government suspected that this was the first step towards a Soviet take-over of part of Iran. They criticised the Soviet occupation at the United Nations. Stalin gave in and withdrew his troops.

> The Council of Foreign Ministers met in Paris in April 1946. The American representative, Byrnes, blocked every Soviet proposal and criticised Soviet policy in Eastern Europe.

> The Soviet navy wished to send ships through the Black Sea Straits and to set up naval bases in the area. Turkey felt threatened by these plans and in August 1946 the US government blocked the Soviet plans. The Americans made it clear that they would use force to resist any Soviet move. American warships were sent to the area to warn off the Soviets.

The crisis of 1947

American policy took shape in the crucial year of 1947. At the beginning of the year there was an economic crisis in Western Europe. The harvest in 1946 was poor and there was food shortage in many places. The winter was unusually fierce and people were cold as well as hungry. In Britain unemployment was soaring and food rationing was more severe than it had been during the war. In Germany people were close to starvation. Millions of refugees had fled to western Germany and this added to the shortage of fuel, food and jobs. In France and Italy discontent led to massive support for the local communist parties; unless conditions improved there was a real possibility that the communists could come to power. By early 1947 it was clear to the US government that their friends in Western Europe could not cope alone. Some Americans had hoped that the return of peace would allow the USA to go back to its isolationist policy. Truman and his advisers realised that this was not possible.

The Truman Doctrine

In February 1947 the British government sent a dramatic message to Washington – Britain could no longer afford to pay for troops in Greece and Turkey. Unless America replaced Britain in Greece and Turkey these countries could easily come under Soviet control. Truman decided to offer American financial help to Greece and Turkey. He went further and declared that American support was available for any people who wanted to fight communism. This became known as the Truman Doctrine. It was based on the idea of containment – the USA would use its wealth and power to stop or contain the spread of communism.

SOURCE A

Truman announced his 'doctrine' in a speech to the US Congress on 12 March 1947.

At the present moment in world history nearly every nation must choose between alternative ways of life. One way of life is based upon the will of the majority, and is distinguished by free institutions, representative government, free elections, guarantees of individual liberty, freedom of speech and religion and freedom from political oppression.

The second way of life is based upon the will of a minority forcibly imposed upon the majority. It relies upon terror and oppression, a controlled press and radio, fixed elections and the suppression of personal freedom.

I believe it must be the policy of the United States to support people who are resisting attempted subjugation by armed minorities or by outside pressures. I believe that we must help free peoples to work out their own destiny in their own way.

Through the Truman Doctrine, the USA had rejected 'isolationism'. America had announced to the world that it would play a leading part in world politics. In Greece and Turkey the doctrine was successful. The communist side was defeated in the Greek Civil War by 1949, and Turkey remained part of the Western pro-American group of countries. Initially, 'the doctrine' was applied in Europe and the Middle East. Eventually, it was extended to the whole world and led to war in Korea and Vietnam.

SOURCE B

A scene from the Greek Civil War: an anti-communist soldier guards communist suspects. Truman intervened to make sure that the communists lost the war. This was the beginning of the Truman Doctrine.

>> Activity

What was the Truman Doctrine? How was the Doctrine different to the traditional American policy of isolationism?

The Marshall Plan

Another strand of American policy emerged in 1947. In Washington there was a belief that communism could only be stopped if Western Europe became wealthy. By the spring of 1947 it was clear that without American help there was little chance of economic recovery.

SOURCE C

Will Clayton, a leading American politician, was sent to Europe in May 1947 to report on conditions.

Millions of people in the cities are slowly starving. Without further prompt and substantial aid from the US, economic and political dislocation will overwhelm Europe.

The USA decided to offer massive economic aid to Western Europe. The project was organised by the American Secretary of State, General George Marshall, and was known as the Marshall Plan. Marshall announced his scheme in a speech at Harvard University in June 1947.

A large amount of American money was made available to those European countries which made an acceptable application. The Soviet Union was, in theory, able to apply for help. However, Stalin saw the plan as an attempt to impose capitalist ideas on European countries. He refused to have anything to do with it. The governments of Poland and Czechoslovkia wanted to join the Marshall Plan but Stalin ordered them not to take part. Stalin was right in thinking that Marshall Plan money would be tied to American-style ideas. The Plan was based on a belief that communism would be much less attractive to ordinary people if they had good jobs and were well paid.

SOURCE D

The American politician, Vandenburg, speaking in 1948, made it clear that the Marshall Plan was part of a strategy to stop the spread of communism.

The Plan is a calculated risk to help stop World War III before it starts. The area covered by the Plan contains 270,000,000 people of the stock which largely made America. This vast friendly segment of the earth must not collapse. The iron curtain must not come to the rims of the Atlantic.

Leaders of 16 West European countries met in Paris between July and September 1947 and wrote a recovery plan. The military governors of western Germany took part. The US accepted the plan and the first American money was transferred. The Marshall Plan was a step towards the division of Germany and this angered the Soviet authorities. Economically, the western area of Germany was now functioning as if it was a separate country from the eastern sector.

The Plan was a great success. Over four years, $13,000 million of help was provided. European countries were encouraged to reduce import taxes and this increased the level of trade. By 1952, when the Marshall Plan officially ended, the countries of Western Europe were well on the road to a period of great economic prosperity. The Plan was also very useful to the USA. By rebuilding Western Europe, America was creating wealthy trade partners who would want to buy large amounts of American goods.

SOURCE E

A Soviet anti-Marshall Plan poster depicting American aid as a menacing influence on the world.

The Soviet response

The Soviet Union organised an international conference in September 1947 in order to condemn the Truman Doctrine and the Marshall Plan. A new organisation was set up to strengthen the links between communist parties in different countries. It was called Cominform (The Communist Information Bureau).

SOURCE F

At the Cominform Conference in September 1947 the Soviet leader, A. A. Zhdanov, bitterly attacked the Truman Doctrine and the Marshall Plan.

The Truman Doctrine and the Marshall Plan are both part of an American plan to enslave Europe. The United States has launched an attack on the principle of each nation being in charge of its own affairs. By contrast, the Soviet Union is tireless in upholding the principle of real equality and independence among nations whatever their size. The Soviet Union will make every effort to ensure that the Marshall Plan is doomed to failure. The communist parties of France, Italy, Great Britain and other countries must play a part in this.

Comecon

Having failed to destroy the Marshall Plan, the USSR created its own economic bloc of countries in Eastern Europe. In January 1949 Comecon (the Council for Mutual Economic Aid) was set up. It was a trading organisation of communist countries but was nowhere near as successful as the Marshall Plan. It did not involve any injection of money into East European countries. Eventually the Soviet Union used it to encourage each country to specialise in different products.

>> Activity

1 What was the Truman Doctrine?

2 What was the Marshall Plan?

3 How did the Soviet Union react to the Truman Doctrine and the Marshall Plan?

SOURCE G

Communists in Western countries were told to try to wreck the Marshall Plan through strikes. There were very large communist parties in France and Italy. In the winter of 1947–8 communist workers in these two countries organised a series of strikes and demonstrations. This attempt to wreck the Marshall Plan did not work. Despite the strikes, American money flowed into Western Europe and eventually the strikes came to an end.

Italian soldiers arrest a lorry-load of communist activists during industrial unrest in 1948. The communists were organising strikes in order to wreck the Marshall Plan.

American motives at the start of the Cold War

The American government responded very energetically to the Soviet take-over in Eastern Europe. The Truman Plan and the Marshall Plan signalled a new stage in the developing Cold War.

Why was the US government hostile towards the Soviet Union?

The world's leading nation

The USA was well-placed to play a leading part in world affairs after 1945. It was in excellent economic condition, unlike almost every other powerful country. At the end of the war the defeated nations of Germany and Japan lay in ruins. Several of the 'winners' also faced great difficulties. Britain and France were in debt and were selling very few goods abroad. As a result they could no longer afford to maintain huge armed forces. Much of the Soviet Union was wrecked by the war. By contrast, the rich USA became even richer in the war years. The output of American factories increased by 50 per cent during the war. By 1945 half of all the manufactured goods in the world were made in the USA. One third of all the world's exports came from the USA. Money flooded in and in 1945 the USA held almost two-thirds of all the gold reserves in the world.

As the leaders of the world's richest and most successful country, American politicians were very confident and expected to have a major say in the way the world was run. Leading Americans were extremely proud of their country and believed that American-style capitalism and free trade was the way forward for all other countries. They were, therefore, annoyed by Soviet communists who tried to stop the spread of American business and said that American capitalism was wicked.

SOURCE A

An advertisement of the late 1940s illustrates the relatively high standard of living enjoyed by many Americans. As the elderly couple cook a meal in their comfortable house, their son arrives in his brand-new car. American leaders were very proud of their economic prosperity.

The nuclear monopoly

The USA was not only rich, it was also powerful. With 1,200 major warships and over 2,000 heavy bombers it had the strongest navy and airforce in the world. The American feeling of power was greatly increased when the atomic bomb was produced in 1945. No other country had this immensely powerful weapon. The Soviet Union produced an atom bomb in 1949, but in 1945 Americans thought that it could be 20 years before any other country caught up with their atomic power. American politicians took a more aggressive line towards the Soviet Union because they thought they could use the bomb as a threat. (This overestimated the importance of the atomic bomb. Stalin rightly thought that the bomb was so terrible that the Americans would hardly ever dare to use it.)

Memories of the 1930s

At the start of 1946 there was a strong feeling in Washington that the US government needed to take a tough line with the USSR. Talks were getting nowhere and Truman became convinced that only the threat of force would stop the Soviets from taking over more land. In January Truman told his advisers that he wanted the USSR to be faced with an 'iron fist'. He added, 'I'm tired of babying the Soviets'.

This hard-line approach was greatly influenced by recent memories. The world had been through great turmoil in the 1930s. In Washington it seemed that the causes of the problem were:

> the rise of evil dictators like Hitler

> the economic crisis of the pre-war Depression.

People in Washington thought that they needed to stop the rise of any more wicked dictators like Hitler. During the war most Americans had a positive view of Stalin. Soon after the war the American Press portrayed him, like Hitler, as a monster and a dictator. The lesson of the 1930s was that appeasement did not work with such people. It would therefore be disastrous if Americans made any concessions to the Soviet Union.

There was also an economic reason for taking a tough line on communism. American politicians were terrified at the idea that there could be another Depression like the one in the early 1930s. Another Depression could only be avoided if American factories were busy. American business was the engine of the world economy and it needed new markets in which to sell its goods. Communist countries were unlikely to buy many American goods. So the spread of communism was a threat to the American economy.

SOURCE B

An American atom bomb test. Until 1949 the USA had a monopoly of the atom bomb and this gave the Americans a sense of superiority over the Soviet Union.

George Kennan and the 'long telegram'

One American expert played a crucial part in encouraging a hostile attitude towards the Soviet Union. His name was George Kennan. In February 1946 Kennan sent a famous report to Washington. He was based at the time at the American Embassy in Moscow and his report gave the American government a detailed view of Soviet motives. The report became known as 'the long telegram'. It made a big impact in Washington. The US government accepted Kennan's views and published hundreds of copies of the telegram for its officials to read. Kennan said that the Soviet government was determined to expand and must be stopped. Kennan also developed the idea of 'containment'. The theory of containment was that the USA should use all means, including the threat of force, to stop Soviet power spreading any further. The USA became committed to containment and this remained its policy until the end of the Cold War in the late 1980s.

SOURCE D

A summary of George Kennan's 'long telegram',
February 1946:

> Soviet policy is a continuation of traditional Russian policy of hostility towards the outside world.

> Russian leaders today, as in the past, feel threatened and insecure because they know that the West is more advanced. In order to remove the threat, Russian leaders are determined to destroy the Western world.

> Communism has made matters worse. Marxist ideas encourage the Soviet leaders to be absolutely ruthless.

> The Soviet Union will use every method possible to smash democracy in the Western world.

> The Soviet leaders are fanatics and can never be trusted.

SOURCE C

George Kennan. He was a young diplomat based in Moscow in the war. He persuaded many people in the American government of the need for a tough line against the Soviet Union.

SOURCE E

A Soviet poster of the 1940s shows the different ethnic groups of the Soviet Union united by communism. Americans were afraid that Soviet communists wanted to spread their revolutionary ideas throughout the world.

Focus

How many different reasons can you find in the following sources to explain why the USA was hostile towards the Soviet Union?

SOURCE F

In 1945 the American ambassador in Moscow commented on the differences between the USA and the Soviet Union.

I am afraid that Stalin does not, and never will, fully understand our interest in free Poland as a matter of principle. It is hard for him to appreciate our faith in principles. It is difficult for him to understand why we should want to interfere with Soviet policy in a country like Poland, which he considers so important to Russia's security, unless we have some ulterior motive.

Averell Harriman

SOURCE G

The US diplomat, George Kennan, in February 1946 said that Soviet leaders wanted to destroy the American way of life.

All Soviet efforts will be negative and destructive in character, designed to tear down sources of strength beyond reach of Soviet control. We have here a political force committed fanatically to the belief that with the US there can be no permanent way of living peacefully together. If Soviet power is to be secure our traditonal way of life must be destroyed and the international authority of our state destroyed.

SOURCE H

Senator E. Johnson made this speech in November 1945:

We can drop, at a moment's notice, atomic bombs on any spot on earth. With vision and guts and plenty of atomic bombs the United States can outlaw wars of aggression.

SOURCE I

President Truman wrote this letter in January 1946:

There isn't a doubt in my mind that Russia intends an invasion of Turkey and the seizure of the Black Sea Straits on the Mediterranean. Unless Russia is faced with an iron fist and strong language another war is in the making. Only one language do they understand: 'How many divisions have you?'

SOURCE J

The American General Eisenhower became President in 1953. In 1951 he commented on American motives.

From my viewpoint, foreign policy is based primarily on one consideration: the need for the US to obtain raw materials and to preserve profitable foreign markets. Out of this comes the need to make certain that those areas of the world where there are essential raw materials are accessible to us.

SOURCE K

William C. Bullitt was a politician and former American diplomat. He made this speech in 1947:

The Soviet Union's assault upon the West is about at the stage of Hitler's manoeuvring into Czechoslovakia. The final aim of Russia is world conquest.

>> Activity

Why was the US government keen to confront the Soviet Union after 1945? In your answer you should mention:

> the wealth and self-confidence of Americans after the war

> the initial monopoly of the atomic bomb

> memories of appeasement

> the influence of George Kennan.

The Berlin Blockade and NATO

In 1948 Stalin tried to starve the people of West Berlin into submission. He failed. The Western allies kept West Berlin supplied through a massive airlift.

What were the consequences of the Berlin Blockade?

Towards a divided Germany

By early 1948 Stalin had control of much of Eastern Europe. The Americans responded by helping to make Western Europe wealthy and pro-American. As part of this process the division of Germany became more and more permanent. The west of Germany had long been the industrial heartland of continental Europe. The US government decided to include western Germany in its plans for a new non-communist Western Europe.

News of a new currency for the west of Germany alarmed Stalin. He saw it as another step towards a divided Germany with the wealthier, larger part of the country closely allied to the USA. Stalin was worried by the idea of a successful, anti-communist government in the west of Germany. In his mind it raised the possibility of another German attack on Russia, as in 1914 and 1941.

In attempting to stop the formation of West Germany, Stalin thought he had one powerful weapon. West Berlin was controlled by the American, French and British forces – but it was a western 'island' deep inside the Soviet sector of Germany. Soviet forces controlled all the land routes into West Berlin. Over 2 million people lived in West Berlin and Stalin could cut off their supplies by simply closing the roads and the railways. As a protest against the currency reforms and the moves towards a divided Germany Stalin decided to put a blockade on West Berlin.

THE EMERGENCE OF WEST GERMANY

> The Marshall Plan for the economic rebuilding of Europe was extended to the western part of Germany but not to the Soviet zone.

> In January 1947 the British and the American governments fused their two zones of Germany into a single administrative unit that was known at the time as Bizonia. In many ways this was the beginning of the establishment of West Germany.

> In June 1948 the Western allies introduced a new currency into their area of control. The new money, known as the Deutschmark, was not used in the Soviet zone.

GERMANY 1945–7

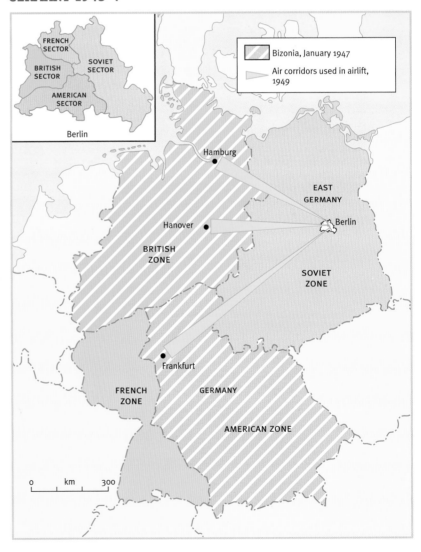

SOURCE A

The blockade began on 23 June 1948 when the Soviet authorities made this announcement:

The transport division of the Soviet Military Administration is compelled to halt all the passenger and freight traffic to and from Berlin at 06.00 hours because of technical difficulties.

The Berlin Airlift

The Western allies were taken by surprise at the start of the blockade. The Americans were initially not sure how to respond. Some advisers thought that the Western powers would have to give way because the 2 million people in West Berlin would starve as long as the roads out of Berlin remained blocked. Another view was that tanks should be used to blast a way through the blockade. The leading American military expert, General Clay, was keen to send his troops down the autobahn towards Berlin. This could easily have led to a full-scale war with the USSR. The government decided on a middle course: not to provoke war by sending troops towards Berlin but to keep the city supplied by aircraft. Never before had a huge besieged city been kept going by an airlift.

SOURCE B

A month after the start of the blockade, Truman ordered General Clay to report to him in Washington to review the Berlin question. In his memoirs, Truman recalled the meeting with Clay on 22 July 1948:

Clay said that the abandonment of Berlin would have a disastrous effect upon our plans for Western Germany. It would also slow down European recovery. The [West] Germans were concerned about the possibility of our leaving Berlin. We should go to any lengths to find a peaceful solution to the situation, but we had to remain in Berlin. He reported that the airlift was more than enough to meet food requirements, but was inadequate to include the necessary amounts of coal.

I asked General Clay if there were any indications that the Russians would go to war. He said he did not think so. What they seemed to be aiming at was to score a major victory by forcing us out of Berlin, either now or after winter weather forced us to curtail the airlift.

I directed the Air Force to furnish the fullest support possible to the problem of supplying Berlin.

SOURCE C

Children from West Berlin watch a US cargo plane bringing in supplies to the besieged city during the Berlin Blockade.

To people in the West, Stalin seemed to be acting with extreme aggression. The attack on Berlin looked like the first step towards a communist march westwards. The Western allies acted firmly in carrying out the airlift. To President Truman it was a test of the new policy of containment: the USSR could not be allowed to take over West Berlin.

>> Activity

Explain in your own words why Stalin decided to impose a blockade on West Berlin.

Stalin ends the siege

Eventually Stalin had to admit that his attempt to starve out West Berlin had failed. In May 1949 the Soviet authorities called off the blockade. The airlift was a triumph for the American and British air forces. During the airlift British and US planes flew nearly 200,000 missions to Berlin. At the end of the blockade the airport in West Berlin was handling an enormous 1,000 arrivals and departures every day. Over 1.5 million tons of food, fuel and equipment was sent in to Berlin. This achievement clearly proved how determined the USA was to resist Stalin. The Berlin airlift showed how far international politics had changed since 1945. Berlin had then been a symbol of defeated Nazism. By 1948 it was a symbol of Western freedom and the struggle with communism.

SOURCE D

Konrad Adenauer, 1949. The blockade strengthened the position of conservative anti-communists like Adenauer. This was the exact opposite of what Stalin wanted when he began the Blockade.

After the blockade: the formation of West Germany

Stalin's attempt to put a stop to the creation of West Germany was a complete failure. The blockade accelerated moves towards a powerful, pro-Western state in much of Germany. As the airlift began, the military authorities in the western zones also organised meetings to work out a constitution for West Germany. The new state was called the Federal Republic of Germany and it was formally founded in May 1949. The Soviet Union responded to this by setting up a new constitution for East Germany. In October 1949 the eastern state was officially established and it was known as the German Democratic Republic.

West Germany held its first elections in August 1949. A political party called the Christian Democrats won the greatest number of seats and dominated the new state. Its leader was Konrad Adenauer, a conservative who hated communism and believed very strongly in linking West Germany to the USA and Western Europe. The development of West Germany under Adenauer was the last thing that Stalin wanted. The idea of a powerful capitalist German state made him feel insecure.

After the blockade: the formation of NATO

The blockade also encouraged the Western allies to form the North Atlantic Treaty Organisation (NATO).

SOURCE E

The North Atlantic Treaty Organisation was set up in April 1949. This is an extract from the treaty.

The Parties to this treaty agree that an armed attack against one or more of them in Europe or North America shall be considered an attack against them all. They agree that, if such an armed attack occurs, each of them will assist by taking such action as it deems necessary, including the use of armed force.

The alliance was dominated by the USA. American influence has been reflected in the fact that every single supreme commander of NATO has been an American. The formation of NATO was a milestone in American foreign policy. Never before had the USA been a member of a peacetime military alliance. The fact that Truman broke with all the traditions of American foreign policy shows how determined he was to stop the spread of communism.

NATO was more than a promise of American help in case of emergency. The alliance was to be supported with large numbers of troops on the ground. In particular, there was a large build-up of NATO forces in West Germany. By 1953, five divisions of US troops were permanently based in Germany.

The Soviet Union felt threatened by this. The sense of threat increased in 1955 when West Germany joined NATO. The Soviet Union responded by setting up its own military alliance in 1955. This was established under a treaty called the Warsaw Pact. For the next three decades NATO and Warsaw Pact forces faced each other and prepared for war.

>> Activity

1 How did the Berlin Blockade end? Was this a victory for the Soviet Union or for the USA?

2 How did the blockade speed up the formation of West Germany?

3 How did the blockade lead to the setting up of NATO?

4 Do you think that Stalin was pleased with the consequences of the Berlin Blockade?

NATO AND THE WARSAW PACT

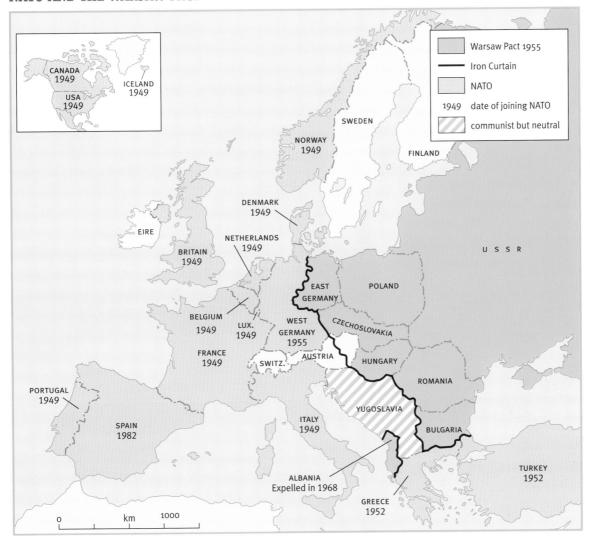

The start of the Cold War

The wartime allies become enemies

Soon after the end of the war the USA and the USSR became hostile towards each other. A period of hostility known as the Cold War lasted until the late 1980s.

YALTA AND POTSDAM

The leaders of the USA, USSR and Britain met twice in 1945 to talk about the world after the war. They had met once before in Tehran, 1943.

Yalta, February 1945

Leaders present: Roosevelt (USA), Stalin (USSR), Churchill (Britain)

Discussed: Poland and the rest of Eastern Europe

Agreed: non-communists to be part of emergency governments

free elections as soon as possible

Outcome: Soviet Union did not allow democracy in Poland

great bitterness caused in the USA

Potsdam, July 1945

Leaders present: Truman (USA), Stalin (USSR), Churchill, replaced by Attlee (Britain).

Discussed: the future running of Germany

Agreed: borders between Germany and Poland

wiping out Nazi influence

arrangements for reparations

Outcome: USA prevented Soviet Union involvement in the rich Ruhr area of Germany and occupied Japan

The Soviet Union blocked American involvement in Eastern Europe

The Soviet take-over

In 1946 Churchill described how an 'iron curtain' was being put across Europe; the iron curtain divided Soviet-style states in Eastern Europe from democratic, capitalist states in Western Europe. Between 1945 and 1948 the Soviet Union imposed communist governments on several East European countries:

> Poland

> Bulgaria

> Romania

> Hungary

> Czechoslovakia

The communist coup in Czechoslovakia in 1948 particularly angered people in the West.

For the Soviet leader, Stalin, the take-over was a defensive move: an attempt to build up a friendly buffer between the USSR and the Western capitalist states.

For the American leader, Truman, the take-over was an offensive move: the first step in a Soviet attempt to impose communism on all the countries of the world.

A US atomic test taking place in the Pacific Ocean near Bikini Atoll on 25 July 1946.

The American response

Between 1945 and 1949 the Americans developed a policy called 'containment'. This involved using the power and wealth of the USA to try to stop or 'contain' the spread of communism, first of all in Europe and later throughout the world.

CONTAINMENT IN EUROPE

1947: The Truman Doctrine

The American President Truman said that the world was being divided into free, democratic countries and undemocratic communist states. Truman promised help for any people who wanted to resist communism and immediate help to anti-communist governments in Greece and Turkey.

1947: The Marshall Plan

The economy of Europe was in ruins at the end of the war. The Marshall Plan, named after General George Marshall, the US Secretary of State, aimed to re-build the European economy so that it could resist communism. In theory, East European countries could join but the Americans made it clear that communist states were not welcome.

1949: the founding of NATO

The USA took the lead in organising a military alliance of non-communist countries in Europe and North America. It was called the North Atlantic Treaty Organisation. All members agreed to defend each other in case of Soviet attack.

1949: the setting up of West Germany

At the end of the war Germany was divided into the British, French, American and Soviet zones. The city of Berlin was also divided into four zones. At first both the USA and the USSR wanted a unified Germany. When the Soviet Union took control of much of Eastern Europe, America moved towards the setting up of a pro-Western state in the British, French and American zones. West Germany, officially known as the Federal Republic of Germany, was established in May 1949.

THE SOVIET REACTION TO CONTAINMENT

Stalin, in turn, saw American actions after 1945 as aggressive and a threat to the Soviet Union. The Soviet response was as follows:

1948–1949: the Berlin Blockade

West Berlin was an island of democracy and capitalism in the Soviet zone. Stalin was worried by the possibility of a strong West German state. In June 1948 Stalin blocked all road and rail transport with West Berlin. This was a failure. Britain and the USA organised an unprecedented airlift to stop West Berliners from being starved out. The blockade was ended in May 1949. The blockade accelerated moves towards a separate West Germany and the NATO alliance.

1949: COMECON

In January 1949 the Soviet Union tried to answer the Marshall Plan by setting up a trading bloc of communist countries. It was called the Council for Mutual Economic Aid or COMECON.

1949: the setting up of East Germany

After the official establishment of West Germany the Soviet zone of Germany was turned into a separate communist state, officially known as the German Democratic Republic.

1949: the Soviet atom bomb

The USA had a monopoly of atomic weapons after 1945. Stalin ordered Soviet scientists to produce an atomic bomb and in 1949 they succeeded.

1955: the Warsaw Pact

In 1955 NATO was expanded to include West Germany. The Soviet Union created a military alliance of communist countries known as the Warsaw Pact.

Communist China

The civil war

There was a bitter struggle for control of China from 1927 to 1949 between nationalists and communists. The nationalists were led by Jiang Jieshi (Chiang Kai-shek); the leader of the communists was Mao Zedong (Mao Tse-tung). At first the nationalists were the more powerful. By 1934 Jiang Jieshi destroyed the communist forces in the east of the country. Mao Zedong re-organised the surviving communists and led them on a famous Long March north to safety in the region of Yanan. The civil war was interrupted between 1937 and 1945 by a war with the Japanese. In 1945 fighting broke out again. At this point the communists controlled only part of northern China and had a smaller army than the nationalists.

Jiang had American backing. However, his government failed to win the support of the ordinary people. Taxes were high and the government had a reputation for corruption. Most Chinese people lived in the countryside. Mao promised the poor country people a fair share of the land. His soldiers fought a skilful guerrilla war against the nationalist armies. By 1946 Jiang lost control of Manchuria. The communist armies swept to victory in 1948–9. In September 1949 Mao announced that the People's Republic of China was now established. The communists controlled all China, except for the large off-shore island of Taiwan. Jiang Jieshi fled to Taiwan.

A new superpower?

As the state with the greatest population in the world the government of China expected to be taken seriously by other powerful countries. China saw itself as an equal of the Soviet Union and the USA. This view was given extra weight when China exploded its first atomic bomb in 1964.

China and the Soviet Union

The relationship between communist China and the Soviet Union was tense from the beginning. Mao was not impressed by the level of support he had received from Stalin during the years of struggle. The Chinese leadership was not prepared to see the USSR as the senior partner in the communist world. After Stalin's death Mao was angered that the Soviet leaders did not consult him before attacking Stalin's memory. These tensions came to the surface in 1960 when the Chinese criticised Khrushchev for being too friendly towards the West. The USSR ordered home many of the Soviet scientists and engineers who were in China. Between 1968 and 1970 the USSR and China came close to war over arguments about the frontier. The two countries remained on poor terms until the time of Gorbachev in the late 1980s.

Young Chinese read the teachings of Mao near an enormous propaganda poster of the Chinese leader. Mao used young followers, called Red Guards, to strengthen his position during the Cultural Revolution.

The Great Leap Forward and the Cultural Revolution

Mao tried to bring about rapid change in the Chinese economy in 1958. Collective farms or 'communes' were set up in the countryside. New factories were built. This attempt to increase output rapidly was called the Great Leap Forward. It was not successful. Mao tried to increase his power by organising a period of turmoil between 1966 and 1969, known as the Cultural Revolution. Young radical followers of Mao, called Red Guards, toured the country terrorising people in senior positions. Amid the chaos Mao was able to remove many opponents from power.

The Cultural Revolution badly damaged the Chinese economy. It also harmed China's relations with the outside world.

China had a very poor relationship with the USA throughout the 1950s and 1960s. After the Cultural Revolution the two countries began to look again at their relationship. The US president in the early 1970s was Richard Nixon and he was keen to build a good relationship with China. Under Nixon the USA 'recognised' the government of China for the first time. Nixon visited China in 1972.

After Mao

When Mao died in 1976 there was a power struggle between radicals and moderates. The leaders of the radicals became known as the Gang of Four, and included Mao's widow, Jiang Qing. The power struggle was eventually won by the moderates, led by Deng Xiaoping. The Gang of Four were blamed for the chaos of the Cultural Revolution and imprisoned. In the 1980s Deng Xiaoping abandoned many of the ideas of communist economics and encouraged free enterprise and competition. At the same time there was no increase in free speech.

A so-called 'pro-democracy movement' developed among students in the early months of 1989. Demonstrators camped in Tiananmen Square, Beijing (Peking) and demanded free speech and free elections. The students were joined by large numbers of ordinary people. On 3 June the Chinese army moved in and used tanks to clear the square. Many thousands of people were killed. Afterwards, leaders of the pro-democracy movement were arrested and imprisoned. The massacre in Tiananmen Square shocked the world and affected the relationship between China and other countries. After Tiananmen, the government continued with its policy of Western-style economics but little political freedom.

An unarmed protester defiantly stands in the way of the tanks of the Chinese Red Army, Tiananmen Square, June 1989. The Chinese government used great force to smash the pro-democracy movement.

Discussion points

> What impact has Mao Zedong had on China in the twentieth century?

> What has been the relationship between communist China and the superpowers?

> How has communist China developed since the death of Mao Zedong?

The Korean War

The Truman Doctrine stated that the USA would help people to fight against communism. In 1950 the USA showed that this was more than words: US troops went to war to stop the spread of communism in Korea.

How successful was the USA in the Korean War?

THE KOREAN WAR

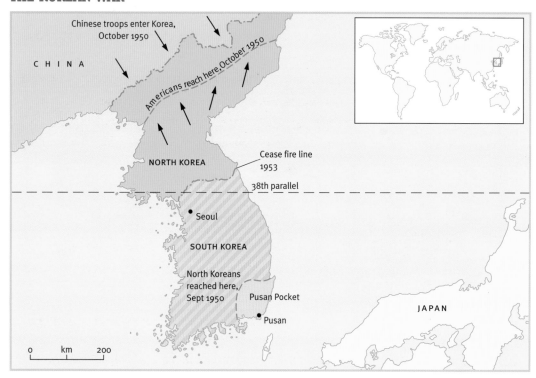

A divided land

The Japanese controlled Korea between 1904 and 1945. At the end of the Second World War Korea was in a situation similar to Germany. Russian forces were in the north of Korea and American troops had landed in the south. Korea became divided in two at the 38th parallel. In 1948 separate Korean governments were set up in the north and south of the country.

A communist, Kim Il Sung, took power in the North. From 1948 the President of South Korea was the anti-communist, Syngman Rhee. He was a corrupt leader and he soon became very unpopular. In April 1950 Rhee did badly in elections. Many of the people of the south voted in favour of unification with the communist state of the north.

Invasion

On 25 June 1950 North Korean troops invaded the South in a bid to re-unite Korea by force. Historians disagree about whether the North Koreans were told to invade by the Russians. Truman believed that the Russians were behind the attack and that it was a test of the US policy of containing communism. The invasion came at a time when many Americans were extremely worried about the challenge of communism. China had recently become a communist state. In September 1949 the Americans found out that the USSR had nuclear weapons. American politicians became convinced that communists wanted to take over the world. On hearing the news from Korea, Truman immediately ordered US forces in Japan, led by General MacArthur, to help South Korea.

Truman asked the United Nations Security Council to back the use of American troops in Korea. At that time the Soviet Union was boycotting the Security Council and was not able to use its veto. As a result the Security Council supported the USA and called on other member states to provide troops. Soldiers from a number of countries fought in Korea, including Britain, Canada, Australia and New Zealand. However, the bulk of the UN forces were provided by the USA.

SOURCE A

General MacArthur, 1949. This US general played a key role in shaping American policy during the Korean War.

The US counter-attack

At first the North Korean attack was very successful. Within four days the Southern capital of Seoul had been captured. The North Koreans conquered all of the country except for a small area in the south around the town of Pusan. In July 1950 MacArthur sent American forces to Pusan and prepared for a counter-attack. The US fight-back began in September. MacArthur organised a successful amphibious attack on the town of Inchon. At the same time US forces broke out of the Pusan area. The counter-attack went extremely well and by 1 October the US troops had reached the 38th parallel, the original border between North and South Korea.

The Americans faced a dilemma. Should they push on and invade North Korea? They now had a chance to go beyond containment and 'roll back' the frontiers of communism. On the other hand, there was a possibility that by invading the North the Americans might provoke China to join the war. MacArthur was keen to go on. Truman approved the change of policy and the US forces crossed the 38th parallel on 7 October. Eventually MacArthur's troops reached the Yalu River, close to the Chinese border. This was the first time since 1945 that Americans had tried to liberate a communist state.

The risk of Chinese intervention

Communist China was a new force in the world. Few people believed that they would risk war with the mighty USA. In early October the Chinese issued a statement that said, 'China will not sit back with folded hands and let the Americans come to the border'. The Americans ignored this warning and continued to march north. On 10 October the Chinese government said that Chinese troops would attack the Americans if MacArthur continued. MacArthur ignored this threat.

SOURCE B

The American view of the dangers of outside help for North Korea was expressed in American magazines of the time.

The danger of Chinese or Soviet intervention if the North Korean Communists are pushed hard to the border is negligible.

Life Magazine, October 1950

If the Chinese should commit their own forces to the struggle in Korea they would do so knowing that they were inviting a general war. That is a price they are not prepared to pay.

The Nation, September 1950

SOURCE C

The communist view was expressed in a Chinese newspaper.

We cannot stand idly by when the American imperialist, a notorious enemy, is now expanding its war of aggression against our neighbour and is attempting to expand the aggressive flames to the borders of our country.

Kung Jen Jih Pao, 13 October 1950

The Chinese intervene

At the end of October Chinese troops went into action and attacked South Korean and American troops. In November the South Koreans and Americans were forced to retreat. Truman and MacArthur were not put off by the Chinese intervention. Britain and France wanted Truman to talk to the Chinese. The advice from these allies was ignored. Instead, MacArthur planned a further push towards the Chinese border. This renewed attack began on 25 November. It went badly wrong. MacArthur made a big mistake: he divided his forces in two and marched north. The Chinese had little difficulty in attacking and destroying many of the US forces. MacArthur had to retreat and the Chinese soon took control of almost all North Korea. Once again it was the turn of the communist forces to push over the border into South Korea. The Chinese offensive continued into the New Year. On 1 January they crossed the 38th parallel, and on 4th January they took the Southern capital, Seoul.

SOURCE D

MacArthur's mistake and retreat was a great blow to the Americans.

There is no doubt that confidence in General MacArthur has been shaken badly as a result of the events of the last few days. Similarly, there is no doubt that the United States leadership in the Western world has been damaged by President Truman's acceptance of the bold MacArthur offensive.

The *New York Times*, 30 November 1950

The success of the Chinese caused great disappointment in America. There were behind-the-scenes arguments about what to do next. General MacArthur recommended extreme action. Truman hinted at a press conference that he might drop the atomic bomb on China.

MACARTHUR'S ADVICE: DECEMBER 1950

> The US should consider all methods to defeat the Chinese; this could include the use of atomic bombs against China.

> The war should be extended to the Chinese mainland in order to cut off supplies to the communist forces in Korea.

> The ultimate aim of the war should be not only the re-capture of North Korea, but also the defeat of communism in China.

The British government was appalled by talk of using atom bombs and invading China. The British Prime Minister, Attlee, flew to Washington and urged Truman to negotiate with the Chinese. Attlee failed to get the Americans to talk to the Chinese but Truman did stop talking about dropping the atom bomb.

SOURCE E

American troops pass through a burning village during the Korean War.

The fall of MacArthur

In February 1951 the Americans launched a further attack on the communist troops. By March the communist forces had been pushed back to the original border, the 38th parallel. At this point MacArthur disagreed with Truman. Truman now abandoned the idea of conquering all of Korea and was considering making peace with China. For a long time there had been tension between Truman and MacArthur. This now reached breaking point. On 24 March MacArthur made a public statement criticising the idea of a deal with the Chinese. Truman was annoyed when he heard this. MacArthur wanted to cross the border again in order to re-conquer North Korea. He sent a message to an American politician explaining his view that America should keep fighting until the Chinese were defeated. Truman was very angry that a general was trying to control the war, instead of obeying his orders, and in April MacArthur was dismissed. This caused a sensation in the United States.

>> Activity

1 Explain what happened in each of the following phases of the Korean War. For every phase decide whether you think the communists or the anti-communists were more successful.

June 1950 – July 1950

September 1950 – October 1950

November 1950 – January 1951

February 1951 – March 1951

April 1951 – May 1951

July 1951 – July 1953

2 Using all the information in this unit decide whether you think American policy in Korea was successful. Give reasons for your decision.

The stalemate

By early summer 1951 the two sides in the Korean War had reached a stalemate. The Chinese launched a huge push south in April and May, but it was not successful. The loss of life on the Chinese side was enormous. In these two months over 200,000 men were killed. Peace talks began in July 1951 but there was no agreed cease-fire. Sporadic but bloody fighting continued. The negotiations soon got stuck over where to draw the border and the exchange of prisoners. As the months passed the situation became similar to the Western Front in the First World War, with both sides dug in to strong defensive positions. This situation continued throughout the second half of 1951 and through the whole of 1952. Soldiers continued to be killed in large numbers on both sides. Between the start of the talks and November 1952, 45,000 American troops were killed or wounded. At the end of 1952 the Americans elected a new President, Ike Eisenhower. The new President took power in January 1953 and he was determined to end the war. An agreement to stop fighting was eventually signed on 27 July 1953.

SOURCE F

Eisenhower. He came to power determined to end the Korean War.

The Cuban missile crisis

Cuba is a large island in the Caribbean. In 1959 a revolution took place in Cuba and Fidel Castro came to power. He introduced a Soviet-style government on the island and he looked to the Soviet Union for support. There was a great uproar in 1962 when the Soviet leader, Khrushchev, placed nuclear missiles on the island.

What happened during the Cuban missile crisis?

The revolution in Cuba was a great blow to America. A communist state had been set up only 90 miles from the USA. In April 1961 the American CIA organised an attack on Cuba. This was carried out by Cuban exiles. Their plan was to land in a remote part of the island and set up a base for guerrilla war against the government of Cuba. They expected that other Cubans would rise up and join the rebellion. The invasion force landed at a place called the Bay of Pigs.

The attack at the Bay of Pigs went disastrously wrong: the Americans had underestimated the strength of the Cuban armed forces and the CIA had misunderstood how popular Castro was. The invasion force was easily defeated by the Cuban government and there was no widespread support for the invasion from among the people of Cuba. The fiasco at the Bay of Pigs was humiliating for the American President, Kennedy.

The struggle for control of Cuba was part of the world-wide Cold War. In early 1962 the Americans placed a number of nuclear missiles in Turkey, within easy range of many cities of the USSR. Shortly afterwards Khrushchev decided to place missiles on Cuba.

THE CUBAN CRISIS, 1962

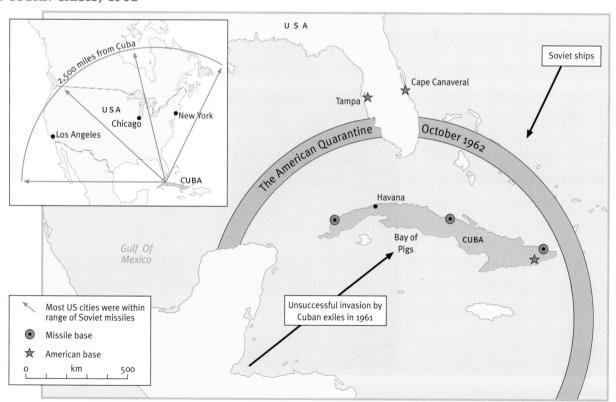

What can we learn from these sources
about why Khrushchev placed the missiles on Cuba?

SOURCE A

Khrushchev speaking in December 1962 to the Supreme Soviet (the parliament of the USSR):

Comrades, everyone still remembers the tense days of October when mankind was anxiously listening to the news coming from the Caribbean. In those days the world was on the brink of a nuclear catastrophe. What created this crisis? The revolution in Cuba was met with hostility from the imperialists in the United States of America. The imperialists are frightened of Cuba because of her ideas. They hate the idea that little Cuba has dared go her own way, instead of trying to please American business. American forces have been doing everything they can, from the first day of the revolution, to overthrow Cuba's government and restore their own control. They set up an economic blockade of Cuba. This is inhuman – an attempt to starve a whole nation. Even this was not enough for them. They decided to use force to suppress the Cuban revolution.

We carried weapons there at the request of the Cuban government. Cuba needed weapons as a means of deterring the aggressors, and not as a means of attack. We sent about forty missiles to Cuba. Naturally, neither we nor our Cuban friends thought that this small number of missiles would be used for an attack on the United States. Our aim was only to defend Cuba.

SOURCE B

Fyodor Burlatsky, Khrushchev's assistant, writing in 1992, recalled how the Soviet leader decided to send missiles to Cuba during a visit to Bulgaria in May 1962:

Khrushchev was walking along a beach on the Black Sea with Defence Minister Malinovskiy, who pointed out to him that American military bases with nuclear warheads capable of wiping out the cities of Kiev, Minsk and Moscow in a matter of minutes were located on the opposite shore in Turkey. Khrushchev then asked Malinovskiy, 'And why then can we not have bases close to America? What's the reason for this imbalance?' And right then and there Khrushchev began to question Malinovskiy about whether or not it would be possible to deploy missiles secretly in Cuba. Malinovskiy assured him that the missiles could be deployed without detection.

The crisis

The Soviets tried to move the missiles secretly to the Caribbean. In public Khrushchev stated that 'no missile capable of reaching the United States will be placed in Cuba'. A U-2 spy plane flew over Cuba on 14 October and took photographs of the missile site. On 16 October 1962 President Kennedy was shown the photographs proving that Soviet missiles were on Cuba. The missiles had only recently arrived and would not yet have been in working order. The Americans spent six days secretly discussing and planning how to respond. They did not consult with their allies at this stage. Even the government of Britain, the closest ally, was not told about the missiles until 21 October, shortly before Kennedy made an announcement to the American people.

>> Activity

The Americans considered a range of options:

> a letter of protest to Khrushchev

> bombing the missile sites

> an invasion of Cuba

> a naval blockade of the island.

Imagine that you are Kennedy's adviser. Which of these options would you recommend? Remember you would want to show Khrushchev that you mean business, but you do not want to provoke all-out war with the USSR.

On the edge of a nuclear catastrophe

SOURCE C

Some of the Cuban missile sites, photographed by an American U-2 spy plane.

Kennedy's response to the news of the missiles was twofold: he decided to get ready for an invasion of Cuba, but first of all to mount a blockade of the island. On 22 October a so-called 'quarantine' was announced – the Americans stated that they would stop and search all ships bound for Cuba. Even at this stage, Khrushchev refused to accept publicly that there were missiles on Cuba. This put the USSR in a difficult position when Kennedy was able to show the world that Khrushchev was lying. Two days later a number of Soviet ships, which probably contained warheads for the missiles, turned back just short of the line of the blockade. This was not the end of the crisis because some warheads were already on the island.

The Americans announced that the missiles must be dismantled immediately or else Cuba would be attacked and invaded. There was a real possibility of a nuclear war breaking out between the USA and the USSR. According to one source, Castro actually suggested to Khrushchev that the USSR should launch nuclear missiles against America to stop the imminent invasion of Cuba. Khrushchev was not impressed by this advice and was horrified to discover that some of his top generals thought it would be better to have a nuclear war than back down. Instead he decided to write an urgent letter to Kennedy. This was sent on 26 October.

SOURCE D

On 26 October Khrushchev sent a letter to Kennedy. It suggested that the missiles could be withdrawn if the USA made a promise not to invade Cuba.

If the assurances were given that the President of the United States would not participate in an attack on Cuba and the blockade lifted, then the question of the removal of the missile sites would be an entirely different question. This is my proposal. No more weapons to Cuba and those within Cuba withdrawn or destroyed, and you reciprocate by ending your blockade and also agree not to invade Cuba.

Before Kennedy had replied to this message Khrushchev sent a second letter on 27 October, with different demands. This second letter demanded that the Americans must take their missiles out of Turkey in return for the removal of the Cuban missiles.

SOURCE E

This an extract from Khrushchev's letter of 27 October.

You are worried over Cuba. You say that it worries you because it lies ninety miles across the sea from the shores of the United States. However, Turkey lies next to us. You have stationed devastating rocket weapons in Turkey, literally right next to us. This is why I make this proposal: We agree to remove the weapons from Cuba. We agree to this and to state this commitment in the United Nations. Your representatives will make a statement that the United States, on its part, will evacuate its similar weapons from Turkey.

The Americans did not know how to respond. The Americans had already considered taking their missiles out of Turkey but Kennedy did not want to be seen to be backing down in the face of Soviet pressure. The American military leaders recommended an immediate air attack on Cuba. Kennedy was unsure. A letter was about to be sent to Khrushchev refusing to do a deal over the Turkish missiles. At this point it was suggested that the Americans ignore the second letter, but reply to the first letter accepting the Soviet proposal that the missiles should be withdrawn in return for an American commitment not to invade Cuba. The President liked this idea and a suitable letter was sent.

The President's brother

Later on the 27 October Robert Kennedy, the brother of the President, went to see the Soviet ambassador. The conversation between Robert Kennedy and the ambassador, Anatoly Dobrynin, was the key to the solution of the crisis. Kennedy gave Dobrynin an ultimatum; he said that if the Soviets did not promise to remove the missiles by the next day the Americans would use force to destroy the missiles. He then made an offer to the Russians – there could be no official deal, but if the Cuban missiles were removed the missiles in Turkey would follow soon after. This message was relayed to Khrushchev, and it was enough for the Russians. On 28 October Dobrynin reported to back to Robert Kennedy and announced that the Russians would withdraw their missiles from Cuba. The crisis was over.

SOURCE F

A few years later, in 1969, Robert Kennedy's account of his crucial conversation with Dobrynin was published.

I said that there could be no arrangement made under this kind of threat or pressure. However, I said that President Kennedy had been anxious to remove those missiles from Turkey and Italy for a long period of time. It was our judgement that, within a short time after this crisis was over, those missiles would be gone.

SOURCE G

Robert Kennedy. The President's brother finally negotiated an end to the crisis with the Soviet ambassador to Washington.

SOURCE I

AFTER THE CRISIS

> The end of the crisis was seen as a victory for Kennedy and a defeat for Khrushchev. The deal over the missiles in Turkey was kept secret so it seemed to the world as if the Soviets had simply backed down. This was good for Kennedy's reputation, but damaging for the Soviet leader. Leading Soviet communists were angry that their country appeared to climb down. This put Khrushchev in a difficult position at home, and contributed to his fall from power in 1964.

> The European allies of the USA were shocked at how little they were consulted during the emergency. It seemed that their opinions was not seen as important by the Americans. The French government of de Gaulle felt this very strongly. As a result de Gaulle eventually pulled France out of NATO and encouraged Western Europe to follow an independent line.

> On the communist side, the Chinese were not impressed by the Soviet performance. They felt that Khrushchev mishandled the crisis and looked cowardly when he removed the missiles. This further encouraged the Chinese to follow an independent line of their own in world politics.

Nikita Khrushchev.

> The most important long-term result of the crisis was that both sides realised the great dangers of direct conflict between the USSR and the USA. Both Soviet and American leaders were shocked at how close they had come to nuclear war. After the Cuban Missile Crisis the Cold War continued but the two superpowers carefully avoided direct hostility. A special telephone 'hotline' was installed so that leaders could communicate easily in any future crisis. The level of tension between the USA and the USSR was never again to be as great as it was in November 1962.

SOURCE H

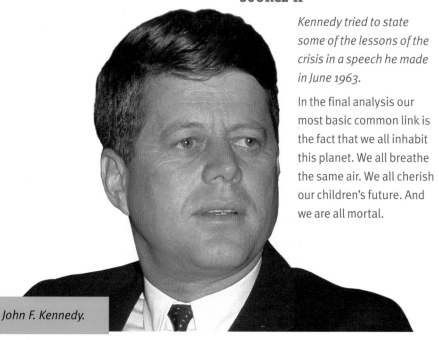

John F. Kennedy.

Kennedy tried to state some of the lessons of the crisis in a speech he made in June 1963.

In the final analysis our most basic common link is the fact that we all inhabit this planet. We all breathe the same air. We all cherish our children's future. And we are all mortal.

>> Activity

Explain in your own words how the crisis:

a appeared to be a victory for Kennedy and a defeat for Khrushchev,

b damaged the relationship between the superpowers and other states,

c led to a period of greater stability in Soviet–US relations.

The Cold War and the Middle East

Israel and the superpowers

Throughout much of the twentieth century there was a bitter argument between Jewish and Arab people over control of the area of the Middle East originally known as Palestine. Until the First World War the territory was part of the Turkish Empire. It was then controlled by the British. After the Second World War the United Nations decided to set up a Jewish state, called Israel, in part of Palestine. As British forces left the area in May 1948, Jewish leaders declared the existence of the new state. Israel was immediately attacked by the neighbouring Arab states of Egypt, Jordan, Syria, Lebanon and Iraq. Fighting came to an end in January 1949 with Israel victorious but this was not the end of the dispute. The two superpowers soon took sides in this conflict. Israel became strongly pro-American, while the Soviet Union became hostile towards Israel.

Suez

There was an upsurge of Arab nationalism in the 1950s supported by the Soviet Union. In 1952 a passionate Arab nationalist called Gamal Nasser took power in Egypt. He turned to the Soviet Union for help in developing the country. In 1956 Nasser seized control of the Suez Canal from the Western powers of Britain and France.

In October 1956 Britain, France and Israel attacked the Suez Canal area. The government of the USA was unhappy about the invasion of Egypt and forced Britain and France to pull out. The Americans got little credit for their actions and radical Arabs increasingly looked to the USSR for assistance. After Suez there was increased Soviet involvement in the Middle East.

War and peace

War broke out again between Israel and the Arab states in 1967 and in 1973. Israel won both these wars and gained control of substantial lands inhabited by Palestinian Arabs. The success of Israel was a blow to the USSR. The Soviets had supplied Egypt and Syria with their weapons but they had lost. Israel was a small country but, with

American help, the Israelis had defeated their hostile neighbours. After 1973 the USA was much more successful than the USSR in influencing events in the Middle East. A new Egyptian leader, Anwar Sadat, broke off relations with the Soviet Union and established a good relationship with the USA. With American help and encouragement the states of Egypt and Israel signed a peace treaty in 1979. In the 1980s the Americans tried to bring Jewish Israelis and Arab Palestinians together. After many years of American pressure the Palestinian leader, Yasser Arafat, signed a peace treaty with the Israeli Prime Minister, Yitzhak Rabin, in 1993. By this time the Soviet Union had fallen apart and the Soviet leaders did not play a significant part in the Middle East peace treaty.

US President Clinton encourages Yitzhak Rabin and Yasser Arafat to shake hands in Washington in 1993.

Discussion points

> Which superpower was more successful in influencing Middle East politics?

The Vietnam War

Between 1965 and 1973 US troops fought a disastrous war against communists in South Vietnam. In the end, the wealthiest country in the world was unable to defeat the Vietnamese fighters.

Why did the USA fight and lose the Vietnam War?

Vietnam divided

Vietnam had been a French colony. After the Second World War, Vietnamese nationalists and communists, led by Ho Chi Minh, fought against the French. In 1954 the French decided to pull out and Vietnam was divided in two. Communists took power in North Vietnam. South Vietnam was ruled by an anti-communist leader called Ngo Dinh Diem. In 1959 the communist government of the North decided to encourage a revolution in the South. Southern communists, who had fled North, returned to fight. These forces were known as the Vietcong.

From 1954 South Vietnam depended on aid from the USA. American policy was based on the 'domino theory': the belief that, because neighbouring states are so interdependent, the collapse of one will lead to the collapse of others. The Americans used this theory as a justification of their involvement in foreign states, particularly in South-East Asia, which they felt were likely to be taken over by the communists. In November 1961 President Kennedy began providing wide-ranging support for the army of the South, including some American soldiers as 'combat advisers'. He hoped that with this help Diem would be able to defeat the communist rebels. This did not happen. The Americans became increasingly unhappy with Diem. In 1963 Diem's government further annoyed the USA by clashing with local Buddhists. With American approval, a group of South Vietnamese generals overthrew Diem in a coup in November 1963.

The Gulf of Tonkin Incident

In 1964 regular North Vietnamese forces marched south along what became known as the Ho Chi Minh Trail to support the Vietcong. Without outside help South Vietnam looked doomed. American involvement increased dramatically after a clash at sea between North Vietnam and the USA in August 1964. An American destroyer near the coast of North Vietnam was attacked by North Vietnamese ships. No serious damage was done in this so-called Gulf of Tonkin Incident. However, the new American President, Johnson, ordered the bombing of Northern naval bases in retaliation. Congress passed a resolution giving the President power to 'take all necessary steps, including the use of armed force' in order to defend South Vietnam. After this Johnson felt he had full authority to step up American involvement in the war.

THE VIETNAM WAR

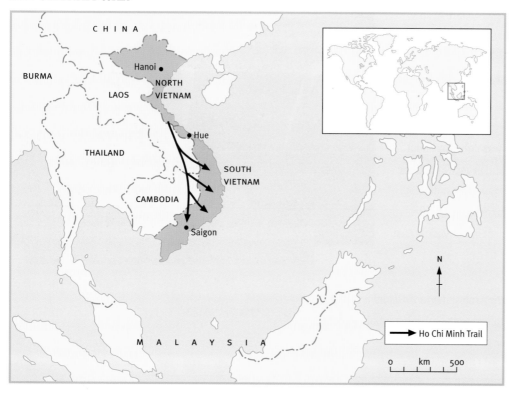

The arrival of US ground troops

By early 1965 American bombers were regularly attacking targets in the North. Johnson did not think that this was enough. He decided that the South Vietnamese needed the help of large numbers of American soldiers on the ground. In July 1965 President Johnson took a fateful step: he agreed to send 180,000 American troops to Vietnam. The number of US troops increased over the next three years until there were 540,000 American soldiers in Vietnam.

SOURCE A

An American B-52 bomber attacks a target near Hanoi, 1966. The US tried to use its massive firepower to force the communists to retreat.

>> Activity

What can you learn from Sources B–D about why the USA got involved in Vietnam?

SOURCE B

Robert McNamara, US Secretary of Defense, March 1964:

We seek an independent, non-communist South Vietnam. Unless we can achieve this objective in South Vietnam, almost all of South-East Asia will probably fall under Communist dominance. Thailand might hold for a period with our help, but would be under grave pressure. Even the Philippines would become shaky, and the threat to India to the west, Australia and New Zealand to the south, and Taiwan, Korea and Japan to the north and east would be greatly increased.

SOURCE C

President Johnson, August 1964:

The challenge that we face in South-East Asia today is the same challenge that we have faced with courage and that we have met with strength in Greece and Turkey, in Berlin, Korea and in Cuba.

SOURCE D

The US government State Department reviewed its policy on Vietnam in February 1965.

South Vietnam is fighting for its life against a brutal campaign of terror and armed attack directed by the Communist regime in Hanoi. This aggression has been going on for years, but recently the pace has quickened and the threat has now become acute. The war in Vietnam is a new kind of war. A totally new kind of aggression has been loosed against an independent people who want to make their own way in peace and freedom. The war in Vietnam is not a spontaneous and local rebellion against the established Government. In Vietnam, a Communist Government has set out deliberately to conquer a neighbouring state.

The people of South Vietnam have chosen to resist this threat. At their request, the United States has taken its place beside them in their defensive struggle. The United States seeks no territory, no military bases, no favoured position. But we have learned the meaning of aggression elsewhere in the post-war world and we have met it. The United States will not abandon friends who want to remain free. It will do what must be done to help them.

The fighting intensifies

The arrival of large numbers of American soldiers stopped the collapse of South Vietnam and strengthened the position of the new South Vietnamese leader, General Thieu. Between 1965 and 1967 there was heavy fighting. The Americans regularly bombed North Vietnam. According to one calculation, more bombs were dropped on North Vietnam than on Germany in the Second World War. American involvement was widely criticised, and many people in the USA were unhappy about the war.

American tactics brought little success. The US forces had the technology to win straightforward battles between tanks or massed infantry. However, the Vietcong and the soldiers of North Vietnam refused to fight this kind of war. Instead they relied on guerrilla tactics: sabotage and sudden ambushes. The American response was to use:

> massive airpower to try to bomb supply lines,

> chemical defoliants to destroy areas of the countryside where communist soldiers might be hiding.

Neither of these methods worked; they simply angered the ordinary people of the Vietnamese countryside and increased support for the Vietcong and Ho Chi Minh.

The Tet Offensive

In January 1968 North Vietnam launched a massive attack at the time of Tet, a religious festival. Communist troops attacked towns all over the country. They struck right in the middle of the Southern capital of Saigon, with attacks on the American embassy. The communists hoped that the Tet Offensive would spark a popular revolution in the South. This did not happen. The losses on the communist side were enormous. About 50,000 communist troops were killed between January and March. The Americans used great force and won back the towns. American guns destroyed the historic centre of the ancient city of Hue, killing many civilians.

What were the results of the Tet Offensive?

The Tet Offensive was a turning-point in the war. Although in the short term it was a failure for the communists, in the long run it helped the North to win the war. The sight of communist fighters in the grounds of the American embassy in Saigon made a mockery of the idea that Americans were close to victory. As a result of the violence of the attack and the clear determination of the communists, many American politicians and people became disillusioned with the war. The anti-war movement in the USA grew in strength. Leading figures in the government began to think that they could not win the war in Vietnam.

SOURCE E

A Vietcong fighter lies dead in the grounds of the US embassy, Saigon, during the Tet Offensive, 1968. This was a turning-point in the war.

>> Activity

Look at the following quotations from the American adviser, Dean Acheson, made before and after the Tet Offensive. What difference is there between the two statements?

SOURCE F

Dean Acheson in November 1967:

We can and will win. We must not have negotiations. When these fellows decide that they can't defeat the South, then they will give up. This is the way it was in Korea. This is the way the Communists operate.

SOURCE G

Dean Acheson in March 1968:

Neither the effort of the Government of South Vietnam nor the effort of the US government can succeed. Time is limited by reactions in this country. We cannot build an independent South Vietnam. The issue is: can we by military means keep the North Vietnamese off the South Vietnamese? I do not think we can.

Johnson bows out and peace talks begin

At the end of March 1968 Johnson admitted that he had failed in Vietnam. Presidential elections were due later in the year; Johnson declared that he would not be seeking re-election. He reduced the level of bombing in the North. He called for peace talks. North Vietnam agreed to negotiate and talks began in Paris in May 1968.

The peace talks got nowhere, but it was clear by the summer of 1968 that the American government was looking for a way out. A new President was elected in November 1968 – Richard Nixon – and he was determined to end the war.

Nixon searches for peace with honour

The challenge for Nixon was to find a way out of Vietnam without humiliation or the clear abandoning of South Vietnam. Nixon tried a number of methods:

1 At the Paris peace talks he tried to persuade North Vietnam that North Vietnamese soldiers should withdraw from the South at the same time as American troops. He threatened a massive attack on the North if they refused to compromise. Nixon was bluffing, and the government of North Vietnam called his bluff. They refused to make a deal but Nixon did not launch an attack.

2 Nixon tried to persuade the USSR and China to use their influence over the government of the North. He told the Soviets and the Chinese that if they helped him over Vietnam the Americans would help them in other areas. This approach did not work. The USSR and China saw no reason to try to help the Americans over Vietnam.

3 Nixon decided to put more of the burden of the war on the shoulders of the government of South Vietnam. He reduced the number of American soldiers and insisted that more of the fighting should be done by South Vietnamese. In April 1969 there were 543,000 American troops in Vietnam. By 1971 the number had gone down to 157,000. This policy of passing responsibility to South Vietnam was known as 'Vietnamisation'.

SOURCE H

A British cartoonist, Nicholas Garland, ridicules Nixon's policy in 1969.
> What point is the cartoonist trying to make?

Atrocities at My Lai

The American war effort was hit by another devastating blow in 1969. It became known that US troops had carried out an appalling atrocity against Vietnamese civilians. On 16 March 1968 American soldiers massacred the villagers of a place called My Lai. The American officer, Lieutenant William Calley, was eventually court-martialled for the murder of 109 civilians. The story of what happened at My Lai horrified many Americans. They had seen their action in Vietnam as a fight against wicked communists. In My Lai all the wickedness was American.

SOURCE J

Murdered women and children at My Lai, 1968.

SOURCE I

In 1969 Time Magazine *reported a series of interviews with American soldiers who had fought at My Lai.*

Varnado Simpson: 'Everyone who went into the village had in mind to kill. We had lost a lot of buddies and the village was a VC [Vietcong] stronghold. We considered them either VC or helping the VC. As I came up on the village there was a woman, a man and a child running away. I told them in their language to stop. They didn't, and I had orders to shoot them down and I did this. This is what I did. I shot them: the lady and the little boy. He was about two years old.

Jay Roberts: 'Just outside the village there was this big pile of bodies. This really tiny kid – he had only a shirt on, nothing else – he came over to the pile and held the hand of one of the dead. One of the GIs behind me dropped into a kneeling position thirty metres from this kid and killed him with a single shot.'

Paul Meadlo: 'We ran through My Lai herding men, women, children and babies into the centre of the village. Lieutenant Calley came over and said, "You know what to do with them, don't you?" And I said, "Yes." and he left and came back about ten minutes later, and said, "How come you ain't killed them yet?" And I told him that I didn't think he wanted us to kill them, just to guard them. He said, "No, I want them dead." So he started shooting them. And he told me to start shooting them. I might have killed ten or fifteen of them.'

Protests against the war

News of the atrocities at My Lai fuelled the anti-war feelings of many Americans. The war was shown on American television and this also caused many people to question why their country was fighting in Vietnam. As the peace talks made little progress in Paris there were increasing numbers of demonstrations in America calling for an end to the war.

SOURCE K

The British journalist, John Pilger, described the scene on 25 April 1971 when a huge demonstration of veterans, or former soldiers, protested in Washington against the war.

'The truth is out! Mickey Mouse is dead! The good guys are really the bad guys in disguise!' The speaker is William Wyman, from New York City. He is nineteen and has no legs. He sits in a wheelchair on the steps of the United States Congress, in the midst of 300,000, the greatest demonstration America has ever seen. He has on green combat fatigues and the jacket is torn where he has ripped away the medals and the ribbons he has been given in exchange for his legs.

Along with hundreds of other veterans of the war, he has hurled his medals on the Capitol steps and described them as shit. And now to those who form a ring of pity around him, he says, 'Before I lost these legs, I killed and killed and killed! We all did! Jesus, don't grieve for me!'

Never before in this country have young soldiers marched in protest against the war in which they themselves have fought and which is still going on.

Did Vietnamisation work?

The South Vietnamese forces were not strong enough to defeat the communists. The government of General Thieu lacked the support and loyalty of the Vietnamese people. Thieu had the backing of landlords and Catholic Church leaders but crucially he had little support from the ordinary Vietnamese people in the countryside.

SOURCE M

When Nixon later wrote his memoirs he recognised the weakness of Vietnamisation.

The real problem was that the enemy was willing to sacrifice in order to win, while the South Vietnamese simply weren't willing to pay that much of a price in order to avoid losing.

As part of Vietnamisation the USA stepped up the bombing of the supply lines of the Viet Cong. This had the effect of spreading the conflict into neighbouring countries of Laos and Cambodia. The attacks on these countries did little to stop the supplies to the communist troops but did manage to encourage local communists. Between 1969 and 1973 the US dropped over half a million tons of bombs on Cambodia. This contributed to the support for the ruthless Cambodian communists, known as the Khmer Rouge. Communists won control of Cambodia in 1975. Similarly, the communist force known as Pathet Lao gained support in Laos and took control of the whole country in 1975.

An American anti-war poster. It shows Uncle Sam as a wounded veteran who has had enough of the war. It is a parody of a First World War recruitment poster.

SOURCE L

The cease-fire: 1973

The peace talks in Paris dragged on for years without achieving anything. By 1972 the communists felt strong enough to launch another all-out attack on the cities of the South, similar to the Tet Offensive. This attack was more successful than the Tet Offensive but the communists were still not able to conquer the main centres of population. After the offensive of the summer of 1972, neither side could see any hope of victory and the peace talks started to make some progress. At last in January 1973 a cease-fire was agreed and the Americans started to take their troops home.

The fall of the South: 1975

The American forces pulled out soon after the cease-fire agreement was signed. This ended US involvement but it did not end the war. Fighting soon resumed between the communists and the Southern forces. Two years after the agreement in Paris the North launched another major offensive against South Vietnam in March 1975. This time, relying only on South Vietnamese troops and without American air support, the Saigon government was not able to resist. The Vietcong and the army of the North swept victoriously through the South. The war effectively ended on 29 April 1975 when the communists captured the southern capital of Saigon. American TV viewers watched in horror as thousands of south Vietnamese people fought to get on the last US helicopters out of Saigon.

After Vietnam: détente and a loss of confidence

American failure to contain communism in Vietnam led to a deep re-assessment of policy towards the communist world. American leaders had been shocked by their failure in Vietnam. The cost had been enormous: 55,000 dead American soldiers and billions of dollars spent. This huge commitment had achieved nothing. Communist governments had taken power not only in North and South Vietnam but also in the neighbouring states of Cambodia and Laos. In addition, Americans had lost the confidence in their mission as the world's leading nation.

The American President who took the US out of the war was Richard Nixon. Together with his adviser, Henry Kissinger, Nixon developed a new foreign policy for the post-Vietnam world. This became known as 'détente' and it involved striving for agreement and peace with the communist world.

>> Activity

Explain why the USA lost the war in Vietnam. In your answer describe:

a American military tactics,

b the impact of the Tet Offensive,

c atrocities such as My Lai,

d opposition to the war in the USA.

SOURCE N

Desperate scenes as the last US helicopters leave Saigon, just before the communist victory in 1975. A US embassy official punches a Vietnamese man who is trying to board the helicopter.

Nixon in China

Nixon tried to get better relations not only with the Soviet Union, but also with communist China. The world was surprised when Nixon announced in 1971 that he would visit China. Since 1949 the US government had treated China with contempt and had refused to 'recognise' the communist government. The visit took place in 1972 and led to much better relations between the two countries.

SOURCE O

The world was astonished when Nixon visited China in 1972.

Arms control

In dealing with the Soviet Union, Nixon emphasised the need for arms control negotiations. The Strategic Arms Limitation Talks (SALT 1) began in 1969 and led to the signing of an agreement on Intercontinental Ballistic Missiles in 1972. Nixon stated that American policy on nuclear weapons was now one of 'sufficiency', rather than 'superiority': this meant that the Americans wanted enough weapons to defend themselves and were no longer committed to having more than the Soviet Union. Détente also increased trade between the superpowers. In 1972 the US government agreed to supply wheat to the Soviet Union and soon a large proportion of all American wheat was exported to the Soviet Union.

In Europe, détente meant a reduction of tension over the divisions of Germany. In 1974 the USA formally recognised East Germany as an independent country. Détente allowed the two German states to establish better relations with each other.

Détente continued after Nixon's fall from office during the Watergate Scandal in 1974. Brezhnev, the Soviet leader organised a conference on the future of Europe in Helsinki between 1973 and 1975. This produced agreements on ways of avoiding confrontation between East and West and economic co-operation. The Helsinki agreements also committed all parties to respect human rights. Communist countries did very little to honour the pledge on human rights.

The end of détente

The US president, Jimmy Carter (in office 1977–80) attempted to achieve more arms reductions through the SALT 2 talks. These talks were very protracted. Carter annoyed Brezhnev by trying to link cuts in weapons to discussions of human rights in the communist countries. A SALT 2 treaty was finally signed in 1979. This set further limits on the number of nuclear weapons that each side could hold. The SALT 2 treaty was never ratified by the US Congress because the Soviet Union invaded Afghanistan in December 1979. The sending of troops into Afghanistan marked the end of the period of détente. The USA boycotted the Moscow Olympics in 1980 in order to show disapproval for the Soviet nation. In 1981, Carter was replaced by a hard-line President, Ronald Reagan, who rejected détente and who started a new arms race with the Soviet Union. The early 1980s have been called the Second Cold War. Reagan attacked Soviet communism in his speeches and talked of the need to oppose an 'evil empire'. His scientists were instructed to explore ways of giving the USA nuclear superiority by developing ways of shooting down Soviet missiles in space. This project was known as Star Wars, or the Strategic Defence Initiative.

>> Activity

Explain in your own words how American foreign policy developed after Vietnam.

Containing communism

After the communist take-over of Eastern Europe, US governments were preoccupied with the need to stop the spread of communism. This policy was called containment.

The fall of China: 1949

Led by Mao Zedong, communists took power in China in 1949. Communist success in China convinced American leaders that they needed to be more energetic in a worldwide struggle against communism. This led to a huge increase in American spending on defence.

The Korean War: 1950–3

At the end of the Second World War, Korea was divided in two at the 38th parallel – North Korea was communist, South Korea was anti-communist. North Korea invaded South Korea in June 1950. The Americans won UN support for a war against the invading North Koreans. General MacArthur led a fight-back that drove the North Koreans out of South Korea. MacArthur then continued to push deep into North Korean territory. This was going beyond 'containment' and became an attempt to 'roll back' communism.

A massive Chinese army invaded to help the North Koreans in November 1950. The US army was driven back close to the original border in early 1951. There was then a military stalemate. MacArthur wanted to widen the war by attacking China itself. President Truman disagreed and dismissed MacArthur. Peace talks dragged on for two years. The war finally ended in July 1953.

The Cuban Missile Crisis: 1962

Led by Fidel Castro, there was a revolution in Cuba in 1959. Castro introduced communist ideas to Cuba. The US attempted to invade and overthrow Castro, but this ended in disaster at the Bay of Pigs in 1961.

In 1962 Khrushchev, the Soviet leader, placed nuclear missiles on Cuba. American spy planes discovered them and the American President, Kennedy, insisted that the missiles should be removed. There was a real possibility of a nuclear war. Eventually Khrushchev gave way and agreed to remove the missiles in return for a US promise to remove missiles in Turkey. The ending of the crisis was seen as a victory for Kennedy and a defeat for Khrushchev.

Fidel Castro.

Restricting Soviet influence in the Middle East

Both the USA and the Soviet Union tried to influence states in the Middle East. The US encouraged the new Jewish state of Israel, set up in 1948. Some Arabs, including the governments of Egypt and Syria and the Palestine Liberation Organisation (PLO), looked for Soviet help in their conflict with Israel. With American money and weapons, Israel was able to defeat its Arab enemies in a series of wars (1948–9, 1967, 1973). These defeats convinced the Egyptian president, Sadat, to break with the USSR. The US government enabled Israel and Egypt to sign a peace treaty in 1979.

The Vietnam War: 1965–1975

Vietnam had been a French colony before the Second World War. The French pulled out in 1954 and Vietnam was divided between a communist state in the North, and and an anti-communist state in South Vietnam. The leader of North Vietnam was Ho Chi Minh.

After 1958 communist guerillas, known as the Vietcong, helped by troops of the regular army of North Vietnam, tried to overthrow the government of South Vietnam. At first the Americans supplied the South with money and weapons and in March 1965 President Johnson sent US combat troops to Vietnam. Eventually there were 540,000 Americans fighting in Vietnam.

The defeat of the USA

The USA was unable to defeat the Vietcong. Many people in the USA were opposed to the war. In January 1968 the Vietcong launched a massive series of attacks called the Tet Offensive. This was not a military success but it convinced American leaders that they would never win in Vietnam. President Johnson was replaced by Richard Nixon, who was determined to pull out of Vietnam. Nixon tried 'Vietnamisation' – a policy of reducing American troops and trying to strengthen the forces of South Vietnam. In 1973 the US signed a peace treaty with North Vietnam and Americans troops left the country. Vietnamisation did not work – without American forces the government of South Vietnam was overthrown by communist forces in 1975. Vietnam became a single, communist state. After the fall of Vietnam several neighbouring countries also became communist.

After Vietnam: détente

The US presidents of the 1970s – Nixon, Ford and Carter – pursued a policy of 'détente'. This involved establishing peaceful relationships with the two great communist powers: the USSR and China.

Defeat in Vietnam reduced American self-confidence.

Further disasters followed:

> The pro-American government in Iran was overthrown in a revolution in 1978. American diplomats were taken prisoner and were held hostage from 1979–81.

> A Soviet army invaded Afghanistan in 1979 to support its new communist government.

Ho Chi Minh.

The end of détente

The new US President, Ronald Reagan, restored some of America's self-confidence in the 1980s. He ended détente. He aggressively challenged the Soviet Union and began a new arms race. This period has been called the Second Cold War. Reagan invested in 'Star Wars' (officially known as the Strategic Defence Initiative). This was intended to be a system for shooting down Soviet missiles in space. The Soviet Union could not compete. Gorbachev came to power in the Soviet Union and established good relations with Reagan. The arms race came to an end and the Soviet Union pulled out of Afghanistan in 1988–9.

Tito and Stalin

Orders from Moscow

After 1945 communists took power in some countries without Soviet help. This happened in Yugoslavia, where a communist leader called Tito led a successful war against occupying German forces between 1941 and 1945. At first, Tito seemed to be highly regarded by Stalin. In April 1945 Tito went on a tour of the USSR and was treated as a great hero. There was, however, an underlying tension between Tito and Stalin. The Yugoslav leader did not see why he should follow orders from Moscow.

Tito, the Leader of Yugoslavia. He successfully defied Stalin.

Tito and Stalin argued in 1948. There were two immediate causes of this rift between Yugoslavia and the USSR:

> Yugoslav foreign policy was at odds with Soviet plans. Tito wanted to control the small neighbouring state of Albania. In late 1947 the Yugoslavs annoyed Stalin by sending their troops into Albania.

> Tito was greatly offended by the way the Soviets recruited agents in Yugoslavia and asked them to report direct to Moscow. Many senior members of the army were asked to become Soviet spies.

'I will shake my little finger'

The conflict between Stalin and Tito was announced to the world in June 1948. Yugoslavia was thrown out of Cominform, the Soviet-led organisation for world communism. Stalin took action to bring Tito into line. Economic sanctions were used – the USSR and other East European states stopped trading with Yugoslavia. Stalin was confident that Tito could be overthrown. At the beginning of the split he said, 'I will shake my little finger and there will be no more Tito'. Stalin hoped that Yugoslav communists would turn against their leader. Tito dealt skilfully with his enemies. Local communists who sided with Stalin were arrested. People in Yugoslavia rallied round their leader.

Tito turns West

Tito believed that the USA and other Western countries would support him in his dispute with Stalin. He was right. Western countries were keen to help Yugoslavia survive the economic blockade. In December 1948 the British provided a $30 million trade deal. Over the next few years the Americans gave considerable financial support. With Western help Tito survived the early days of the split with Stalin. Having failed through other means Stalin began, in 1949, to threaten war. In the early 1950s the West began to give direct military help, as well as money. In 1951 the Americans provided the Yugoslav armed forces with equipment worth $60 million dollars.

Stalin spent his final years making sure that no other East European leaders tried to follow Tito. Some were accused of 'Titoism' and executed. According to some sources Stalin was making plans to have Tito poisoned when he himself died in 1953. After the death of Stalin, the new Soviet leader, Khrushchev, ended the dispute with Yugoslavia in 1955. This was a victory for Tito, who continued with his independent foreign policy.

Discussion points

> Why did Tito and Stalin argue?

> How successful were Stalin's attempts to destroy Tito?

The Red Army in Budapest and Prague

In 1956 the Soviet Union shocked the world by sending troops to overthrow the government of Hungary. A similar invasion of Czechoslovakia took place in 1968.

Why did the Soviet Union invade Hungary and Czechoslovakia?

>> Activity

Imagine that you were working for the United Nations in 1956. You have been asked to write a report on why the Soviet Union invaded Hungary. In your report you should discuss:

> why Hungarians disliked Soviet rule

> how the death of Stalin created a new situation in Eastern Europe

> the impact on Hungarians of events in Yugoslavia and Poland

> how the Soviet Union reacted to changes in Hungary.

Hungary and the Soviet Empire

The Hungarians were a proud nation with a strong sense of identity. Before 1918 they played a key part in the running of the vast Austro–Hungarian Empire. Hungarian nationalists did not like being part of a Soviet Empire after the Second World War.

Stalin's actions increased anti-Soviet feelings in Hungary. Free elections were held in November 1945. The communists got less than 20 per cent of the vote. Stalin ignored the decision of the Hungarian people and imposed a government on the country in which communists had many of the most important posts. In August 1947 another election was held in Hungary. This time the Soviet Union made sure that the

SOURCE A

Cardinal Mindszenty, leader of the Catholic Church in Hungary. As an opponent of Soviet communism he was sentenced to life in prison.

election was rigged so that the communists won. Between 1949 and 1953 Hungary was badly treated by Stalin. Opponents of Soviet power were dealt with ruthlessly. In 1949 the leader of the Roman Catholic Church in Hungary, Cardinal Mindszenty, was sentenced to life imprisonment. Even Hungarian communists were attacked if they showed any signs of disagreeing with Stalin. The leading communist, Laszlo Rajk, was put on trial and hanged in 1949 because he was too independent-minded.

After Stalin

The death of Stalin in 1953 created a new uncertain situation in Eastern Europe. During the Stalinist years, Hungary had been ruled with considerable brutality by Mátyás Rákosi. Rákosi managed to hang on to power after 1953, but he was forced to invite a reformer called Imre Nagy to join his government. The two men got on badly and in 1955 Rákosi got the upper hand and threw Nagy out of the government and the party.

Hungarians were not sure how far the new Soviet leadership would allow Hungary to operate as an independent country. For a number of reasons Hungarians hoped that they might be able to have greater independence:

> The new Soviet leadership was friendly to Tito's Yugoslavia. Yugoslavia had successfully broken away from Soviet control in 1948. People in Hungary thought that other countries could now follow the Yugoslav path.

> Stalin was criticised by the new Soviet leader, Khrushchev, in a famous speech in February 1956. Hungarians hoped that Khrushchev would be very different from Stalin and would be happy with a new, independent Hungary.

> In June 1956 there were anti-Soviet demonstrations in Poland. Khrushchev looked for a compromise. He allowed reforms and he appointed Gomulka, a man who had been imprisoned by Stalin, as the new leader of the Polish Communist Party.

The news from Poland seemed like further proof that the bad old days of Soviet control were over. In fact this was a mistake: the new Soviet leaders still wanted to control the countries of the Warsaw Pact. Hungarians listened to radio broadcasts from the West that criticised communism. Some felt that if Hungary challenged Soviet power they could expect help from the USA. Back in 1948 the Truman Doctrine had stated that the USA would help any people fighting against communism. In practice, the US theory of containment meant that America would only threaten force to stop the spread of communism; countries that were already communist could expect sympathy but no help.

SOURCE B

In 1955 Khrushchev visited Yugoslavia to make friends with Tito. He made a speech claiming that the USSR no longer wished to interfere in other states.

True to the teaching of the founder of the Soviet State, Lenin, the government of the Soviet Union bases its policy towards other countries, big and small, on the principle of peaceful co-existence. We believe in equality, non-interference, respect for sovereignty and national independence. The Soviet Union rejects aggression and believes that any invasion of another state is not to be permitted.

Alarm in Moscow

There was an air of excitement in Hungary in the summer of 1956. People heard the news from Poland. They wanted even more change in Hungary. They talked about Hungary breaking away from the Soviet bloc and becoming a neutral country. This was too much for Khrushchev. He could accept some changes but not Hungarian neutrality. If Hungary left the Warsaw Pact, other countries might follow. The protective buffer of friendly countries built up by Stalin might fall apart.

The Soviet leaders tried to stop the disturbances in Hungary by changing the leadership of the Hungarian communists. Realising that Rákosi was extremely unpopular, the Soviet leadership forced him to resign in July 1956. The new ruler was Ernó Geró. However, Geró was seen as a Stalinist by many Hungarians and the change of leader made little difference.

On 6 October 1956, Laszlo Rajk, the leading victim of Stalinist terror, was re-buried with a state funeral. A huge crowd turned out to show their support for the memory of Rajk and the idea of reform. Further demonstrations called for the removal of Geró and the reinstatement of the popular reformer Nagy. On 24 October Nagy became Prime Minister. Khrushchev had hoped that this would end the disturbances. It did not. Across the country, workers set up revolutionary councils. They demanded a complete end to the Soviet system in Hungary. They called for free multi-party elections, a free Press and for Hungary to leave the Warsaw Pact. Nagy agreed to accept these reforms. At this point Khrushchev decided to invade.

SOURCE C

Laszlo Rajk, on trial for his life. Stalin was afraid that this communist leader would copy Tito and break away from Moscow. Stalin ensured that Rajk was executed.

SOURCE D

The Soviet leader, Khrushchev, expressed his anxiety over Hungary in July 1956.

If the situation in Hungary gets still worse, we here have decided to use all means at our disposal to bring the crisis to an end. The Soviet Union could not at any price allow a breach in the front in Eastern Europe.

SOURCE E

The Soviet Foreign Minister, Shepilov, explained Soviet actions to the General Assembly of the United Nations on 19 November 1956.

We could not overlook the fact that Hungary is a neighbour of the Soviet Union. A victory of the reactionary forces would have converted that country into a new jumping-off ground for an aggressive war not only against the Soviet Union but also against the other countries of Eastern Europe.

>> Activity

1 Look at Source B. Why do you think that Hungarians who wished for independence were encouraged by Khrushchev's speech in 1955?

2 Look at the Sources D and E. What do they tell us about Soviet motives in invading Hungary?

The Soviet invasion

The Soviet forces reached Budapest on 4 November 1956. The Red Army forces comprised 200,000 soldiers and 2,500 tanks. The Hungarians fought against the invaders. At least 3,000 Hungarians were killed (some estimates are much higher). Despite Nagy's desperate appeal (Source G) neither the United Nations nor the USA did anything to help. The powerful Soviet forces took control of Hungary and imposed a new pro-Soviet government.

SOURCE F

Hungarian nationalists engaged in street fighting in Budapest, 4 November 1956.

SOURCE G

When he heard of the invasion, Imre Nagy, the Hungarian Prime Minister, appealed to the United Nations for help.

Reliable reports have reached the government of the Hungarian People's Republic that further Soviet units are entering Hungary. The Hungarian government immediately repudiates the Warsaw Treaty and declares Hungary's neutrality, turns to the United Nations, and requests the help of the great powers in defending the country's neutrality. I request Your Excellency to put on the agenda of the forthcoming General Assembly of the United Nations the question of Hungary's neutrality and the defence of this neutrality by the great powers.

AFTER THE RISING

> The new communist government of Hungary was led by a man called János Kádár. Under Kádár economic conditions in Hungary gradually improved.

> The supporters of the Rising were severely punished. Imre Nagy was executed in 1958.

> The Hungarian Uprising showed East Europeans that they could expect no help from the USA if they rose up against Soviet control. The US policy of 'containment' meant that the Americans would fight to stop the spread of communism but would not interfere if a country was already communist.

> There was a period of uneasy peace in Eastern Europe for the next 10 years. It was not until the mid-1960s that people in the satellite states once again challenged Soviet control. In 1968 the government of Czechoslovakia decided to develop a new form of communism that was much more liberal than Soviet communism.

> Communists around the world were dismayed by the way the Soviet Union used force against the Hungarian people. In Western Europe many communists were disillusioned. In China the leaders became more wary of Moscow.

> The invasion was a blow to the reputation of the United Nations. It did nothing to stop an act of aggression by one member state on another member state.

Czechoslovakia: 1968

Economic problems were a major cause of calls for reform in Czechoslovakia. The country had been economically successful before the Second World War. By the mid-1960s many people were very disappointed with the standard of living under Soviet-style communism. Czechoslovakia had also been a democracy before the war and people resented their lack of freedom of speech under the Soviet system. In 1966 there were student demonstrations and public criticism of the way the Soviet Union controlled the economy of Czechoslovakia. The student protesters called for greater democracy and free speech.

In January 1968 a new communist leader, Alexander Dubček, was appointed. He was determined to improve communism. His plans were described as 'socialism with a human face', and the early months of 1968 have become known as the 'Prague Spring'. Dubček began to introduce a number of reforms:

> the Soviet system of state planning would be altered to give more responsibility to farms and factories,

> trade unions would be given greater freedom,

> more foreign travel to the West would be allowed,

> censorship of the Press would be abolished so that people could say and write what they liked,

> criticism of the government would not be seen as a crime.

At the same time Dubček was still a communist. He did not want to introduce Western-style capitalism. Dubček knew what had happened in 1956. He tried to re-assure the Soviet leaders that his reforms were less radical than those called for during the Hungarian Uprising. He stated repeatedly that he wanted Czechoslovakia to remain a loyal member of the Warsaw Pact. He insisted that changes in Czechoslovakia were no threat to the security of the Soviet Union.

Brezhnev, the Soviet leader, did not accept these assurances from Dubček. He was afraid that once the communist system allowed free speech the country would become chaotic. Brezhnev felt that the Czechoslovak reforms were the first step towards the country leaving the communist bloc and becoming a Western-style country, allied to the USA. He was not prepared to allow this. Czechoslovakia was in an important strategic position. If it was allied to the USA, it would provide a corridor along which American forces could march from West Germany to the Soviet Ukraine. Brezhnev was also under pressure from hard-line communists in East Germany. They argued that if free speech was allowed in Czechoslovakia, people in all other Eastern bloc countries would demand the same rights. This would weaken the power of the communist parties throughout Eastern Europe.

SOURCE H

Dubček during the early days of the Prague Spring.

Help from the USA?

Brezhnev, the Soviet leader, began to plan an invasion of Czechoslovakia. By late July Soviet tanks and troops were massed on the Czechoslovak border. Brezhnev was encouraged by developments in the West. The American government was in crisis in the summer of 1968. There were race riots in the black districts of several cities. The war in Vietnam had gone disastrously wrong for the USA. Brezhnev calculated that there was no possibility of America taking any action to stop the invasion. The Vietnam crisis distracted attention from Czechoslovakia, just as in 1956 the Suez crisis reduced the impact of the invasion of Hungary.

SOURCE I

A letter of warning was sent by the Soviet leadership to the Czechoslovak Communist Party, 15 July 1968.

Developments in your country are causing deep anxiety among us. We are convinced that your country is being pushed off the road of socialism and that this puts in danger the interest of the whole socialist system.

We cannot agree to have hostile forces push your country away from the road of socialism. We cannot accept the risk of Czechoslovakia being cut off from the socialist community of countries. This is something more than your own concern. It is the common concern of all communist parties and states. It is the common concern of our countries, which have joined in the Warsaw Treaty to place an insurmountable barrier against the imperialist forces.

At great sacrifice the people of our countries achieved victory over Hitlerian fascism and won the opportunity to follow the path of socialism. The frontiers of the socialist world moved to the centre of Europe. And we shall never agree to these historic gains and the security of our peoples being placed in jeopardy. We shall never agree to imperialism making a breach in the socialist system of countries.

SOURCE J

Dubček's response to the Soviet threat made matters worse. He invited Tito, the independent communist leader of Yugoslavia, to Prague. Tito arrived on 9 August. To Brezhnev this seemed like a signal that Dubček was moving away from the Warsaw Pact and towards the same independent position taken by Yugoslavia. Dubček also entered into negotiations with the Romanian leader, Nicolae Ceauşescu. A pact of friendship between Czechoslovakia and Romania was signed. The Romanian leader also resented control from Moscow. The closer ties between these two countries seemed like an attempt to undermine Soviet control of the Warsaw Pact.

The Warsaw Pact forces invade

Soviet forces crossed the Czechoslovak frontier on 20 August 1968. They were joined by token forces from East Germany, Poland and Bulgaria. A day later the Warsaw Pact forces were in Prague, the capital of Czechoslovakia. Large-scale loss of life was avoided because the Czechoslovak government decided not to resist the invading army. People took to the streets to protest but there was none of the bloody street fighting that had taken place in Budapest in 1956. The Soviet troops took Dubček to Moscow and ordered him to abandon his reforms. He was finally removed from office in 1969. A pro-Soviet leader called Husák took his place. Soviet power was demonstrated in May 1970 when a Soviet–Czechoslovak treaty was signed. In this the Czechoslovaks were forced to thank the Soviets for the invasion.

Rioting in Prague as Soviet tanks take over the city. In contrast with Budapest, there was relatively little bloodshed in Prague.

THE AFTERMATH OF CZECHOSLOVAKIA 1968

After the invasion Brezhnev said that the Soviet Union was not prepared to let any communist country abandon communism. If a state did try to give up communism, the Soviet Union claimed the right to impose communism by force. This view became known as the Brezhnev Doctrine. The doctrine was finally abandoned in the 1980s.

The way the Soviet Union dealt with Czechoslovakia was less bloody than the treatment of Hungary after 1956. Nagy was executed. Dubček was thrown out of the communist party in 1970. He spent the 1970s and 1980s working as a forestry inspector. However, he kept his life and his freedom.

The government of China was unhappy at the invasion and it led to a further deterioration in relations between the two communist superpowers. The Chinese disliked the way the Soviet Union treated other communist countries. Afterwards, Mao encouraged Yugoslavia and Romania to remain independent of Moscow. There were border clashes between Soviet and Chinese troops in the months after the invasion.

The invasion disillusioned communists around the world. In Western Europe many communists stopped looking to Moscow for guidance. In the 1970s the powerful Italian and French communist parties called for a new style of communism that allowed free speech and free elections.

>> Activity

1 Explain in your own words why Brezhnev decided to invade Czechoslovakia in 1968.

2 Look back at the whole of this unit. What similarities and differences were there between the Hungarian Uprising and the invasion of Czechoslovakia? Think about the following aspects of each event:

> the causes of unrest,

> the aims of the people wanting change,

> the reasons why the Soviet Union found these changes unacceptable,

> the way the Soviet Union invaded,

> the treatment of the leadership after the invasion.

Building the Berlin Wall

In 1945 Berlin was divided into American, British, French and Soviet zones. Berlin itself was deep inside the Soviet zone of eastern Germany. This created a curious situation in Berlin. The American, British and French zones joined together to form a single area known as West Berlin. It became an island of Western capitalism in the middle of the communist sea of East Germany. In 1961 a wall was built to separate East and West Berlin. This became the most famous symbol of the Cold War.

Why was the Berlin Wall built?

BERLIN AND MOSCOW

The existence of West Berlin was very annoying to Soviet leaders in Moscow:

> It was much more prosperous than communist East Germany and was an advertisement for the economic success of Western Europe.

> Western governments used Berlin as a headquarters for their spying activities.

> German people could move freely from communist East Germany to West Berlin. Many decided to flee via West Berlin. Between 1949 and 1960, 3 million East Germans fled to the West through Berlin. These people were often young, talented and well-educated. The communist government could not afford to lose its future managers and leaders.

The crisis over Berlin was not simply about the problems the city posed for East Germany. It was part of the wider Cold War struggle between the USA and the USSR. In the early 1960s both countries had confident, aggressive leaders. The Soviet leader was Nikita Khrushchev and the American leader was John F. Kennedy. Each one was convinced that his side was right and each one was ready to threaten war to get what he wanted.

Khrushchev and the Soviet challenge

Nikita Khrushchev had emerged victorious from the power struggle that followed the death of Stalin in 1953. Khrushchev was confident that Soviet communism would eventually triumph over Western democracy and capitalism. He believed that the communist world was just about to overtake the West in wealth and scientific research. In October 1957 the Soviets launched the world's first ever satellite, called Sputnik. Khrushchev thought that this proved the strength of the communist world. Convinced of the increasing power of communism, Khrushchev decided to extend communist influence in Europe. He chose Berlin as the place for a trial of strength.

SOURCE A

In speeches made in 1958, Khrushchev expressed his view that Soviet communism was overtaking the West.

The launching of the Soviet sputniks first of all shows that a serious change has occurred in the balance of forces between socialist and capitalist countries, in favour of the socialist nations.

January, 1958

We are firmly convinced that the time is approaching when socialist countries will outstrip the most developed capitalist countries in the volume of industrial production.

October, 1958

Khrushchev calls for a neutral Berlin

The crisis that led to the building of the wall started in 1958 when Khrushchev called for the end of the four-power control of Berlin. He set a time limit of six months for the settlement of the future of Berlin. There was a vague threat of war if the matter was not resolved. His own plan was that Berlin should become a neutral free city and Western troops should withdraw. The Western powers were divided about how to react to Khrushchev. The West German leader, Konrad Adenauer, was strongly against any deal. By contrast, The US President, Eisenhower, was ready to negotiate over the future of Berlin. As the deadline approached Eisenhower made it clear that he did not want to risk a war over Berlin. Khrushchev dropped his ultimatum. At a summit meeting in September 1959 Eisenhower said that he was prepared to make concessions on the future of Berlin.

SOURCE C

Eisenhower's views at the 1959 summit:

We must remember that Berlin is an abnormal situation. It has come about through some mistakes of our leaders – Churchill and Roosevelt. There must be some way to develop some kind of free city which might somehow be part of West Germany. Perhaps the UN would become a party to guaranteeing the freedom, safety and security of the city. Berlin would have an unarmed status except for police forces. The time is coming, and perhaps soon, when we would simply have to get our forces out.

The U-2 spy plane incident

So far, Khrushchev had been very successful. Through threatening war he had divided the Western allies and won a promise of change from the US President, Eisenhower. Khrushchev and Eisenhower agreed to meet for further discussions about Berlin in May 1960.

This meeting did not take place. Just before it was due to start, an American U-2 spy plane was shot down over Soviet territory. The pilot, Gary Powers, was taken prisoner and put on trial. Khrushchev demanded an apology. Eisenhower refused to apologise. Khrushchev cancelled the summit meeting. As a result he missed his chance to do a deal over Berlin.

SOURCE B

An exhibition about Gary Powers and his U-2 spy plane, held in Moscow in 1960. The US government was extremely embarrassed by the U-2 incident.

A change of president

Eisenhower retired at the end of 1960. The new President was the young John F. Kennedy. In his election speeches Kennedy said that he was going to be tougher with the Soviets than Eisenhower.

SOURCE D

Extracts from John F. Kennedy's campaign speeches in 1960:

The enemy is the communist sytem itself – unceasing in its drive for world domination. This is a struggle for supremacy between two conflicting ideologies: freedom under God versus ruthless, godless tyranny.

We will mould our strength and become first again. Not first if. Not first but. Not first when. But first period. I want the world to wonder not what Mr Khrushchev is doing. I want them to wonder what the United States is doing.

The threat of war

Kennedy brought a new firm approach to the argument over Berlin. Kennedy and Khrushchev met in Vienna in June 1961. This was unfriendly and unsuccessful. Khrushchev demanded that Berlin should become neutral. He angrily talked about the danger of war if the USA refused to pull out of Berlin. Banging his hands on the conference table, Khrushchev said, 'I want peace, but if you want war, that is your problem.' Kennedy ended the conference by saying, 'It's going to be a cold winter.'

SOURCE E

Kennedy and Khrushchev at the summit meeting in Vienna, 1961. At this meeting both sides threatened war.

Afterwards Khrushchev repeated his demands in public and insisted, as he had done with Eisenhower, that the USA must act within six months. At the same time he increased Soviet spending on defence by 30 per cent. Unlike Eisenhower, Kennedy was in no mood to do a deal. At the end of July Kennedy announced a complete rejection of the Soviet demands. He ordered a massive increase in the American armed services: the number of troops was increased by 15 per cent, spending on defence was increased by $3 billion and many new aircraft and warships were ordered. In public speeches both Kennedy and Khrushchev suggested that they were ready for war over Berlin:

SOURCE F

Kennedy made a television and radio speech to the American people on 25 July 1961.

I have heard it said that West Berlin is militarily untenable. Any dangerous spot is tenable if men – brave men – will make it so. We do not want to fight – but we have fought before. We cannot and will not permit the Communists to drive us out of Berlin, either gradually or by force. There is peace in Berlin today. The source of world trouble and tension is Moscow, not Berlin.

SOURCE G

In late July 1961 Khrushchev spoke to an American diplomat and threatened war:

If your troops try to force their way to Berlin, we will oppose you by force. War is bound to go thermonuclear, and though you and we may survive, all your European allies will be completely destroyed.

Behind the angry words it seems that neither side was really willing to start a nuclear war over the future of Berlin.

SOURCE H

On his way back from the Vienna summit Kennedy described his private thoughts.

It seems particularly stupid to risk killing a million Americans over an argument about access rights on an Autobahn or because the Germans want Germany reunified. If I'm going to threaten Russia with a nuclear war, it will have to be for much bigger and more important reasons than that.

Building the wall

While Khrushchev threatened nuclear war, he secretly planned a different solution to the Berlin crisis. The continued uncertainty over Berlin increased the number of East Germans who fled to West Berlin. Every day over a thousand East Germans entered the Western part of the city. In the early hours of 13 August 1961 barbed wire and barricades were erected all around West Berlin. When the people of West Berlin woke up their city was sealed off from East Germany. The barbed wire was later replaced by more substantial barriers; the Berlin Wall was created.

SOURCE I

An 18-year-old builder, Peter Fechter, shot dead behind the East Berlin side of the wall while trying to escape to the West.

WHO GAINED AND WHO LOST FROM THE BUILDING OF THE BERLIN WALL?

> The flow of refugees from East to West stopped almost completely. This allowed the communists to consolidate their control over East Germany.

> Enemies of communism could argue that communism was so awful that people had to be walled in to make sure that they did not run away from communism.

> Between 1948 and 1961 there was a real possibility that arguments about Berlin would lead to a Third World War. This possibility stopped with the building of the Berlin Wall.

> People in East Germany who did not support communism were now trapped. Those who tried to get over the wall were shot.

> The building of the wall was the beginning of a period of calm in Europe. On both sides people accepted that there was no immediate prospect of change and the level of tension went down.

>> Activity

Explain why the Berlin Wall was built. In your answer mention:

> how West Berlin came to exist,

> why West Berlin annoyed Soviet leaders,

> why Khrushchev was keen to confront the USA,

> the different reactions of Eisenhower and Kennedy to Soviet threats.

155

Solidarity

In 1980 a remarkable new development took place in Eastern Europe. Since the communist take-over in the 1940s Moscow had not allowed any real political opposition to communism in the countries of Eastern Europe. In Poland, in 1980, this changed. A powerful non-communist organisation called Solidarity challenged the government.

What part did Solidarity play in the decline of Soviet power?

The challenge of Poland

With a population of 35 million, Poland was, after the Soviet Union, the largest country in Eastern Europe and there were several reasons why the Soviets had problems controlling Poland:

1 Much of Poland had been ruled by Russia since the eighteenth century. Most Poles were proud of their nation and disliked Soviet communism.

2 The Second World War increased the Poles' hatred for Soviet Russia. Stalin had carved up their country with Hitler in 1939. In 1940 Stalin massacred thousands of Polish Army officers and buried them at Katyn. In 1944 the Soviet Red Army deliberately allowed the Warsaw Rising to fail, with huge loss of Polish life.

3 Most Poles were Catholics. The Catholic Church, which was too well-organised to be broken by the communists, encouraged Polish nationalism. In 1978 a leading Polish churchman became Pope John Paul II.

4 Ordinary Polish people had more power than in other communist countries. Polish farmers successfully held on to their own farms. Among Polish factory workers there was a strong tradition of using strikes against the government. In 1956 and 1970 strikes had forced the communist government to change both its leaders and its policies.

The birth of Solidarity

Polish living standards were poor in the 1970s. The communist government had large international debt. In July 1980 new price rises led to widespread unrest and strikes. Strikers were particularly active at the Lenin shipyards in the town of Gdansk (formerly Danzig). The workers at Gdansk were led by a remarkable man, an electrician called Lech Walesa. He was a brilliant speaker. In August the striking workers set up a new trade union called Solidarity. Unlike all other trade unions in communist states, Solidarity was not controlled by communists. Soon it had 9 million members and was demanding not only better conditions for workers, but also more political and religious freedom. Unrest spread throughout Poland. The communist leader, Gierek, was replaced in September as the communist party tried to find a way out of the crisis. In November, judges in the Polish Supreme Court sided with Solidarity and declared that the union was legal.

SOURCE A

Lech Walesa, the Solidarity leader, speaking at Gdansk, 1980.

Once Solidarity was formed and became a national force, the Polish communist leaders were in an impossible position:

> If they tried to destroy Solidarity they would be despised by the great majority of the Polish people.

> If they accepted the existence of a non-communist opposition force they risked provoking an armed invasion by the USSR.

Send in the tanks?

In December 1980 and March 1981 the Soviet leaders considered sending troops into Poland to impose Soviet power, just as they had done in Hungary in 1956 and Czechoslovakia in 1968. They decided against immediate armed intervention but urged the Polish communists to destroy Solidarity before it got out of control. A new Polish Prime Minister was appointed called Wojciech Jaruzelski. He was a communist and an army general. The Soviet leaders made it clear to him that he must control Solidarity or expect a Soviet invasion.

SOURCE C

Speaking in 1995, Jaruzelski described the pressures that were put on him in 1981.

At first the Soviets gave us an ultimatum: either bring the situation under control or we will cut off supplies of oil, gas and other raw materials. I was summoned three times to the Soviet Union. On the last occasion, in September 1981, I was shown army manoeuvres all along the Polish border. The Soviet army leader, Marshal Ustinov, informed me that what was happening in Poland was intolerable. We had to convince our allies that we would not undermine the Warsaw Pact or allow the state to be de-stabilised. The introduction of martial law allowed us to avoid military intervention.

SOURCE B

General Jaruzelski. The communist leader knew that if he did not control Solidarity, Soviet tanks could invade Poland.

Martial law

Jaruzelski tried to negotiate with Solidarity but the talks were not successful. In December 1981 he took the advice from Moscow and declared a state of martial law in Poland. This meant that the army had emergency powers. The leaders of Solidarity and thousands of its supporters were arrested and held without trial. Meetings and demonstrations were forbidden. Many supporters of Solidarity lost their jobs. In October 1982 the government tried to replace Soldarity with new communist unions.

Jaruzelski's attempt to destroy Solidarity did not work. Walesa was imprisoned but this made him seem even more of a hero. The movement survived underground. No one took the new unions seriously. Communist party members left the party in huge numbers. Almost a year after the declaration of martial law, in November 1982, Walesa was released from prison.

SOURCE E

A British newspaper later summed up the impact of martial law on Walesa while in prison:

Walesa waited, his message to the government the same, 'You will have to talk to us again. Without the public consent, which only Solidarity can deliver, your economic reforms can never succeed.' The claim was the simple truth.

He emerged from prison to a surprising discovery – Poland was not a political wasteland. In addition to the Solidarity underground network there were new groupings producing an extraordinary range of newspapers, journals and books. Far from being snuffed out, the opposition to Communist rule had been broadened and strengthened.

The *Observer*, 'Tearing down the Curtain', 1990

SOURCE D

In 1983 Walesa was awarded a Nobel Prize for his work for Solidarity. In the same year the Pope visited Poland and was greeted with great enthusiasm. He was another symbol of hope for Polish opponents of communism. In 1984, Polish people were outraged to learn that Father Jerzy Popielusko, a priest who supported the union, had been beaten to death by secret police. The continuing support for Solidarity was shown when a quarter of a million people attended his funeral.

Huge enthusiastic crowds turned out to greet Pope John Paul II during his visit to Poland in 1983.

The impact of Gorbachev

In 1985 the political mood in Poland began to change because of the rise to power of Gorbachev in the USSR. By calling for greater freedom in the Soviet Union Gorbachev undermined old-style communism in Eastern Europe. The threat of Russian tanks also began to disappear.

Jaruzelski introduced reforms similar to those being tried in the USSR under Gorbachev. Jaruzelski held a referendum in November 1987 asking for backing for his economic reforms. He failed to win enough votes which was a great blow to his authority. In 1988 Walesa and the still illegal Solidarity organised a nationwide series of strikes against price rises. Walesa called for talks with the government and finally Jaruzelski agreed. As a result of these talks Solidarity was once again legalised and elections were organised for June 1989.

Solidarity triumphs in elections

For the first time since the 1940s free elections were being held in Eastern Europe but the freedom was limited. They were organised so that 65 per cent of seats in the main chamber of the Polish Parliament were reserved for communists. Nevertheless, the elections were a disaster for the communists. So few people voted for them that they looked ridiculous. Almost all leading communists failed to get elected. The Polish people voted massively for Solidarity. In the Polish Senate, the second chamber of the Polish parliament, there were no restrictions and Solidarity won 99 out of 100 seats. Weeks of chaos followed as the discredited communists tried and failed to form a government. Eventually, Jaruzelski agreed that Solidarity could help to form a government. In August, Tadeuz Mazowiecki, a leading member of Solidarity, became the Prime Minister of a coalition government that included both communist and Solidarity ministers. In less than a year Solidarity had gone from being illegal to being the leading part of the government. The remaining communist ministers soon resigned and the Solidarity take-over was complete.

SOURCE F

Bronislaw Geremek was a leading Solidarity activist. He reacted emotionally when in August 1989 Solidarity helped to form a government:

For the first time in 45 years, a Polish government is to be formed, on Polish soil, by non-Communist forces. The monopoly of the Party which ruled Poland against the will of the people has been broken.

>> Activity

1 Explain in your own words why the Soviet Union had always found it difficult to control Poland.

2 Why were the leaders of the Soviet Union worried when Solidarity was set up in 1980–81?

3 How successful was the introduction of martial law?

4 How did Solidarity take power in 1989?

SOURCE G

A Solidarity demonstration in 1989. In that year Solidarity triumphed in elections.

Gorbachev and the fall of the Soviet Empire

Between 1985 to 1991 Mikhail Gorbachev was the leader of the USSR. In 1989 Soviet control of Eastern Europe collapsed. In 1991 the Soviet Union fell apart.

Was Gorbachev responsible for the collapse of communism in Europe?

Focus

Look at the following information about the Soviet Union and Eastern Europe before Gorbachev came to power. What were the long-term causes for the collapse of communism?

The standard of living

In the early 1960s, communists had been convinced that communism was better than capitalism and that the communist states would soon produce more goods than in the USA and Western Europe. By the 1980s it was clear that communism had failed to deliver high living standards. Most people in the Soviet Union and Eastern Europe were much poorer than the people of Western Europe. Some basic goods, such as sugar, were rationed. The gap between communist and capitalist economies was growing all the time. The Soviet Union and its allies were not able to compete with the West in the new industries of the 1980s – computers and telecommunications.

By the 1980s Soviet farming had failed. The Soviet Union had rich land at its disposal but it could not produce enough food to feed its people. Many people worked on the land but they were very inefficient. In the 1980s farming employed over 20 per cent of the workforce, compared with 3 per cent in the USA. On average each American farmer produced seven times more food than each Soviet farmer. As a result the USSR had to import millions of tons of grain, much of it from the USA.

SOURCE A

Leonid Brezhnev.

Corruption and the decline of communism

The founders of communism promised a new kind of state based on fairness and equality. Under the leadership of Brezhnev, Soviet communism moved a long way from these ideals and became more corrupt. As a result ordinary people had less respect for communism. It was widely known that the family of Brezhnev was corrupt. Leading communists had luxurious country houses or 'dachas' built for themselves. According to one joke that circulated in the Soviet Union at the time, Brezhnev showed his own mother round a new luxury house that he had just had built; his mother commented 'It's wonderful, Leonid. But what happens if the communists come back to power?'

A second Cold War

With the communist economies in trouble, the cost of the Cold War became more and more unbearable. The price of weapons was constantly increasing. By the 1980s a single bomber cost the same as 200 bombers built during the Second World War. America and its allies could afford these higher costs because their economies were doing well. The Soviet Union could only keep up with the USA by diverting a huge proportion of its national income to defence. People suffered even lower living standards as tanks were built instead of cars and televisions.

The cost of the Cold War began to increase when the US President, Ronald Reagan, came to power in 1981. He rejected the idea of detente and encouraged a policy of confrontation with the Soviets. He took the view that communism was wicked and needed to be approached with great firmness. Reagan increased military spending and challenged the USSR to join a new arms race.

The early 1980s have been called the 'Second Cold War' because there was heightened tension between the USA and the Soviet Union. The competition between the superpowers was symbolised by Reagan's 'Star Wars' project (officially known as SDI: the Strategic Defence Initiative). This project involved research into ways of giving America nuclear superiority by destroying Soviet missiles in space.

War in Afghanistan

Brezhnev made a big mistake in December 1979. Soviet troops invaded Afghanistan to support its communist government. The invasion was widely criticised and lost the USSR many friends. It led to a widespread boycott of the Olympic Games that were held in Moscow. Afghanistan was a Muslim country and the USSR was criticised by much of the Islamic world. The Afghan rebels received help from the USA and the invasion encouraged Reagan to take a tough anti-Soviet stance when he became president in 1980.

The Soviet military action was a failure. The official Afghan army was not strong enough to win alone and once the Soviet forces had become involved it became very difficult to withdraw. With Soviet help the Afghan government controlled Kabul, the capital, and other large towns, but the rebels controlled much of the countryside. More and more Soviet troops were needed to prop up an unpopular government. In the early 1980s there were about 125,000 Soviet troops in the country.

The situation of the Soviets in Afghanistan was similar to that of the Americans in Vietnam a decade earlier. The 10-year war led to the death of about 15,000 Soviet troops. It also damaged the Soviet economy: one estimate is that the war cost the USSR about $8 billion dollars a year. The last Soviet troops finally left Afghanistan in February 1989.

SOURCE B

Soviet troops fighting anti-communist forces in Afghanistan. The war in Afghanistan damaged the international reputation of the Soviet Union.

Andropov and Gorbachev

The ideas of Gorbachev were not completely original. By 1980 there were many younger, idealistic communists who were disgusted by corruption and wanted to reform the system. Several reformers gathered around the head of the KGB, Yuri Andropov. Gorbachev was one of this group. Brezhnev died in 1982 and Andropov became the new Soviet leader. Within a few months he became desperately ill and he died in February 1984. Although he was not in power long, Andropov introduced some policies that were later developed by Gorbachev:

> He called for an end to the arms race, and offered to reduce the Soviet stockpile of weapons in return for American reductions.

> He attacked corruption at home.

Andropov made a number of offers to Reagan. One of these was revolutionary – this was a plan to abandon the Brezhnev Doctrine and to promise never again to invade other Warsaw Pact countries. Reagan did not take this offer seriously and it came to nothing. Although Andropov had many original ideas he did little to provide more freedom for the people of the Soviet Union. As the KGB Chairman from 1967–82 he had played a key role in the persecution of dissidents, nationalists and different religious groups. After the death of Andropov, the new leader of the Soviet Union was Konstantin Chernenko. He had little interest in reform. Like Andropov, Chernenko did not live long enough to have much impact. He died in 1985 and his replacement as General Secretary was the reformer Mikhail Gorbachev. He introduced policies of 'glasnost' or 'openness' and 'perestroika' or 'economic restructuring'.

One critical difference between Gorbachev and Andropov was in the way glasnost gave new freedom to the people of the Soviet Union. This was a radical change. Control of ideas had always been a central part of the Soviet system. Under glasnost, people were told an increasing amount about the atrocities committed by the government when Stalin had been in power. Thousands of political prisoners were released. The leading dissident Andrei Sakharov was released in 1986.

THE GORBACHEV AGENDA

> The economy was failing. The communist system needed to be reformed but not replaced. This would be done by a process called 'perestroika' or 'restructuring'.

> Perestroika would require a new honesty on the part of people in the Soviet Union. Free speech should be allowed. There should be a new spirit of 'glasnost' or 'openness'. There should be an end to the persecution of the dissidents.

> Corruption must be stamped out.

> A key cause of the economic problems was the amount of money being spent on defence. To reduce this the Soviet Union should:

pull out of Afghanistan

negotiate arms reductions with the USA

stop interfering in the affairs of other communist countries.

Another distinctive feature of the Gorbachev leadership was the energy and imagination with which he pursued the idea of disarmament with the US president, Reagan. Unlike Andropov he was able to persuade Reagan that he genuinely wanted an end to the Cold War. The two men met, face-to-face, at a series of summit meetings. The main focus for these discussions was arms control. The result was a major disarmament treaty in 1987. Both the USA and the Soviet Union agreed to remove medium-range nuclear missiles from Europe within three years.

Withdrawal from Afghanistan

As soon as he was in office, Gorbachev began to explore ways of ending the war in Afghanistan without destroying the communist government in that country. In February 1988 he announced publicly that the Soviet army was going to pull out of Afghanistan. The withdrawal began in May 1988. By February 1989 the last Soviet troops had left.

Failure at home

Gorbachev had many triumphs in foreign policy but he was less successful at home. By encouraging free speech, Gorbachev simply brought problems out into the open. He wanted to make the Soviet system of centrally planned production more efficient. This did not happen. The levels of corruption and inefficiency in the economy were too great. The managers of the Soviet economy saw the reforms as a threat to their jobs and they blocked the changes.

>> Activity

1 What similarities and differences were there between the policies of Andropov and those of Gorbachev?

2 What can you learn from Sources C and D about the motives of Gorbachev?

SOURCE C

Gorbachev 1987:

I want to put an end to all the rumours in the West, and point out once again that all our reforms are socialist. We are looking within socialism, rather than outside it, for the answers to all the questions that arise. Those who hope that we shall move away from the socialist path will be greatly disappointed.

SOURCE D

In 1992, after he had lost power, Gorbachev tried to make sense of his years in control:

I knew that an immense task of transformation awaited me. Engaged in the exhausting arms race, the country, it was evident, was at the end of its strength. Economic mechanisms were functioning more and more poorly. Production figures were slumping. Scientific and technical developments were cancelled out by an economy totally in the hands of the bureaucracy. The people's standard of living was clearly declining. Corruption was gaining ground. We wanted to reform by launching a democratic process. It was similar to earlier reform attempts.

SOURCE E

Gorbachev and Reagan, 1987. The two men established a warm personal relationship and agreed to substantial disarmament.

The end of the Brezhnev Doctrine

Another foreign policy breakthrough came in December 1988, when Gorbachev spoke at the United Nations. He announced huge cuts in the Soviet armed forces. Gorbachev also made it clear that the Brezhnev Doctrine was now abandoned: the countries of Eastern Europe could do what they liked. There would be no more Soviet tanks rolling into Prague or Budapest.

SOURCE F

Gorbachev, speaking to the United Nations on 7 December 1988:

Force or the threat of force neither can nor should be instruments of foreign policy. The principle of the freedom of choice is mandatory. Refusal to recognise this principle will have serious consequences for world peace. To deny a nation the choice, regardless of any excuse, is to upset the unstable balance that has been achieved. Freedom of choice is a universal principle. It knows no exception.

SOURCE G

1989: year of revolution

When it became clear that the Soviet Union was no longer ready to use force to control its Empire, there was rapid change. In May 1989 the Hungarian government opened the frontier with Austria; there was now a gap in the Iron Curtain. In June free elections were held in Poland. Solidarity won and in August led a new non-communist government. Gorbachev expressed support for a peaceful hand-over of power. The rolling back of communism in Eastern Europe had begun. Many young East Germans made their way to Hungary and passed though Austria into West Germany. This made a nonsense of the Berlin Wall.

In October 1989 Gorbachev visited East Germany for the celebration of the fortieth anniversary of the state. Behind the scenes Gorbachev explained to East German leaders that he had no intention of using Russian force to stop reform. A month later, on 10 November, the Berlin Wall was torn down. The most famous symbol of the Cold War had been destroyed. On 17 November a series of massive anti-communist demonstrations took place in Czechoslovakia. By early December the Czechoslovak communist government had collapsed. On 21 December a revolution began in Romania. The Romanian dictator, Ceauşescu, was executed on Christmas Day. Throughout Eastern Europe there was no popular support for communism and, without the threat of Soviet tanks, communism fell apart. In 1990 the two halves of Germany were re-united and a single pro-Western state was established.

The collapse of European communism was symbolised by the fall of the Berlin Wall, November 1989.

The last days of the USSR

After 1989 Gorbachev was in a difficult position. His plan to reform communism had failed. Communism had been rejected by Eastern Europe and different nationalities demanded independence from the Soviet Union. The call for independence was strongest in the Baltic republics of Latvia, Lithuania and Estonia. In Russia itself, the heart of the USSR, many people demanded an end to communism. On 4 February 1990, 250,000 people demonstrated in Moscow against communism.

With his plans in ruins Gorbachev responded by drawing back from reform and trying to make an alliance with old style, hard-line communists. On May Day 1990, demonstrators humiliated Gorbachev by shouting at him in public during the traditional communist march.

The rise of Yeltsin

Boris Yeltsin became the leader of the reformists. He had been a communist boss in the city of Moscow until he was dismissed in 1987 by Gorbachev because of his radical views. In May 1990 Yeltsin was elected President of Russia. The USSR was divided into separate republics and Russia was the largest of them. A month later Yeltsin left the communist party and joined forces with those who wanted to destroy Soviet communism. Gorbachev was losing control of events.

In the autumn of 1990 Gorbachev tried to stop the disintegration of the USSR by using force against nationalists in the Baltic republics. At the same time Gorbachev appointed more old-style communists to key positions of government. This new hard line from Gorbachev was not a success. He began to lose many of his long-standing friends and supporters. In December 1990 the Soviet Foreign Minister, Eduard Shevardnadze, resigned and complained of a move towards dictatorship. This was a great blow – Shevardnadze had been one of Gorbachev's allies for many years.

The fall of Gorbachev

The struggle for control of the USSR came to a head in 1991. Yeltsin attacked the power of the communist party in the daily life of Russian people. He banned the party from operating at all places of work. The Russian Parliament that Yeltsin controlled became more powerful and challenged the central government of Gorbachev. Gorbachev did not know which way to turn. In August 1991 a group of hard-line communists tried to seize power. They arrested Gorbachev and declared a state of emergency. The coup was opposed by Boris Yeltsin and it soon collapsed. After the coup, the authority of Gorbachev was damaged. In December 1991 the individual Soviet republics became independent and Gorbachev resigned as Soviet leader. The Soviet state, born in the 1917 revolution, no longer existed.

SOURCE H

Boris Yeltsin at the time of the 1991 coup. Yeltsin took power in Russia as the Soviet Union fell apart.

>> **Activity**

Explain the part that Gorbachev played in the collapse of communism in Eastern Europe and the Soviet Union. In your answer discuss:

a the long-term causes of the crisis for communism,

b the personal contribution of Gorbachev.

The Soviet Empire 1948–91

The split with Tito

The Yugoslav communist leader, Tito, liberated Yugoslavia from German control without help from Moscow. He argued with Stalin and refused to take orders from Moscow. In 1948 Yugoslavia was expelled from Cominform, the international grouping of communist parties. The Soviet Union imposed a trade ban on Yugoslavia but they survived due to support from the USA. Stalin dealt ruthlessly with other East European countries between 1949 and 1953. He was worried that they might try to copy Tito. Leading communists with independent ideas were imprisoned or executed.

TURMOIL IN THE COMMUNIST WORLD AFTER STALIN

> After Stalin's death in 1953 people in Eastern Europe hoped for more freedom from Soviet control.

> The new Soviet leader, Khrushchev, established friendly relations with Yugoslavia in 1955. Hungarians hoped to copy Yugoslav independence.

> In 1956 unrest in Poland led to reforms and concessions by the communist government. This encouraged Hungarians to demand reforms.

The Hungarian Uprising

In October 1956 unrest in Hungary led to the appointment of a new Prime Minister, the communist reformer, Imre Nagy. People demanded that Hungary should leave the Warsaw Pact and become neutral. Nagy agreed but in November 1956 Soviet troops invaded Hungary and imposed a new pro-Soviet government. There was fierce street fighting in which thousands of people were killed. Nagy was arrested and later executed. The USA did nothing to help the Hungarians: people in the West were preoccupied with the Suez crisis.

The Prague Spring

Economic problems caused unrest in Czechoslovakia in 1967. A new communist leader, Dubček, took power in January 1968. He introduced democratic reforms while remaining communist. In August 1968 Soviet troops invaded Czechoslovakia to end the reforms. Dubček lost his job in 1969 and a pro-Soviet government was put in place. Afterwards the Soviet leader, Brezhnev, announced the 'Brezhnev Doctrine': the Soviet Union would use force to keep communists in power in any country.

1956 AND 1968 COMPARED

> In both cases the Soviet Union used force to end reforms in East European countries. New pro-Soviet governments were imposed.

> The Hungarian government wanted to break with the Soviet Union, leave the Warsaw Pact and become neutral. The Czechoslovak government wanted much more democracy at home but promised to stay in the Warsaw Pact.

> In both cases the USA did nothing to help. The West was preoccupied with Suez in 1956 and Vietnam in 1968.

> The Hungarians fought against the Soviet invasion – thousands were killed. The Czechoslovak people offered non-violent resistance. The Hungarian leader, Nagy, was executed; the Czechoslovak leader, Dubček, lost his job but remained alive and free.

The Berlin Wall

Between 1958 and 1961 there was a dispute between the Soviet Union and the USA over Berlin. The Soviet leader, Khrushchev, said that Western forces should leave the city and that it should become neutral. The US president, Eisenhower, was prepared to compromise but he was replaced in 1961 by President Kennedy. Kennedy refused to compromise and both leaders publicly threatened war over Berlin. In 1961 the crisis was resolved, and the threat of immediate war disappeared, when a wall was built around West Berlin to stop East Germans fleeing the communist state.

Poland and the rise of Solidarity

Shipyard workers in Gdansk went on strike in 1980 in protest against rising prices. They were led by Lech Walesa and formed a new non-communist trade union called Solidarity. Millions of workers joined Solidarity. The Soviet government considered invading Poland in order to crush the union. To avoid this the Polish communist leader, Jaruzelski, banned Solidarity in December 1981. He declared martial law and imprisoned Solidarity leaders without trial but failed to destroy the union. Solidarity did well in elections in 1989 and formed a non-communist government.

SOVIET COMMUNISM IN DECLINE

The Soviet Union was in crisis by the early 1980s:

> The economy had failed to match the economies of America and Western Europe.

> The arms race further reduced living standards.

> There was widespread corruption.

> The Soviet Union was fighting a disastrous war in Afghanistan.

The second Cold War

After the Vietnam War the USA pursued a policy of detente with the Soviet Union. This involved peaceful co-existence and some arms reductions. Ronald Reagan became president of the USA in 1981 and he ended détente and began a new arms race with the USSR.

Gorbachev

Mikhail Gorbachev, a reformist communist, took control in the Soviet Union in 1985. He wanted to improve the Soviet Union by 'perestroika' – 'restructuring' or reforming the economy – and 'glasnost' – greater 'openness' and freedom of speech. His reforms undermined the position of old-style pro-Soviet leaders in other countries. He renounced the 'Brezhnev Doctrine' of interference in other countries.

The whole of communist Europe was swept with revolution in 1989. One by one, the communist authorities were overthrown. The Soviet Union led by Gorbachev did nothing to stop this process. The Berlin Wall was torn down in November 1989. In 1991 the Soviet Union fell apart. After a failed communist coup in August, the republics that made up the USSR declared their independence. Gorbachev resigned. Russia became a separate state ruled over by Boris Yeltsin.

Crowds outside the Reichstag celebrate the reunification of Germany, 3 October 1990.

The United Nations

Towards the end of the Second World War the victorious allies decided to set up a world organisation to replace the failed League of Nations. The United Nations was founded in 1945. From 1952, the UN had a permanent headquarters in New York.

POWER IN THE UN

The Secretary General

The person in charge of the day-to-day running of the United Nations is called the Secretary General.

The General Assembly

All member states send representatives to a General Assembly. This is a place for the discussion of world problems. By 1995 there were 185 members of the General Assembly. It has no real power. It can make recommendations but they are not binding on members. Before 1960 the USA had great influence over the General Assembly. This changed as more and more former colonies became independent. The newly independent countries were often critical of US policy.

The Security Council

Power in the UN lies in the hands of a small committee of member states called the Security Council. This originally had representatives from eleven countries; the number was increased to fifteen in 1965. Five powerful countries had permanent membership: the USA, the USSR (Russia since 1992), China, Britain and France. Each permanent member of the Security Council has a veto over any decisions. The veto rule can stop the Security Council from being effective. In the days of the Cold War the Americans and the Soviets rarely agreed on major issues. The USSR repeatedly used its power of veto. Other countries took turns at having membership of the Security Council.

The UN in action

The UN has been effective on some occasions when the use of force had the full backing of the USA. The Korean War (1950–3) and the Gulf War (1990–91) were both fought by the USA in the name of the UN. If two sides in a conflict were ready to talk, the UN was able to mediate and bring them together. In this way the UN helped to bring about ceasefires at the end of wars such as the Iran–Iraq War (1980–88). Like the League of Nations before it, the United Nations has no armed forces of its own. The UN had great difficulty in peace-keeping during the civil wars that started in 1991 in the former Yugoslavia.

While the UN has only had limited success in peace-keeping, it has done much good in many other areas of life. There are a large number of UN agencies that aim to help different groups of people across the world. The World Health Organisation runs projects in many poor countries in order to improve people's health. The Food and Agriculture Organisation encourages farmers in poorer countries to develop farming methods. The United Nations High Commission for Refugees provides basic help to people who have had to flee their homeland.

Discussion points

> How is the United Nations organised?

> How successful has the United Nations been?

The General Assembly of the United Nations.

The UN in action: Korea and the Congo

The United Nations was set up by the winners of the Second World War. Like the League of Nations after the First World War it was intended to ensure an end to war. The UN faced many challenges in the following years, such as conflicts in Korea and the Congo.

How successful was the United Nations in the Korean and Congo crises?

When the United Nations was founded in 1945 its members signed a document, known as the Charter of the United Nations, that set out the aims and principles of the organisation.

SOURCE A

The opening words of the United Nations Charter, signed in June 1945, set out the main purpose of the United Nations:

We are determined to save succeeding generations from the scourge of war, which twice in our lifetime has brought untold sorrow to mankind.

The United Nations and the Cold War

How would the UN ensure world peace in the way described by Source A? How would it avoid repeating the failures of the League of Nations? The founders of the UN hoped that it would be an effective force for peace because it would be led by the same powerful countries that had been able to unite and destroy Hitler. The League of Nations had been fatally weakened by the absence of the USA and other powerful countries. The UN did not have this problem. Its membership included the most powerful countries in the world: the USA, the USSR and Britain. The American President, Roosevelt, hoped that these three states could act together in leading the United Nations, just as they fought together against Hitler.

The organisation of the United Nations reflected the fact that the wartime allies intended to work together to impose peace on the world. Under their joint leadership, the UN was intended to be a 'policeman' for all of humanity. The Security Council had a special responsibility for international peace. It was controlled by its permanent members, which included the wartime allies. The UN Charter described how the Security Council could try to stop countries from attacking other states. It could order trade sanctions: member states would stop selling goods to any aggressive country. If sanctions failed, the Security Council could order military action by United Nations forces. A Military Staff Committee was set up to control any United Nations force and it had members from each of the five permanent member-states.

The plans of the wartime leaders – Roosevelt, Stalin and Churchill – did not work out very well in practice. The organisation of the United Nations was based on the assumption that the most powerful countries would continue to co-operate after the war but this did not happen. The Cold War soon developed and the two superpowers, the USA and the USSR, became extremely hostile towards each other. The Cold War disrupted the work of the Security Council. The Americans and the Soviets constantly disagreed and this stopped the Security Council from acting effectively to stamp out wars. American proposals were consistently vetoed by the Soviet Union; Soviet suggestions were blocked by the American veto. The result was deadlock. In both the Korean and the Congo crises the work of the UN was influenced and distorted by superpower rivalry.

The UN in Korea

The United Nations used armed force against North Korea and China during the Korean War, 1950–53. Communist North Koreans invaded South Korea. A UN army, led by the USA, invaded Korea and tried to drive the communists back. When it seemed that the UN forces might conquer the whole of Korea, the North Koreans were reinforced by troops from communist China. The war eventually led to stalemate and Korea remained divided into communist North Korea and non-communist South Korea. There are at least two possible interpretations of the role of the UN in the Korean War:

Interpretation A

The Korean War was a success for the United Nations. It showed that the UN could take firm action against aggression.

Interpretation B

The Korean War was a failure for the United Nations. The UN forces were completely dominated by the USA. The Korean War showed that the Cold War had ruined the original idea of the United Nations.

>> Activity

Look back to pages 124–7 to find out the detail of what happened during the Korean War. Using that unit and the following information and sources, decide which of the two interpretations, A or B, you think is correct.

Divisions in the Security Council

Communists took power in most of China in 1949. The Americans would not allow the new communist government to join the Security Council. Instead the Chinese place on the Security Council remained occupied by the non-communist nationalists who, by 1949, only controlled the Chinese island of Taiwan. The argument about who should represent China became another episode in the bitter Cold War. The Soviet Union demanded that the nationalist Chinese should leave the Security Council and give way to the communist Chinese. In protest, the Soviet representatives walked out of the Security Council in January 1950. In June 1950 North Korea invaded South Korea and the Security Council met to discuss its response. The absence of representatives from the Soviet Union meant that they were not able to veto the American proposal to help South Korea.

A UN army or an American army?

The UN army that fought against the communists in Korea was dominated by the USA and was led by the US General MacArthur. The government of the United States controlled the war and simply reported its decisions to the Security Council. Another 15 countries supplied troops to the UN but they were a small minority of the total UN force. Leaders of countries such as Britain which sent troops became annoyed at the way General MacArthur and President Truman failed to consult them about important decisions in the war.

SOURCE B

HISTORY DOESN'T REPEAT ITSELF

This cartoon by David Low, from the early days of the Korean War, approves of the firm action taken by the USA and sees UN action as an improvement on the work of the League of Nations.

The Congo Crisis 1960–64

The Congo is today known as Zaire. Before 1960 it was a Belgian colony. It became independent on 30 June 1960 and the country was soon thrown into chaos. The Belgian government had done very little to prepare the Congo for independence. All the important jobs in government, industry and the army were performed by white Belgians. For example, there was not a single black doctor in the whole country. This created a very difficult situation for the Prime Minister of the newly independent state, Patrice Lumumba. Almost immediately, trouble broke out. The white Belgian officers in the national army refused to promote any black Congolese men to join them as officers. The soldiers mutinied and attacked both their officers and other white people.

The problems faced by Lumumba soon increased. The Belgian government sent paratroops to defend European people in the Congo. At the same time the copper-rich province of Katanga broke away from the rest of the Congo. The Katangan leader, Moise Tshombe, declared Katanga to be an independent state. Tshombe used white mercenaries to build up a new army in Katanga. He received support and encouragement from many Belgians and from Belgian mining companies who still wanted to have a presence in the new state.

Lumumba turned to the United Nations for help. The Secretary-General of the UN was Dag Hammarskjöld. He was keen to take action because he wanted to show that the UN could bring peace to the trouble spots of the world. Following his advice, on 13 July 1960 the Security Council agreed to restore order in the Congo and 4,500 UN soldiers immediately flew out to the troubled African country. Eventually there was a force of 8,000 UN troops in the Congo. The Security Council ordered Belgium to withdraw its troops. The Belgians agreed to pull out of much of the country but they refused to leave Katanga. The UN forces were successful in restoring order in much of the country but they were not able to stop the fighting between the forces of Lumumba and those of Tshombe. Lumumba soon had a bitter argument with the UN about their role in the Congo. He wanted UN soldiers to attack Katanga and end Tshombe's breakaway government. Hammarskjöld was not happy at the idea of the UN becoming involved in a civil war and he refused to invade Katanga.

SOURCE C

Patrice Lumumba became Prime Minister of Zaire in 1960 when it became independent from Belgium.

SOURCE D

Moise Tshombe, the leader of the break-away Katangan state.

SOURCE E

The Secretary-General of the UN, Dag Hammarskjöld.

Superpower mischief

The position of Hammarskjöld was undermined by each of the two superpowers. They insisted on pursuing their own policies, independent of the Security Council. The Soviet leader, Khrushchev, publicly criticised Hammarskjöld for not offering enough help to Lumumba. The USSR wanted to show itself to be a friend of newly independent countries and it strongly supported Lumumba. In August Lumumba ignored the United Nations, turned directly to the Soviet Union, and tried to invade Katanga with Soviet help. Despite being a member of the Security Council, the government of the USSR disregarded UN policy and provided Lumumba with military aircraft for his invasion plan but the attack failed.

A month later, in September 1960, Lumumba was overthrown by one of his own army officers, Joseph Mobutu. The US government gave secret support to Mobutu in his bid for power because they thought that he would be more pro-Western than Lumumba. Lumumba was eventually captured by the forces of Tshombe and murdered in January 1961.

The debate about how the UN should act in the Congo led to angry scenes at the United Nations General Assembly meeting in September 1960. Khrushchev argued that Hammarskjöld's job should be abolished. Despite these criticisms, Hammarskjöld remained in his post.

The end of the emergency

By early 1961 UN intervention had not brought peace to the Congo. With the help of white mercenaries, Tshombe remained in control of the breakaway region of Katanga. The Security Council tried to stop a civil war by announcing in February that, except for the UN forces, all foreign troops must leave the country. Tshombe refused to co-operate. Hammarskjöld was killed in an air accident in the Congo in September. The new Secretary-General was a Burmese man called U Thant. He took a tougher line with Tshombe and in December 1961 UN troops began fighting the white mercenaries and other Katangan forces. By the end of 1962, after periods of negotiation and renewed fighting, the UN succeeded in expelling the mercenaries. In January 1963 the Katangan leader, Tshombe, went into exile and the Congo was reunited. The UN had, at last, brought peace to the country but its own reputation had suffered. Some of the UN soldiers acted with brutality during the fighting in Katanga. People were unhappy at the sight of 'peacekeepers' involved in fighting. The UN forces left the Congo in 1964 and a year later Joseph Mobutu became President of the united country. The Congo crisis was over but people have disagreed ever since about whether the UN operation was a success or a mistake.

SOURCE F

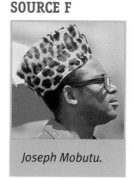

Joseph Mobutu.

THE CONGO CRISIS 1960–64

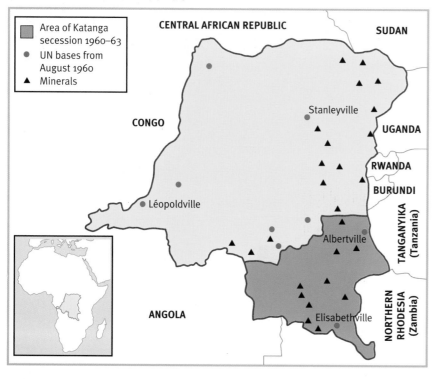

Area of Katanga secession 1960–63
UN bases from August 1960
Minerals

CENTRAL AFRICAN REPUBLIC
SUDAN
CONGO
Stanleyville
UGANDA
RWANDA
BURUNDI
Léopoldville
TANGANYIKA (Tanzania)
Albertville
ANGOLA
NORTHERN RHODESIA (Zambia)
Elisabethville

>> Activity

1 Explain in your own words why trouble broke out in the Congo in 1960.

2 What did the United Nations do to end the crisis in the Congo?

3 How did the superpower leaders undermine the efforts of the UN Secretary-General, Dag Hammarskjöld?

4 How did UN policy change after the death of Hammarskjöld?

5 In what ways did UN action succeed or fail in the Congo?

The work and success of the UN

The UN was set up in 1945 by the winners of the Second World War. The main features of the organisation were:

> a large General Assembly with little power;

> a powerful Security Council with five permanent and ten (originally six) temporary members.

PURPOSE AND PROBLEMS

The aims of the United Nations were stated in the United Nations Charter of June 1945:

> to encourage peace and avoide war;

> to develop international co-operation;

> to encourage economic and social progress;

> to promote respect for human rights.

The UN has not been very successful in peace-keeping. The Security Council has been stopped from taking firm action because of the right of veto held by permanent members and the Cold War conflict between the USA and the USSR.

UN AGENCIES

In addition to peacekeeping, the UN has run a number of organisations to ensure economic and social progress and deal with a whole range of global problems. This aspect of the work of the UN has been more successful than the its peacekeeping activities. Organisations include:

> UNESCO – the United Nations Educational, Scientific and Cultural Organisation;

> UNICEF – the United Nations International Children's Emergency Fund;

> ILO – the International Labour Organisation;

> WHO – the World Health Organisation;

> UNHCR – the United Nations High Commissioner for Refugees.

The changing face of the United Nations

In the late 1940s and 1950s the General Assembly was dominated by the United States. This began to change in the late 1950s as more African and Asian colonies became independent and joined the UN. In 1945 there were 51 members, by 1965 there were 118. Some of the new states were sympathetic to the USSR, many others were 'non-aligned'. It became much more difficult for the USA to dominate the General Assembly. The influence of the non-aligned countries increased in 1971 when communist China joined the United Nations. Non-aligned countries played an increasing role in the agencies of the UN. In the 1980s the US government claimed that these agencies were anti-American.

The UN in Korea and the Congo

A UN army, led by the USA, fought the Korean War, 1950–53, against communist North Korea and communist China. UN support for the war was only possible because the USSR was boycotting the Security Council in 1950. The UN forces drove the communists out of South Korea but were unable to conquer North Korea.

The African state of the Congo (modern Zaire) was a Belgian colony. After independence in 1960 it was torn apart by civil war. A UN force was sent to bring peace to the Congo. The leader of the breakaway province of Katanga, Tshombe, defied the UN. The UN was criticised by the USSR for not doing enough. In 1961 the UN took a tougher line with Katanga and finally reunited the Congo in 1963.

Index

Nobel Peace Prize, 40, 158
'non-aligned' movement, 93
nuclear weapons, 124, 128–32, 141, 142, 154
    atomic bombs, 91, 102, 113, 121, 122, 126

oil, 47, 58, 59
Ottoman Empire, 22, 23

Pakistan, 92, 93
Palestine, 23, 133
Palestine Liberation Organisation (PLO),
    142
Paris Conference (1919), 12–17
Passchendaele, Battle of, 8
Pearl Harbor, 90
'perestroika', 162, 167
Petrograd (St Petersburg), 10, 11
Philippines, 91, 92, 93
Pilsudski, Jozef, Marshall, 29
PLO (Palestine Liberation Organisation), 142
Poland, 12, 14, 19, 21, 22, 27
    agreements affecting Poland, 40–41,
        96–100
    and communism, 105, 120, 146, 166
    Second World War, 82, 87, 88, 97
    Solidarity, 156–9, 164, 167
    Vilna, 29, 37
Polish Corridor, 19, 24, 26, 27, 41
Portugal, 93
posters
    America, 13, 139
    France, 16, 42
    Germany, 8, 45, 48, 76
    Soviet Union 11, 32, 107, 110, 115
    United Nations Association, 99
Potsdam Conference (1945), 102–3, 120
Powers, Gary, 153
Princip, Gavrilo, 7
prisoners of war, 37, 90, 99
protectionism, 46, 86
Prussia, 4, 16, 19, 24, 27

Rabin, Yitzhak, 133
racial discrimination, 30
Rajk, Laszlo, 145, 146, 147
Rákosi, Mátyás, 146
Reagan, Ronald, President, 162,
    163, 167
    Second Cold War, 141, 143, 161
rearmament, 42, 49, 50, 75, 87
Red Army (Soviet Union), 11, 74, 90, 97,
    104, 145–51
Red Guards (China), 122, 123
refugees, 37, 62, 108, 168, 155
reparations, 22–3
reparations: Germany, 13, 15, 27, 28, 103
    arguments about, 16, 19, 20, 24, 26, 33
    Dawes and Young Plans, 38
Rhee, Syngman, 124
Rhineland, 16, 19, 27, 41–2
    German invasion, 61, 64–5, 86
Ribbentrop, Joachim von, 79, 83
Romania, 8, 22, 29
    and communism, 105, 120, 150, 151, 164
Rome–Berlin Axis, 57, 61
Roosevelt, Franklin D., President, 47, 74,
    153
    Yalta Agreement, 96, 98, 99, 100, 101
Ruhr area, 28, 33, 38, 45, 103

Runciman, Lord, 68, 69
Russia, 5, 7, 8–9, 14, 21, 52
    decline of communism, 162, 165
    Treaty of Brest-Litovsk, 9, 11, 26
Russian Revolution, 9, 10–11, 56, 94
    see also Soviet Union

Saarland, 16, 19, 27, 37
Sadat, Anwar, 133, 142
SALT (Strategic Arms Limitation Talks), 141
samurai, 52
Sarajevo, 6, 7
Sazonov, Sergei, 7
Schuschnigg, Kurt von, 66
Second World War, 57, 60, 82–91
self-determination, 13, 18, 22, 27
Serbia, 7, 8
Shevardnadze, Eduard, 165
Slovak people, 29, 68
socialism, 24, 56, 57, 149, 163
Solidarity, 156–9, 164, 167
Somme, Battle of the, 8
South Africa, 17, 18, 73, 92, 93
Soviet Union, 11, 29, 39, 160–67
    armed forces, 11, 74, 78, 81, 82, 148
    and China, 122–3, 132, 148, 151
    Congo, 172, 173
    Korea, 170, 173
    League of Nations, 32, 55, 63
    and Middle East, 163
    Nazi–Soviet Pact, 76–81, 87
    Second World War, 88–91, 99
    United Nations, 168, 169–73
    see also Cold War; Russia
Speer, Albert, 83
Sputnik, 152
Sri Lanka, 92, 93
Stalin, Joseph, 11, 43, 74, 76–81
    Eastern Europe, 104–7, 116–18, 120–21,
        144–6, 166
    Second World War, 89, 96–100, 102
Stalingrad, 90, 106
'Star Wars' (Strategic Defence Initiative),
    141, 143, 161
Strategic Arms Limitation Talks (SALT), 141
Stresa Front, 58, 61, 87
Stresemann, Gustav, 38, 40, 41
submarines, 9, 20, 58
Sudetenland, 29, 68–71, 86, 87
Suez Canal, 150, 166
Sweden, 37, 63
Switzerland, 30, 40, 62
Syria, 23, 92–3, 133, 142

Tardieu, André, 16, 19
Taylor, A.J.P., 84, 85
Tehran Conference (1943), 98, 120
Tet Offensive, 136, 143
Thant, U, 172
Thomas, Albert, 37
Tiananmen Square, 123
Tito (Josip Broz), 144, 146, 150, 166
trade ban: League of Nations, 33, 62
    not effective, 35, 53, 55, 58, 86
trade ban: Yugoslavia, 144, 166
Treaties, Locarno, 40–42, 87
Treaty, Washington, 39
Treaty of Brest-Litovsk, 9, 11, 26
Treaty of Lausanne, 23, 27

Treaty of London, 12
Treaty of Neuilly, 22, 27
Treaty of Rapallo, 39
Treaty of St Germain, 22, 27
Treaty of Sèvres, 23, 27
Treaty of Trianon, 22, 27, 29
Treaty of Versailles, 18–21, 24–7, 45, 49, 84
    breaches of, 49, 58, 64–7, 86
    see also League of Nations
Trotsky, Leon, 11
Truman, Harry, President, 101–3, 107, 113,
    117, 120, 124–6, 142, 170
Truman Doctrine, 109, 111, 121, 124, 146
Tshombe, Moise, 171–2, 173
Turkey, 23, 27, 108–9, 128–32, 142
    empire, 7, 14, 17, 18, 21, 23

U-boats (submarines), 9
Ukraine, 11, 78
unemployment, 46, 50, 51, 86, 108
    Germany, 38, 45, 48, 49
United Nations, 108, 125, 133, 148, 164,
    168–73
    structure, 37, 99, 168
Upper Silesia, 16, 19, 27
USA (United States of America),
    see America
USSR (Union of Soviet Socialist Republics),
    see Soviet Union

Vandenburg, Arthur, 110
Verdun, Battle of, 8
Vichy Government, 89
Vietnam, 18, 92, 93
Vietnam War, 134–40, 143, 150, 166
Vyshinsky, Andrei, 105

Walesa, Lech, 156, 158–9, 167
Wall Street Crash, 46, 86
    see also Depression
war debts, 13, 16, 20, 51, 112
war guilt, 20, 24, 26, 27
Warsaw Pact, 119, 121, 151
Warsaw Uprising, 97, 156
Washington Conferences (1921–2), 39
Weimar Republic, 28, 45, 49
West Germany (Federal Republic of
    Germany), 116, 118, 119, 121, 164
Wilhelm I, Kaiser, 4
Wilhelm II, Kaiser, 4, 7
Wilson, Sir Horace, 70–71
Wilson, Thomas Woodrow, President, 12, 13,
    24–7
    Fourteen Points, 14–15, 21, 26
    League of Nations, 17, 18, 21, 31–4, 62
women, 57, 75
world economy, 46, 113
World Health Organisation, 37, 168

Yalta Agreement, 96–100, 102, 107, 120
Yeltsin, Boris, 165, 167
Young, Owen, 38
Young Plan, 38
Yugoslavia, 12, 22, 29, 168
    and communism, 144, 146, 151, 166

Zaire, 92, 93
Zimbabwe, 92, 93